Wild Horse Vacations

Wild Horse Vacations

Your Guide to the Atlantic Wild Horse Trail

With Local Attractions and Amenities

Volume 2

Ocracoke, NC • Shackleford Banks, NC • Cumberland Island, GA

Written and illustrated by

Bonnie U. Gruenberg

QUAGGA PRESS

Wild Horse Vacations: Your Guide to the Atlantic Wild Horse Trail with Local Attractions and Amenities, Volume 2

Library of Congress Control Number: 2015952709

ISBN 13: 978-1-941700-13-6

Published by Quagga Press, an imprint of Synclitic Media, LLC • 440 Schoolhouse Rd • New Providence,, PA 17560 www.quaggapress.com

Also by the author

Wild Horse Vacations: Your Guide to the Atlantic Wild Horse Trail with Local Attractions and Amenities, Volume 1 (Quagga Press, 2016)

The Wild Horse Dilemma: Conflicts and Controversies of the Atlantic Coast Herds (Quagga Press, 2015)

The Hoofprints Guide Series (Quagga Press, 2016) Assateague • Chincoteague • Corolla • Ocracoke • Shackleford Banks • Cumberland Island

Wild Horses of the Atlantic Coast: An Intimate Portrait, Kindle Edition (Quagga Press, 2014)

Hoofprints in the Sand, Kindle Edition (Quagga Press, 2014)

The Midwife's Journal (Birth Guru/Birth Muse, 2009)

Birth Emergency Skills Training (Birth Guru/Birth Muse, 2008)

Essentials of Prehospital Maternity Care (Prentice Hall, 2005)

Hoofprints in the Sand (as Bonnie S. Urquhart; Eclipse, 2002)

Forthcoming

Wild Horses! The Kids' Guide to the East Coast Herds (Quagga Press, 2017)

Birth Emergency Skills Training, 2nd Edition (Synclitic Press, 2017)

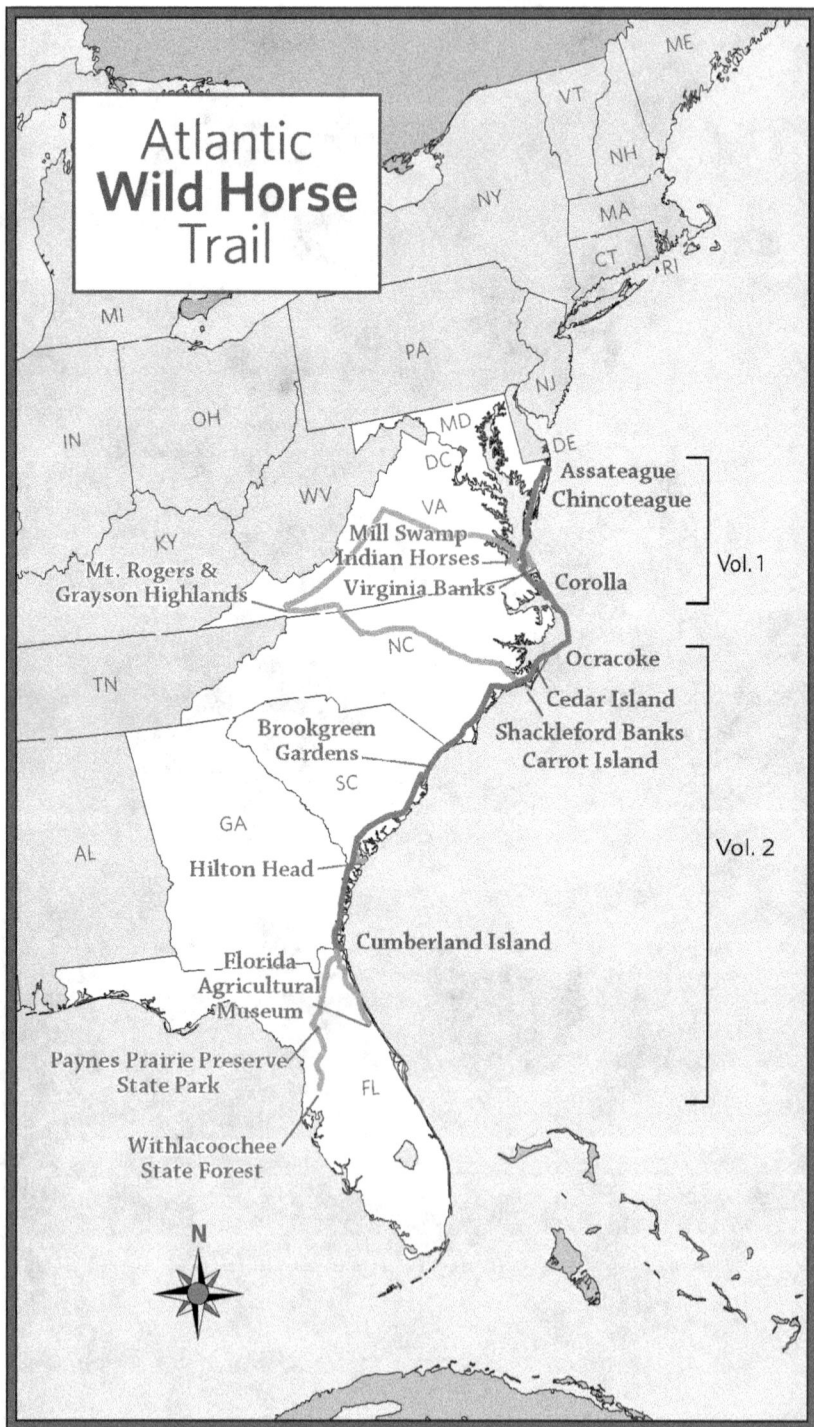

Atlantic
Wild Horse
Trail

ME
VT
NH
NY
MA
CT
RI

MI
PA
NJ
OH
MD
IN
DC
DE
WV
VA
KY
Mt. Rogers &
Grayson Highlands
Mill Swamp
Indian Horses
Virginia Banks
Corolla

Assateague
Chincoteague

Vol. 1

NC

TN
Ocracoke
Cedar Island
Shackleford Banks
Carrot Island

Brookgreen
Gardens
SC

GA
AL
Hilton Head

Vol. 2

Cumberland Island

Florida
Agricultural
Museum

Paynes Prairie Preserve
State Park
FL

Withlacoochee
State Forest

N

The
Atlantic Wild Horse Trail

The Atlantic Wild Horse Trail, spanning six states and more than 1,700 miles of highways, bridges, and ferry routes, is a horse-watchers' avenue to a lifetime of enjoyment and learning. It links all seven wild herds of Colonial Spanish Horses that survive on the East Coast and several other important horse populations into a chain of vacation destinations that appeal not only to horse lovers, but also to hikers, photographers, campers, day-trippers, nature enthusiasts, and families seeking quality time outdoors. The Trail lacks markers, marketing, or official recognition, but you can follow it easily through the directions in *Wild Horse Vacations*. For the latest news about the Trail as it develops, visit www.wildhorseislands.com

Happy watching.

Introduction

I disembarked from the boat taxi on Carrot Island, but saw no horses. I hiked the length of the island—a grassy hillock, really—in existence for centuries, but fortified by sand dredged from estuarine bottom to keep the waterways open. From the crest of a dune, I could see boats docked along the Beaufort waterfront, bobbing like pelicans on the lapping waves. In another direction, I could almost visualize the waters covering the remains of *Queen Anne's Revenge*, the flagship of the notorious pirate Blackbeard, yet I couldn't spot a herd of horses on a small marshy island. I began to worry that perhaps the herd had suffered another population crash, like the wrenching die-off in the 1980s that reduced its size by more than half. But, no. Well-grazed marsh, uncountable hoof prints, and clumps of drying manure indicated recent visitation by horses, though even from my elevated vantage, I was unable to spot them.

Following a trail to the water's edge, well worn by wild equine hooves, I finally spotted the entire Rachel Carson Reserve herd congregating on a grassy spit some distance away. I hiked though a quarter mile of tepid shallows, across marsh and submerged fans of shifting sand, and set up my camera a respectful distance from the horses. They rested in small groups, organized by social hierarchy, cooled by the sea breezes that fingered their manes and discouraged biting insects.

As the hours passed, I gained insights into their behavior, their body language, their friendships and rivalries, and their relationships with the other species sharing their barrier island habitat. My pulse slowed to the rhythm of the waves and the gentle winds. I was no longer observing the scene, I was part of it. The simple act of watching these fellow creatures on their territory and on their schedule reminded me that some of our best moments happen when we surrender the need to control or predict the world around us. If the horses had really died off and left the island forever, as I had feared for a moment, the ecosystem would have lost some of its key players, and we humans would have lost something of inestimable value.

Although wild horses are usually found in small bands of 3-8, the hot day and relentless biting insects drove the entire Rachel Carson Reserve herd to congregate on a cool grassy spit near deeper, open water. There, horses were able to rest while stiff breezes kept the horseflies from alighting.

Horses have lived as wild on barrier islands and peninsulas of the Atlantic coast for hundreds of years, probably longer than mustangs have roamed the American West. In spite of this fact, or maybe because of it, they are the topic of heated controversy.

Scientists, laypeople, politicians, land managers, and other stakeholders label and categorize them, define their roles, and assign meaning to their presence. Some see the horses as historically significant living symbols of freedom. Some view them as feral nuisances that disrupt the ecological balance. Some devote their lives to protecting the free-roaming survival of these horses; others, to their confinement, restriction, and removal. On both sides, opinions are put forward as Gospel, and deeply held beliefs are entwined with intense emotion. Meanwhile, the horses live much as they have through the centuries, while people colonizing their home ranges clash or coexist with them.

These herds present a unique opportunity for people to view horses in their natural state. Even people who are knowledgeable about domestic horses are surprised and amazed when they observe the behavior of equids living true to their wild nature. A domestic horse is persuaded to accept circumstances that would be incomprehensible to his wild kin. He learns to seek shelter from the elements under a roof, whereas a wild horse turns his tail to the wind and endures. He finds

Ponies cavort on the Chincoteague National Wildlife Refuge after returning to Assateague at the end of a Pony Penning festival.

security in confined quarters, whereas a wild horse feels safest in open spaces with many potential avenues of flight. He offers partnership and camaraderie to a predatory animal perched on his back, whereas a wild horse would flee in panic if a human leaped aboard.

The family unit is the hub of social structure for a wild herd. A wild stallion's motivation to defend his band and maintain a harem, central focuses of his life, are largely driven by testosterone. The domestic male horse is usually castrated and lives most of his life in a hormonal limbo that is neither male nor female. This sexlessness makes him easier to manage and allows him to focus more easily on human priorities, such as training and riding. If he remains a stallion, he is allowed to breed when and if his owner permits reproduction. His sexual interludes are choreographed by the handler at the end of his lead rope, and may involve an upholstered "dummy" mare and semen specimens shipped great distances to impregnate mares that he will never meet.

We ask our companion horses to sort cattle, jump fences, run grueling races, and pull heavy loads, and we feed them concentrated foods to meet the increased energy requirements. We train them to disregard their instincts and accept a rider's demands. In exchange, we provide them with abundant, easily accessed food and water, protect them

Most male domestic horses are gelded. Consequently, most equestrians are unfamiliar with the natural behavior of stallions. Wild-horse watching offers the opportunity to learn about the true nature of horses.

from diseases, and help them to live longer, sometimes more comfortable lives.

Under natural conditions, horses are exposed to disease, severe weather, famine, and drought, but in return, they know freedom and independence. Wild horses follow their own internal rhythms, their behavior shaped by millions of years of evolution and interaction with their environment. Many of the choices they make daily relate to the survival of the individual, the herd, and the species, in that order.

Most of the wild horses in North America live in the West on U.S. Bureau of Land Management property or other federal or private ranges. This book, however, will focus on the smaller, but perhaps older herds along the Atlantic coast of the United States: Assateague Island, MD and VA; Corolla, NC; Ocracoke, NC; Shackleford Banks, Cedar Island, and Carrot Island, NC; and Cumberland Island, GA.

Why visit the wild horses of the Atlantic Coast? While Western mustangs are usually shy and live in remote ranges, the horses of the East Coast barrier islands are habituated to human visitors and offer exceptional opportunities for observing horse behavior in the wild. Additionally, all these coastal horse ranges lie within a day's drive of much of the East Coast population. There are many activities to enjoy on and near the islands where the horses reside. This book will tell you about the horses and where to see them, as well as where to go, where to stay, what to do, and what to avoid.

There is somethinng about the sight of a wild horse on a pristine seashore that stirs the senses. On most of the east coast islands that support wild horse herds, it is possible to get dramatic photographs with a simple camera that lacks a telephoto lens.

As a child, I was well acquainted with the classic book *Misty of Chincoteague,* and I knew that wild ponies lived on the island of Assateague. When I first visited Cape Hatteras, NC, in 1993, I was astounded to find that wild horses also lived on several nearby barrier islands and had been there for centuries.

I learned that small herds remained along the coast of Georgia; on Sable Island, off Nova Scotia, Canada; and on Great Abaco Island in the Bahamas. I became increasingly curious about the barrier island herds, their behavior, and their relationship to their environment, wildlife management programs, and local and national politics. Year after year, I hauled my growing sons to Assateague to camp among horses and to the Outer Banks to research the wild herds of North Carolina. I spent long hours in libraries and salt marshes separating fact from myth, and ultimately wrote *Hoofprints In The Sand: Wild Horses of the Atlantic Coast* (Eclipse Press, 2002).

In 2009, I updated and revamped my initial body of research and began work on a comprehensive—and prize winning!—volume titled *The Wild Horse Dilemma: Conflicts and Controversies of the Atlantic Coast Herds* (Quagga Press, 2015).

Even people who have extensive experience with domestic horses are surprised by the behavior of wild horses. After nine straight days of heavy rain, the deluge ceased and the ground began to dry. A band of Assateague horses, unable to lie down to rest while the ground was flooded, took the opportunity to nap on the drying grass near Bayside Campground—all at once. Despite the lack of predators on the island, one or two horses always remained standing, as sentries.

Many readers were inspired to view these herds for themselves and wrote to ask for advice on how to find them, where to stay, and what to do nearby. Because so many people showed an interest, I collected my experiences and investigations into the informative, practical, and abundantly illustrated travel guide before you.

The purpose of *Wild Horse Vacations* Volumes 1 and 2 is to stream-line your wild horse odyssey. They are organized by region and include nearby attractions and side trips. There is much to be said for taking the time to get to know each herd, but I have tried to make the routes and recommendations equally useful to ambitious travelers who plan to visit some or all of the herds in whirlwind trips.

Wild-horse sightings are unpredictable. On one visit you may see many horses without having to search. On the next, you may look for hours and find only two or three, and those some distance away. Horses have their own agendas, and it is difficult to predict their whereabouts, though with some knowledge of their habits it is easier to find them on any given day. Where horse ranges have visitor centers, staff can advise where you are most likely to see horses.

As with any guidebook, certain caveats are in order. The herds, their circumstances, the people who manage and protect them, even the islands they inhabit are in continual flux. At this writing, Assateague is a single island. But it has been a chain of islands and a peninsula at various times in the last 100-odd years, and it may revert to either configuration overnight. The maps in this guide are for general orientation, not for navigation. Distances are approximate, and some directions may already be obsolete. You are more likely to reach your intended destination without bother if you rely on recent detailed roadmaps or information from your global positioning device, though they, too, may not be completely reliable.

A Few Words about End-of-Chapter Lists

To the best of my knowledge, the information on lodging, dining, attractions, and activities that follow the main text of each chapter was accurate at the time of publication. By the time you visit, any business listed may have changed management, changed name, changed physical or Internet address, changed phone numbers, changed prices, or shut down. Government agencies and nonprofit entities are more stable in some respects. Chincoteague National Wildlife Refuge has occupied roughly the same acreage under the same name since 1947, though policies, goals, hours, fees, regulations, staff, concessionaires, and public relations have been fluid.

The end-of-chapter information offers a representative selection of noteworthy or reputable establishments, and is not meant to be comprehensive. For brevity, I've omitted *http://* from URLs where it precedes *www*. I've avoided listing national chain restaurants, though many of them can provide excellent dining experiences. I do include national chain hotels and motels, largely because they have absorbed many local competitors. You can see the latest listings, maps, videos, and other useful material at www.WildHorseIslands.com If you have suggestions for businesses to include in future editions of the book, contact me at info@WildHorseIslands.com.

I once owned a Connemara gelding known as Mr. Pone. Everyone agreed that he was a pony with great wisdom and insight who could see things the rest of us could not. At least that's how we generously explained his tendency to spook at the invisible. When I've had a posi-

Often desired, but seldom awarded, the Pone of Approval is the highest honor that the author bestows on restaurants, lodgings, and attractions.

tive experience with a business or institution, I've given it the Pone of Approval and included a brief review. I don't necessarily endorse the other restaurants, lodgings, or activities listed in this guide, though I comment on many that have not won the POA.

Any recommendation or review can reflect the personality or biases of the reviewer or the circumstances of the visit more than it reflects the quality of the establishment. Many of my research trips are solo adventures, but I also travel with my husband; so I often shift between *I* and *we* in the text. In the interest of transparency, I'm obliged to add that our children are grown, and as middle-aged empty-nesters we gravitate toward peaceful, relaxing settings and quietude. While I have included venues that appeal to athletic adventurers, youthful partiers, and families with small children, we might not have experienced these activities ourselves, at least not recently.

To broaden perspective, I've included rankings (usually high) or referred to reviews (usually positive) from a variety of external sources in the entries for lodgings and restaurants. (See the sample entry above.) Please remember that rankings can change rapidly for a variety of reasons. For a better idea of how recent travelers have experienced the places mentioned here, look over posts on sites such as TripAdvisor, Oyster, and Zomato.

In hope of improving the potential utility of lodging and dining information, I've added price-range indicators ($, $$, and $$$), explained below.

Information about the Wild Horse Ranges

This section includes phone numbers and other details about agencies controlling a herd's territory and entities operating within it.

Amenities, such as campgrounds, situated mostly or completely in the horse ranges are broken down as under Nearby Points of Interest, immediately below.

— SAMPLE ENTRY —

Castle in the Sand Hotel
3701 Atlantic Ave.
Ocean City, MD 21842
Toll free 800-552-7263
410-289-6846
www.castleinthesand.com
$$
Frommer's 2 stars, Oyster #10, TripAdvisor # 21, *U.S. News* #6
    175 oceanfront rooms, efficiencies, apartments, and suites; 25-meter Olympic pool; meeting rooms; restaurant; lounge; golf packages. Kid-friendly, as the name suggests. Pets allowed. 11 mi.

Nearby Points of Interest

    Listings include approximate road distances from some convenient location. Pone of Approval winners appear at the beginning of a category; the remaining entries are in alphabetical order.

Camping

    Camping comes first because it's a compact subject, because campgrounds are often inexpensive and close to the horses' ranges, and because readers who willingly hike through flooded marsh for a glimpse of wild horses seem likely to enjoy or tolerate some degree of roughing it.

Bed and Breakfasts

    B&Bs follow for utterly different reasons: Some B&Bs are distant from the equine action, and all are costlier than campgrounds, though many B&Bs are price-competitive with hotels and motels. But superior B&Bs can reward their guests with seclusion, pampering, or the proprietors' unique perspectives on local nature and culture.

Because B&Bs are both public accommodations and private residences, they may be smoke-free by law or by owners' preference. Many put restrictions on children, some make limited provisions for the mobility-impaired, and not every policy or constraint is crystal-clear. It never hurts to ask before you book.

Hotels and Motels

Quite a few hostelries close in the off season, and dates of operation vary with location and market forces. For brevity's sake, I usually make note only of those that stay open all year. If the entry doesn't address the topic, the establishment operated seasonally when the book went to press.

Rates were complex and changeable long before intermediaries such as Groupon and Hotwire appeared, but *relative* pricing is fairly constant over the long term. Although promotions can create amazing deals, an oceanfront hotel with valet parking and a spa won't consistently undercut a landlocked Super 8.

In this book, *$$$*, *$$*, and *$* denote the top, middle, and bottom thirds of the price range *in a particular area*, as near as rank can be determined. The average and spread of prices for $$ motels in one area may differ from those in another.

Dining

While avoiding vague cuisine labels, e.g., *coastal Southern*, I try to hoist a flag over anything out of the ordinary—for example, Right Up Your Alley in Chincoteague, VA, a taco stand that does business in a literal alley.

Hours vary, so I use *breakfast* (until ~11 a.m.), *lunch* (~11 a.m. to ~4 p.m.), *dinner* (~4 to ~9 p.m.), and *late* instead. Crabcakes and iced tea served at sunrise count as breakfast.

A number of national and regional restaurants cater to the 20 million or so Americans who avoid gluten. Although these enterprises receive little space in other parts of the series, their appreciation of this issue has earned them sole possession of Appendix 6 in volume 2.

As with lodgings, *$$$*, *$$*, and *$* indicate the top, middle, and bottom thirds of the local price range. McDonald's and other inexpensive national chains make up much of the $ tier.

Consequently, many $$ and $$$ establishments can be surprisingly merciful to the debit card.

Each dining section includes bits of locavore lore dealing with some distinctive, unexpected, or underappreciated aspect of an area's cornucopia.

Horse-Related Activities

These pertain to domestic horses and include riding, boarding, racing, and showing.

Other Attractions

Though biased toward nature and art, I've tried to feature a variety of interesting places and activities to enjoy when horse-watching is impossible. In some chapters, this category is divided for convenience.

Events

The goal here is to capture local color and point out significant occurrences without setting down a whole year's doings.

Outlying Destinations

Places more than 20 road miles from the reference location used with Nearby Points of Interest (which see). Outlying Destinations and Nearby Attractions both follow the organizational scheme shown here, but may not include every category.

Local Contacts

These include, but aren't limited to, chambers of commerce, tourist bureaus, historical societies, horse-welfare advocates, and environmental-protection groups.

More Information

A short list of sources, such as books, periodicals, and Web sites, that may enhance your horse-watching or help you pass the time when it's raining buckets.

Listings that accompany side trips (see below) are similar to these, but shorter, free of headings, and sometimes arranged geographically.

The last items in each chapter are always

The One Thing . . .

A place, vista, program, or event that can round out a visit, no matter whether it's your first or your twentieth.

Getting to . . .

A set of driving directions and tips with an accompanying small-scale map. Although this information was current at the time of publication, it can't compete with real-time traffic reports or with the most recent data for your GPS device.

and

One or more side trips. These cover a wide range of distances and themes; not all of the latter are strictly equine.

Chapter 1

General Recommendations

for Barrier Island Horse Watching

Wild-horse observation builds indelible memories and deeper understanding of many things, not just horses. For those of us who spend too much time indoors juggling deadlines and commitments, it is extremely therapeutic to hike a fertile salt marsh and fall into the rhythms of tide and season, sunrise and sunset, footfalls, breathing, sea breezes, and heartbeats. Horse-watching is an activity that can be enjoyed by all, from serious naturalists and adventurous hikers to

Regulations aside, watching horses or any other wildlife from a distance keeps the animals from becoming overly tame. Binoculars and telephoto lenses allow the observer to witness routine and drama in great detail without jeopardizing safety or affecting natural behavior.

I was photographing Dominic, an alpha male on Shackleford Banks, NC, from a presumably safe distance (about 70 feet) with a telephoto lens, when he suddenly locked his eye on me, turned and galloped toward me, jaws open to bite. I ran, and he dropped the chase.

time-challenged sightseers. Even those unable to walk great distances, including toddlers, pregnant women, and disabled persons, can enjoy horse-watching. Active people with no physical limitations can gain access to any of the East Coast islands that support wild horse populations and hike to their remote reaches.

All the stewards of east coast herds have rules against petting and harassing the horses. Assateague Island National Seashore requires visitors to stay 10 feet away from the wild horses—about a car's length. Failure to do so can result in a $175 fine per incident. It is also unlawful to pull off the roadway to watch or photograph the horses. Cumberland Island NS does not specify a distance, but imposes fines on anyone who harasses or makes contact with wildlife.

In and around Corolla, NC, it is illegal to approach within 50 feet (about one and one half school bus lengths) of a wild horse, and transgressors are fined $500 per incident. The penalty for being within 50 feet of the horses is the same whether you approached the horse or the horse approached you. If you see people approaching, tormenting, or feeding the horses, please call the Corolla Wild Horse Fund at 252-453-8002.

"It wasn't me!" A pony appears to feign indifference by examining something on the ground while the Park Service ranger approaches a car. This family earned a $175 fine for feeding ponies from their vehicle. When visitors lure horses into the road for a treat or a pat, they are much more likely to cause a deadly accident.

Feeding, touching, teasing, frightening, or intentionally disturbing *any* wildlife on Shackleford Banks, NC, can result in a $5,000 fine and 6 months in jail. The National Park Service recommends keeping "a safe distance of 50 feet" from the horses, but that isn't always enough. I was about 70 feet from a stallion who was annoyed with a mare when he suddenly turned and charged me! Fortunately, he dropped pursuit when I ran. If he had injured me, I might have lain undiscovered on an island with few visitors and patchy cell phone reception until the ferry came to pick me up the next day—if the ferry captain sent someone out to look for me.

Respect these horses as wildlife. If a horse approaches you, move away. If she follows, move away again. The goal should be to watch the horses, appreciate them, and learn from them, but not interact with them. If what you are doing interferes with the horse's natural behavior, you need to change what you are doing.

At the Maryland end of Assateague, ponies range everywhere, and it is usually easy to observe them even if your time is limited. Assateague has paved roads that allow visitors to see wildlife from their vehicles and trails to suit both the meek and the daring. In the summer, the

Even people with limited mobility can enjoy horse-watching at Assateague Island National Seashore in Maryland. The author took this photograph from the road through an open car window.

horses often take to the beach to escape the heat and biting insects, dozing on the shore alongside beach umbrellas and sand castles. On cool, breezy days or in light rain they are often on the marsh. We usually drive up and down the roads until we spot ponies, then hike in for a better look. The Maryland end of Assateague offers both developed sites and wilderness camping options, including locations accessible by kayak or canoe, but be forewarned that summer visitors must reserve sites months in advance. Prime spots beside the ocean are often reserved a year in advance.

On the Virginia end of Assateague, sometimes you can see ponies from your vehicle on the way to the beach. As of this writing, the Chincoteague Natural History Association runs a 90-minute bus tour from the Chincoteague National Wildlife Refuge Visitor Center to the north end of the Refuge, but locals inform me that it might close in 2016. Numerous tour-boat operators offer excursions that bring the visitor relatively close to the ponies and other wildlife. Ponies come and go on their own schedule and can be difficult to spot. The Woodland Trail on the south end of Assateague provides a platform overlooking part of the pony range, and ponies may be seen grazing in the distance.

Shackleford Banks, NC, is easily accessible by active, able people for hiking, beachcombing, and camping; but the island has no buildings and is not negotiable by wheelchair, walker, or crutches.

Pony Penning week (the last week in July) is the optimal time to see the Chincoteague ponies up close, albeit in a more domesticated setting. Each July the entire herd is corralled and swum across a channel to the island of Chincoteague so the foals can be sold at auction. While they are penned on Assateague and at the Chincoteague Fairgrounds, you can watch their clashes and camaraderie up close.

On the Currituck Banks of North Carolina, the Corolla Wild Horse Fund offers a 2–4-hour off-road vehicular tour with a wild horse specialist. When you take your tour with this organization, every dollar you spend directly benefits the wild horses themselves. The Corolla Wild Horse Fund has a museum in Corolla Village and offers seasonal

In and near the marshlands, mosquitoes are a merciless scourge during the warm season on all of the East Coast horse ranges, and often bite ruthlessly though autumn. The thick hair of the horses offers some protection from the bloodthirsty mosquitoes, but biting flies torment both people and horses from May to October. Around midday, horses often rest near deep, open water, where cool winds thwart biting insects.

events such as pony rides on a trained once-wild horse. Commercial tour companies also take groups and individuals north of Corolla Village to view wild horses. You can also walk or drive the beach yourself or rent a beach house and watch wild horses graze in the yard or scratch themselves on your bumper.

On Ocracoke Island, NC, you can observe horses safely and with minimal effort from a handicapped-accessible boardwalk and viewing platform. This herd has not run wild since the 1950s, but its ancestors lived free on the island for hundreds of years. The roadside Ocracoke Pony Pen is managed by the National Park Service, and ranger programs illuminate the history and management concerns of this unique herd.

The herds on Shackleford Banks, NC, and those ranging on the Rachel Carson Estuarine Reserve off Beaufort, NC, are accessible only by water. Concessionaires and guides can show you the herds via tour boat, or drop you off at either location to explore on your own. Both islands are undeveloped, with no water, rest rooms, or other facilities, so visitors should prepare to hike unassisted. If you want to learn from the experts, Cape Lookout National Seashore offers horse tours with

Wild horses escape the onslaught of biting insects by catching breezes on the beach, a strategy that also works well for people. During a heat wave, horses often nap on the beach, relatively safe from ferocious flies.

the staff biologist. These excursions fill quickly, so call well in advance to book a spot. The herd at Cedar Island ranges on private land, but you can sometimes glimpse the horses when you take a beach ride at Outer Banks Riding Stable, or if you follow the shoreline in your own boat.

Cumberland Island, GA, is accessible only by concessionaire ferry or charter boat. Horses frequently graze near the ferry dock and may be immediately visible when you arrive. Otherwise, you can usually find them grazing in colorful groups if you hike toward the ruins of the Dungeness compound. It is about a mile from the first ferry dock to the beach, some of it deep sand, and all of it potentially very hot in summer. Cumberland Island offers both developed and wilderness camping options.

At any of the locations, hikers and campers should be prepared for the harshness of the barrier island environment. In the warm season, intense sunlight fries skin quickly, especially when reflected by sea and sand, and sunburn is a hazard even on cloudy days and in winter (when the earth is about 3.7 million miles closer to the sun than in summer). Frequent applications of sunscreen with a high SPF can save a vacation and lessen the risk of subsequent skin cancer. Summertime heat can be scorching, leaving tent campers no respite. At many of the destinations, shopping excursions or midday movies can bring air-conditioned relief when the heat becomes oppressive. If you visit the islands before

Ponies range though the state park and national seashore campgrounds on the Maryland part of Assateague. Anything edible (and some things that are not!) left at campsites become fair game for hungry ponies. Like hooved raccoons, they open coolers, collapse tents, and sort through trash bags for tasty morsels.

10 a.m. or after 3 p.m., you will find the indirect sun to be kinder, and the crowds at the beach thinner.

Barrier islands are home to the most dangerous animals on earth. For that matter, so is your back yard. East coast mosquitoes are host to a wide array of life-threatening diseases, including West Nile virus and several types of encephalitis.

Some people are "mosquito magnets" owing to a quirk of genetics. Mosquitoes are particularly attracted to people who have high concentrations of steroids or cholesterol on their skin, have high blood levels of uric acid, or exhale large quantities of carbon dioxide. Larger people and pregnant women emit more carbon dioxide, which attracts mosquitoes from great distances. Movement, heat, and the lactic acid present in exertional sweat also attract mosquitoes.

DEET is among the most effective mosquito repellents, and it has been in use for more than 40 years. It has a good safety record if not grossly overused. A repellent with 23.8% DEET gives adequate protection for about five hours. Picaridin, the active ingredient in Cutter® Advanced, has been used worldwide since 1998. Picaridin is as effective as DEET, but is odorless and feels lighter and cleaner. Parents can safely apply repellents with DEET concentrations of 10% or less and those that contain picaridin on babies over 2 months old.

Metofluthrin, sold as DeckMate Mosquito RepellentTM, comes in a paper strip, which can be placed in outdoor areas such as campsites and decks. Alternatively, it can be worn as a cartridge clipped onto a belt

Camping on Shackleford Banks in a backpacking tent pitched on a dune afforded wonderful views of grazing horses and the Cape Lookout Lighthouse. Drinking water was the heaviest thing in my pack, but I was glad I brought more than I thought I would need. Extra-long stakes penetrated deeply into the sand and anchored the tent against wind gusts.

or clothing, the repellent wafted by a battery-powered fan into the air surrounding the wearer.

Natural alternatives include soybean oil-based repellents, citronella, cedar, peppermint, lemongrass, and geranium. These natural oils are somewhat effective, but must be reapplied every hour or two. Oil of eucalyptus products, available under the Repel® brand name, may confer protection similar to repellents with low concentrations of DEET and can be used by children older than 3. While Avon® Skin So Soft has not been proven to repel mosquitoes, its Skin So Soft Bug Guard line, which includes products containing picaridin and IR3535, can be effective.

Surprisingly, mosquitoes feed primarily on nectar, which provides adequate nutrition for their bodily maintenance, but not enough for reproduction. When a female is ready to reproduce, she must ingest a meal of blood to support the development of her 200–300 eggs. Males do not drink blood. Two to three days after emergence from her pupa as a new adult, a female mosquito takes her first blood meal. She mates only once and stores the sperm in her body so that she may lay fertile eggs several times. She lays her eggs in ponds, puddles, containers— anything that holds water. Shady, dark water high in organic content is preferred over clear, sunny, or flowing water. Eggs are deposited just above the water surface, and they are stimulated to hatch when flooded by water warmer than 60°F. If the water is cool, the eggs remain dormant and can even hatch the following spring. Larvae live in the water for one or more weeks, depending on water temperature and the amount of food present.

The intensity of mosquito harassment varies from year to year and from season to season. Mosquitoes are most virulent during hot, wet years and are minimally vexing during dry years, in prolonged cool weather, and on windy days. When barrier island mosquitoes are moderate, repellent will keep them at bay. During a bad mosquito season, however, they descend in a black veil and envelop potential victims in a frenzy of bloodlust. There have been times when I set out along a trail saturated in insect repellent, intending a half-day hike, only to run back to the car minutes later, swatting frantically at the voracious scourge that alighted on my skin.

Hikers must carry adequate water and drink it often. Especially in summer, it is easy to become dehydrated while hiking, and potable water sources do not exist in the wilder areas.

Appropriate footwear is essential for anyone who decides to brave the backcountry in search of horses (or anything else). Hiking boots are best, but work boots or sneakers with good treads are acceptable. Hikers who plan to cover long distances should bring a blister kit. Barefoot hikers are vulnerable to crabs, rays, jellyfish, sharp shells, and broken bottles. The sandy areas behind the dune line are studded with sandburs and sandspurs—round, prickly pods that are virtually unnoticeable until bare feet find them. My much-loved Vibram 5-Finger® shoes—which offer some protection while retaining the advantages of bare feet—were easily penetrated by sandburs and cacti on Cumberland Island, forcing me to stop every few strides to pull spines out of my feet. On Currituck Banks, they were practical and comfortable, though an encounter with prickly pear cacti would have proved painful.

Poison ivy is an important food source for deer and ponies, but it is a bane to hikers and campers. All parts of the plant can cause a rash in all seasons. Poison ivy accidentally burned in a campfire can trigger a severe allergic reaction in anyone exposed to the smoke.

The sea is most turbulent during and following a storm. When the surf is rough, swimmers are frequently tumbled by the waves, sustaining sand abrasions, shoulder dislocations, and even broken necks. Riptides can pull a swimmer out to sea. To escape the current, swim

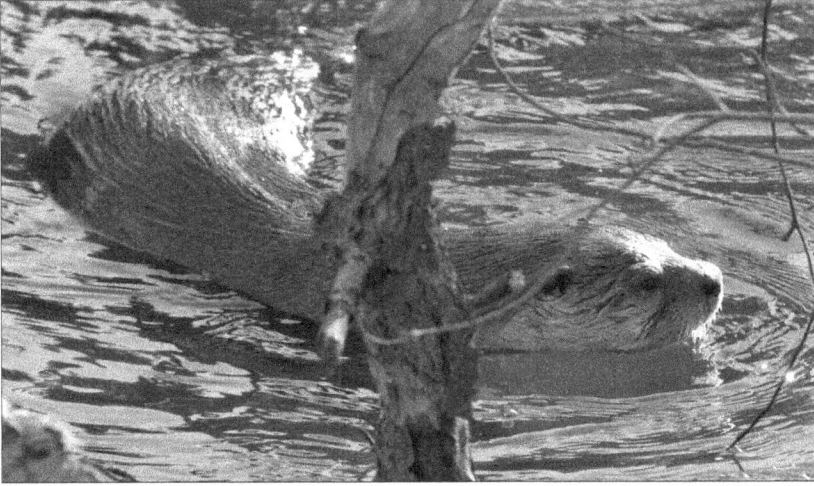

River otters romp in creeks on many of the East Coast barrier islands. This otter was one of a pair the author photographed on the Chincoteague National Wildlife Refuge. Any mammal can carry rabies—another good reason to observe wildlife from a safe distance.

parallel to shore until you are free, then swim back to the beach. If you fight the current, you may become exhausted and drown.

Tideline treasures are most readily found following a storm. Shells, beach glass, and all manner of odds and ends are most abundant on the beach after the angry tide has ebbed.

When camping on barrier islands, anchor your tents with extra-long stakes. The standard variety uproots easily from loose sand. Improperly secured tents can catch the gusty barrier island winds and behave like giant kites, soaring great distances while unattended. (My kids have fond memories of fishing our tent out of a duck pond on Hatteras.) Car campers should also consider bringing a screen tent to provide blessed shade.

Often visitors do not realize that wild horses can be dangerous. They may appear as tame as their counterparts at a petting zoo, but these are 600-plus-pound animals that are used to doing as they please. If it pleases them to take proffered treats and enjoy scratching, they stand quietly. Then with unpredictable suddenness, two horses may squabble over a tidbit, catching the person in the middle with a powerful kick capable of breaking bones. Fingers may be fractured by crushing teeth when horses bite the hand that feeds them. Domestic horses are carefully trained not to bite, kick, or trample people, but wild horses receive no such training and have their own agendas.

It is also possible to catch serious diseases from close contact with wild horses. The flies that feed on horse blood before biting humans can spread encephalitis. The horses themselves can transmit rabies. Foxes, bats, and raccoons pose the greatest risk; but about 100 cases of rabies in horses and burros are reported every year in the United States, and the mortality rate is 100 percent. Horse-to-human transmission has not been documented, but it is possible. The ponies carry deer ticks, which in turn can carry Lyme disease, and these ticks easily migrate from horse to human (or from horse to underbrush to human). Dr. Ronald Keiper writes that a pony-watcher can pick up 40–60 ticks an hour. On one trip I disregarded the no-contact edict to comfort a dying foal abandoned by his herd. Without a cell phone, I could not summon help. He spent his last hours with his head in my lap. Back on the mainland, taking a much-needed shower, I discovered five ticks implanted in the skin of my abdomen and another two on my arm.

Deer ticks are tiny. The nymphs are only about the size of a fleck of pepper. Ideally, hikers should wear long, light-colored clothing and inspect themselves and one another for ticks regularly. Ticks are easy to miss, and an infected one can transmit Lyme disease if it attaches. I caught Lyme disease myself from a deer tick while photographing horses on Assateague. Many infected people never see a tick or a tick bite, and 20–50 percent do not develop the characteristic bulls-eye rash. Symptoms of Lyme include flu-like discomforts, headaches, disabling fatigue, palpitations, and painful or swollen joints.

The East Coast barrier islands present endless opportunities for people to see horses living wild. Most of the herds are tolerant of people, and the visitor can get close enough to watch them foraging, playing, and reinforcing social bonds. The seashore is an idyllic setting, and many other family-friendly activities are available near all the wild horse islands.

Wild horses inspire hot arguments, and with each population the question resurfaces—should they be allowed to remain on these islands, living as their ancestors have done for hundreds of years? Their destiny is in our hands. Whatever we choose to do or not to do will determine their fate. Having spent 20 years studying and observing the wild herds of the Atlantic coast—as well as some herds in the Western states—I have come to believe that these animals have value simply because they are wild horses, and they are valuable to us because they reawaken the wildness in our own souls.

Side Trip 1

East Coast Greenway

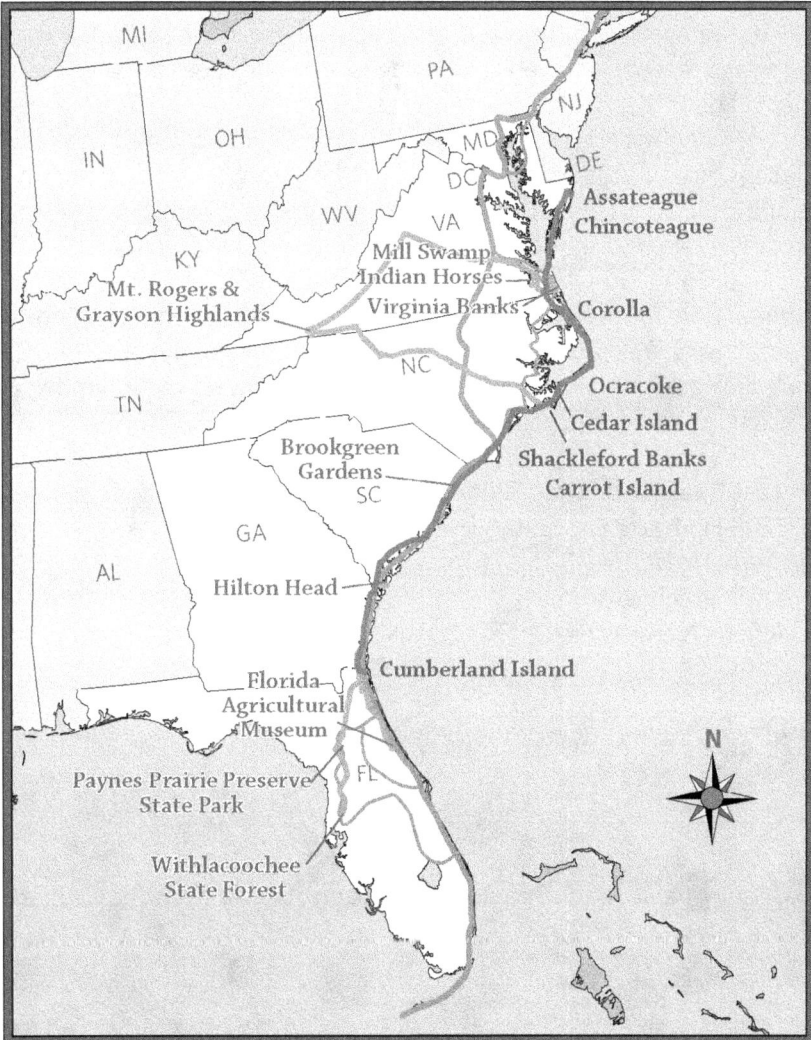

The East Coast Greenway, shown here with the Atlantic Wild Horse Trail, is an evolving system of hard-surface routes for cyclists and pedestrians that combines features of the Appalachian Trail and the Interstate Highway system. Since its inception in 1991, it has grown to nearly 3,000 miles of actual and proposed routes from Calais, ME, to Key West, FL. At this writing, about 27 percent of its length—including purpose-built sections, pre-existing park infrastructure, railroad rights-of-way, and historic canal towpaths—is free of vehicular traffic. Off-road components are mostly discontinuous for now, and some are as yet unpaved. The "interim" remainder of the ECG coincides with highways, streets, and vehicular bridges, many of them busy, some of them in densely populated urban areas.

The Greenway crosses the Atlantic Wild Horse Trail in several places, most notably St. Marys, GA, the gateway to Cumberland Island. It also passes near Corolla, Shackleford Banks, and other horsey destinations. The ECG is a wonderful resource worthy of exploration if you want to walk, run, hike, or bike. If you add other intersecting or nearby routes, such as the Captain John Smith Chesapeake Trail, a water route with interpretive buoys; the 1,400-mile Florida Trail; and the equestrian trails covered in Appendix 2, you'll have enough potential adventures for several lifetimes.

East Coast Greenway Alliance
5315 Highgate Dr., Suite 105
Durham, NC 27713
www.greenway.org
info@greenway.org

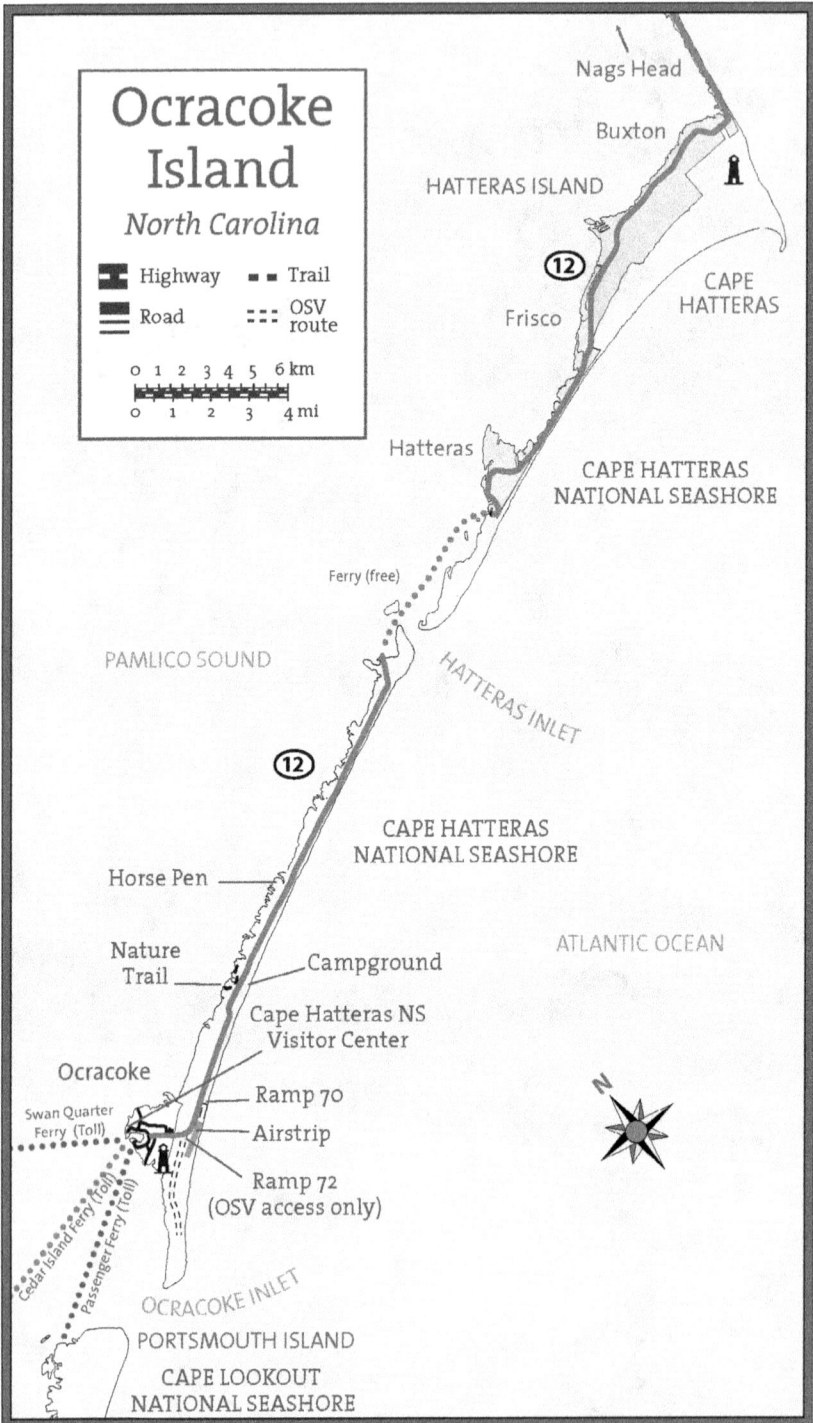

Ocracoke Island
North Carolina

Highway ·· Trail
Road ··· OSV route

0 1 2 3 4 5 6 km
0 1 2 3 4 mi

Nags Head

Buxton

HATTERAS ISLAND

CAPE HATTERAS

12

Frisco

CAPE HATTERAS NATIONAL SEASHORE

Hatteras

Ferry (free)

PAMLICO SOUND

HATTERAS INLET

12

CAPE HATTERAS NATIONAL SEASHORE

Horse Pen

ATLANTIC OCEAN

Nature Trail

Campground

Cape Hatteras NS Visitor Center

Ocracoke

Ramp 70

Swan Quarter Ferry (Toll)

Airstrip

Cedar Island Ferry (Toll)

Passenger Ferry (Toll)

Ramp 72 (OSV access only)

OCRACOKE INLET

PORTSMOUTH ISLAND

CAPE LOOKOUT NATIONAL SEASHORE

Chapter 2

Ocracoke

North Carolina

On March 22, 2010, a Banker mare named Spirit made national news by giving birth to a fuzzy bay-and-white filly named Paloma on the remote Outer Banks island of Ocracoke. The filly's instant celebrity went well beyond the public's fascination with whiskery new foals. Before 2009, the Ocracoke herd mostly comprised elderly horses and those unsuitable for breeding. It appeared that this historic herd was spiraling toward inevitable extinction. Under the advice of Dr. Sue Stuska of the National Park Service, two stallions and two mares from Shackleford Banks arrived to invigorate the genome with new bloodlines from a very old breed. When Spirit became romantically involved with Wenzel, a diminutive bay Shackleford stud, the result was Paloma. Since then, the herd has seen the births of Rayo, full brother to Paloma in 2012; Capitan, a chestnut colt to Shackleford mare Jitterbug and Corolla stallion Alonzo in 2013; and in 2015, Sacajawea, a Shackleford mare, foaled a bay filly named Hazelnut to Rayo.

Free-roaming Banker horses were an integral part of the culture of Ocracoke for hundreds of years. Historically, these horses were born in the wild and spent their lives running free, deliberately handled by human beings only during annual gathers.

July Fourth pony pennings were a long-anticipated celebration, a festival of hard work and hard play for the Ocracokers and the visitors that traveled great distances to watch. Each Ocracoke family had its own brand, and foals were matched to mothers and emblazoned with an owner's logo. They were beautiful animals with long, flowing manes and tails, easy-going, smooth-gaited, and easy to train.

Gary Dunbar, in his 1958 book *Historical Geography of the North Carolina Outer Banks*, wrote, "The Ocracoke ponies are quite useful as a tourist attraction. Not to be classed with 'banks ponies' and 'tackies,' these horses have recently been improved and are eminently photogenic." "Recently been improved" denotes addition of some outside

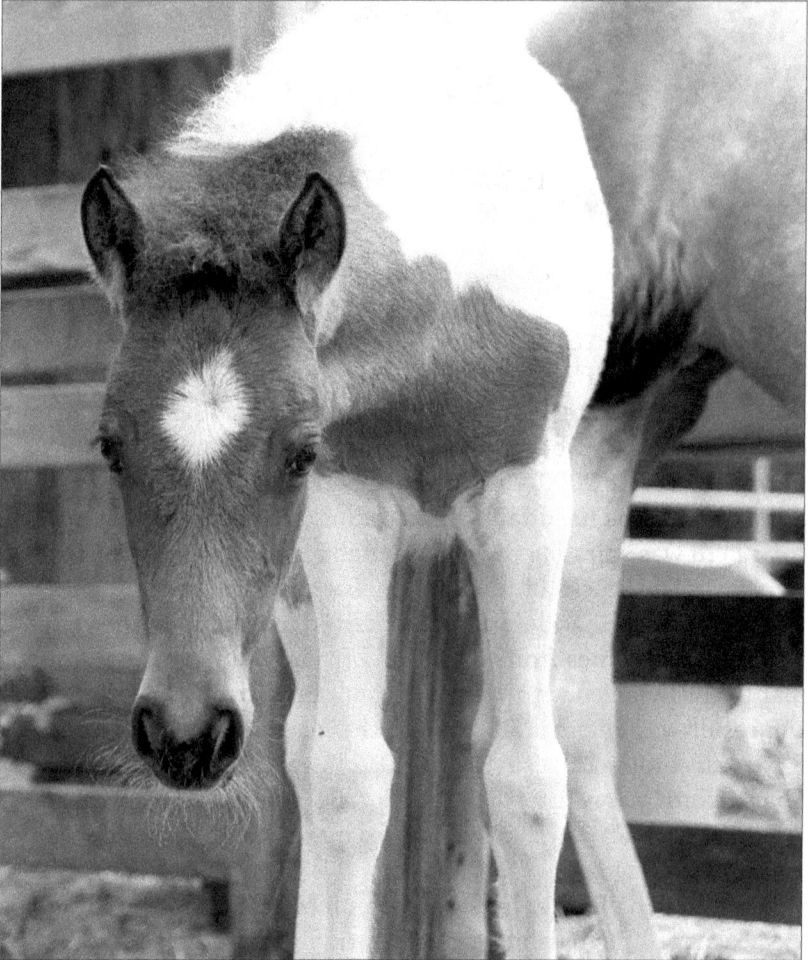

Spirit, born to the Ocracoke herd in 2010, represents a cross between two strains of Banker horse. Her sire is a Shackleford, and her mother is an Ocracoke. The Ocracoke lineage has been infused with the genes of outside breeds in recent decades and is no longer pure Banker.

genes—evidently non-Banker blood was added to the herd sometime before this.

Traditionally, the annual round-up began on July 3, when a handful of Ocracoke's skilled horsemen would ride north to where free-roaming horses grazed in places with such fanciful names as Scrag Cedars, Great Swash, and Tar Hole Plains. The horsemen would camp overnight near the sound, and in the morning the round-up would begin.

Ocracoke horses in the wild, circa 1950s. Courtesy of Ocracoke Preservation Society.

The men swept through the ranges, grouping horses together in one great drive—hundreds of horses damp with sweat and fighting among themselves in the scorching heat of July. Horse Pen Point was the destination for many years, though other locations were also favored throughout the 20th century.

Buyers sometimes preferred to have their horses ridden by the cowboys to accustom them to handling before their stressful shipment to the mainland. The riders obliged swiftly and effectively. They would chase the horse into an individual pen, crowd him against the rail, grasp his tail through the fence, tie his head to a post, and place a blindfold over his eyes. Then the men could work a saddle onto his back.

A cowboy would mount to take the ride. Off came the blindfold, and the horse was released. The frantic pony would run, buck, pivot, twist, rear, and sunfish, but the tenacious cowboys could not be dislodged. At last the pony would decide that fighting was futile and acquiesce to carrying a rider.

Homer Howard, a renowned Ocracoke cowboy, was celebrated for his skill in breaking the willful, powerful wild stallions that ruled the herds. Homer would slip between the mares and youngsters until he was close enough to vault to the back of a stallion with a sudden leap. With one strong hand clamping off the airway just above the stallion's nostrils and the other hand clutching the pony's thick mane, Homer would stay aboard despite the stallion's indignant, infuriated bucking.

After about a half-hour, the stallion would admit defeat. At the first sign of submission, Homer Howard would release his grip. If the stal-

Above and below: images from the Ocracoke pony penning, July 1939. From the photograph collection of the N.C. Department of Conservation and Development in the N.C. State Archives.

An Ocracoke boy and his Banker Horse, circa 1950s. Photo courtesy of the Ocracoke Preservation Society.

lion resumed his battle, Homer would again cut off his wind. It did not take long for the stallion to realize that Homer would stop tormenting him as long as he tolerated a rider on his back. It was an exciting display to watch, and Homer Howard's stallion-breaking was often one of the highlights of pony penning.

Most of the time, though, Banker horses were trained in a gentler fashion, tempted with sweets, petting, and scratching the itchy spots. Sometimes the first mounting was accomplished in the sound, with the horse belly-deep in water. This way, the horse's movements were

In the 1950s, Ocracoke was home to the world's only mounted Boy Scout troop. The boys would frequently race down the beach, often without a saddle, seemingly at one with their mounts. Photo courtesy of Ocracoke Preservation Society.

restricted, and a thrown rider would meet with a soft landing. Horses gentled before riding was attempted often put up no resistance.

Shipping the horses off Ocracoke was not always easy. Ocracoke is thirty miles from the mainland, and the ponies were transported on flat barges, freight boats, and fishing boats. In one incident, two horses broke into the engine room of a fishing boat when a storm panicked them. Sometimes the animals would fall off the barges and drown.

The ponies were pesky at times, but their presence was enjoyed by most of the Ocracokers. The ponies would sometimes wander into town looking for handouts. One apparently developed a taste for fried fish and would reach his head into open windows to devour the family supper. They would intrude into gardens and devour the vegetables if the gates were left open. Occasionally a family would be awakened long before dawn by an odd noise only to find an itchy pony scratching himself on the corner of the house. Occasionally a herd would stampede through town.

Boy Scout Troop 290 parading down the beach before admiring onlookers. Photo courtesy of Ocracoke Preservation Society.

In the early 1900s, locals added horses of other breeds, mostly stallions, to the free-roaming population to expand the gene pool and improve the breed. Homer Howard's personal mount, a gray Arabian named White Dandy, reportedly sired foals from Ocracoke mares.

In 1925, David Keppel brought a tall dun English Thoroughbred stallion to Ocracoke and kept him in a study pen for several years for breeding to Ocracoke mares. In 1922, the young stallion had sold at Tattersall's Bloodstock Auction House in central London for 61 guineas, and was subsequently imported to America. His foals were popular, and most were sold to mainlanders for riding and polo.

In 1938, more spectators than ever flocked to the pony penning to bid on these foals. At this time there were fewer than 200 ponies on Ocracoke, half of them wild, the rest broken and trained. Jeannetta Henning, who helped to manage the herd in the 1970s, maintains that the blood of Beeswax has been lost to Ocracoke over time, and none of his Thoroughbred genes remain in today's Banker herd.

The Coast Guard used Banker ponies to patrol the beaches during World War II. But the war years of the 1940s marked the beginning of the end of Ocracoke pony pennings. The wild ponies were left alone during the war years, and after the war, pony pennings were never as big or exciting. The number of ponies on the island was declining rapidly as well, from 300–400 in the 1800s to 70 in 1956, to an all-time low of nine individuals in 1976.

Major Marvin Howard retired from his military career to his home on Ocracoke Island and organized the first and only mounted Boy Scout troop in the world. Major Howard, who found great satisfaction in working with both children and horses, founded Troop 290 in 1954, and most of the boys on the island enthusiastically joined. For the next decade, Howard served as Scoutmaster to about fourteen boys at a time and advised them in the care and training of their once-wild mounts.

For the freckle-faced, barefoot boys of Ocracoke, the Scout troop and the ponies were the focus of their lives. Each boy began by selecting a wild pony to catch, train and ride. Each pony, though living free, technically had an owner. The price was $50 per pony, a steep sum for a young boy on a remote island in the 1950s. Fortunately, there were jobs available for any boy willing to work hard mowing lawns or assisting fishermen with the day's catch.

Usually two boys set out after the chosen pony, which had no desire to be captured. The herds evaded the boys at every turn, often venturing out into the water or the muddy marshes to escape. The preferred mount was a stallion, even though (or maybe because!) young stallions were the most difficult to capture and train. Stallions in general have four things on their minds—dominance, mating, looking out for predators or threats to the herd, and satisfying bodily needs such as hunger and thirst. Gelding a colt allows him to focus his attention on his rider's wishes and makes him more tractable. Most male horses are gelded young, but not the mounts of these boys.

It is a tribute to their skills as horsemen that they were able to ride these once-wild stallions bareback in a group. The feisty ponies were used to having their own way and often resisted domestication, especially at first. Stories abound among current residents. One time, so the tale goes, a rowdy stallion aptly named "Little Teach" bucked a scout from his back, kicking him in the head for emphasis. A vacationing doctor, in a slightly inebriated condition, successfully sewed up the scalp wound with 44 stitches.

The Scouts followed many time-honored Ocracoke techniques of horse breaking, including mounting blindfolded horses as they stood belly-deep in the sound. They experimented with filling an old pair of pants with sand and tying it around the pony so that he could expend his bucking energy on an inanimate object rather than a scout. Unfortunately, the ponies usually dislodged the pants and trampled them. The Scouts realized that it was best not to reinforce trampling a rider.

Howard coached the boys in training methods and horsemanship, and they met most of their Scouting requirements on horseback. The boys also had the opportunity to show off their skills at the Pirates' Jamboree, featuring races and other tests of riding ability. Annually the troop would compete in the horse races held on the beach at Buxton and at Hatteras. This was no small undertaking.

The boys would set out early, for they had to ride a total of 26 miles to get there. To cross Hatteras Inlet, eighteen boys would lead their stallions onto the little ferry and hold them on the open deck for the 40-minute crossing, while the boat rocked and groaned underfoot, a situation that would panic most other horses. After the long ride to Buxton, the boys would race in four quarter-mile heats, often besting stiff competition that included Arabians and Quarter Horses.

About 500–600 head of cattle still roamed Ocracoke Island during this period, and the scouts became skilled at cattle round-ups and pony pennings, showing off their superb horsemanship skills for the benefit of the visitors. Branding was done with a hot iron. The fee for filing a brand with the County Register of Deeds was the same as it had been for 200 years—ten cents.

The Scouts also helped around town and served as mounted honor guards for the Coast Guard. During the summer, the boys helped keep Ocracoke's mosquitoes at bay by spraying the marshes with insecticide.

Celebrated O'cokers, "from-heres" and "come-heres," include

- Steel tycoon Sam Jones, who built many of the island's largest structures and had himself buried at Springer's Point beside his favorite horse, an Ocracoke pony named Ikie D

- Charles Temple, an English teacher at the K–12 Ocracoke School, who won the first *Jeopardy!* Teacher Tournament in 2011

- The pirate Edward Teach, a.k.a. Blackbeard. Although Blackbeard lost his head in Ocracoke Inlet, he wasn't a North Carolinian, he lived in the colony less than a year, and he spent very little time on the Outer Banks alive or dead.

Astride sure-footed marsh ponies, they were able to penetrate the wide flats of muck far more easily than anyone else.

The Ocracoke mounted scouts often captured national attention. They were featured in *Boy's Life* magazine and in a children's novel titled *Wild Pony Island*, by Steven Meader.

Aside from the $50 investment to purchase the pony, it cost the boys little to maintain their mounts. They could be released when not being used and caught later. They remained sleek and well-fleshed on a diet of marsh grass. Most of the boys opted to build stalls in their back yards to keep their horses close at hand, however. It cost about twelve dollars a month to feed and house a back-yard pony, and the boys earned the funds by working odd jobs around town.

When the boys attempted to supplement their horses' diet with sweet feed, a tasty grain-and-molasses mixture that most horses relish, the ponies were confused. The boys initially had to place it in their mouths until they noticed the sweet flavor and realized that it was food. It was not long before they discovered the pleasure of other flavors as well. Many Scout ponies developed a taste for soda pop.

The horses often had a close bond with their owners, and when set loose to run free would visit them in the village to seek human companionship. Many learned to respond to the sound of their owner's whistle.

When Cape Hatteras National Seashore took over Ocracoke Island, it was a mixed blessing. The new status of National Park would allow Ocracoke to remain wild and beautiful and would offer some protection against the condominiums and tourist attractions that had overtaken many East Coast beaches. But the Park Service did not want free-roaming horses competing with the native wildlife that it was established to protect. Cattle, pigs, sheep, and goats that roamed the island were removed by the late 1950s, and the Park Service saw no reason why horses should be treated any differently

Ocracokers loved their horses, though, and asserted that free-roaming ponies were an important element of the character of the island. Lawmakers argued that not enough was known about their past to support claims that they had historical value. There were high emotions on both sides of the argument.

Major Howard put relentless energy into saving the Ocracoke horses. His family had been involved with Banker horses since the 1700s. His primary argument was the lack of juvenile delinquency on Ocra-

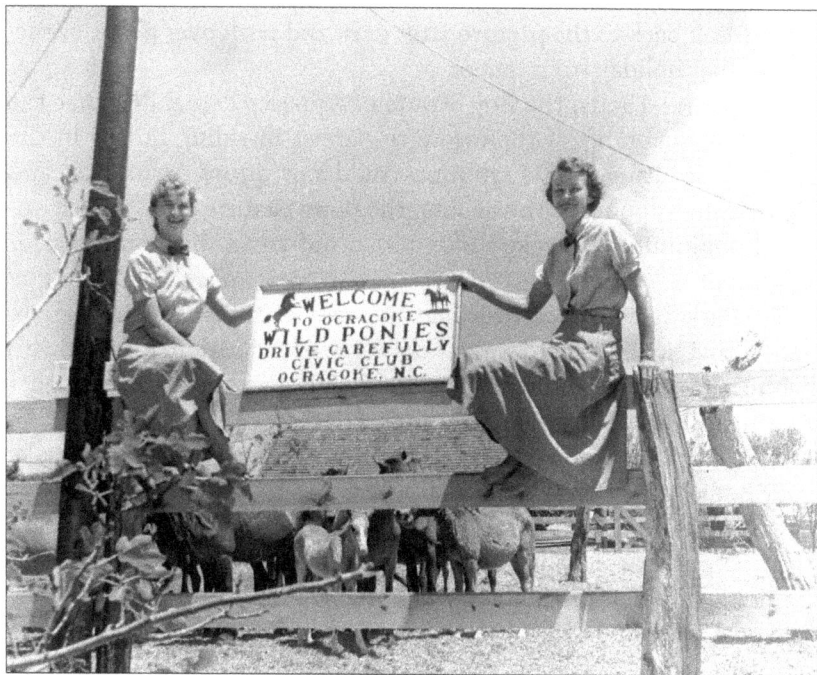

Banker ponies safe behind a sturdy fence, circa 1959. From the Aycock Brown Collection, courtesy of the Outer Banks History Center.

coke, which he saw as a direct result of involvement with the ponies.

When NC Highway 12 was opened on Ocracoke in 1957, the posted speed limit of 50 mph posed a new danger to the horses. The scouts petitioned to fence a large pasture for the horses as a sort of compromise—the horses would not roam entirely free anymore, but they would remain on the island to be enjoyed as a reminder of Ocracoke's bygone days.

The Park Service eventually granted a special-use permit and provided fence posts. Money for fencing was raised, along with the funds for the first year of supplemental feeding. The State of North Carolina also contributed funds toward the ponies' new lifestyle for the first year. The animals were finally penned in 1959.

It was a fairly easy task to fence the herd, but getting them to stay fenced was a different story entirely. When the ponies wearied of confinement, they simply knocked over the posts and broke the wire. The Scouts would be released from school to recover the ponies and mend fences. The scouts enjoyed this task—so much, in fact, that they would often sneak back to the pasture after dark and push over posts, ensuring another holiday from school.

In the mid-1960s, the Boy Scouts of America demanded that the boys carry insurance if they were to persist in riding horses in the name of Scouting. These children could not afford insurance, and without the support of the Scouts, the pony pasture grew too expensive to maintain. Ocracoke's mounted scout troop dismounted after only about ten years.

The Park Service took over management of the ponies in the late 60s. By this time, the herd was on the verge of extinction, having dwindled to a low of nine individuals in 1976. This rare breed was in danger of being lost entirely.

In 1973, Park Ranger Jim Henning was transferred to Ocracoke from Bodie (pronounced "Body") Island. He took an interest in the magnificent herd stallion, also named Jim, and with his wife, Jeannetta, whole-heartedly devoted himself to the resurrection of the herd. The ponies were a sorry bunch when the Hennings first arrived. They were malnourished, full of parasites, and in dire need of veterinary care. Dr. Jasper Needham, a veterinarian on Hatteras Island, vaccinated the animals, trimmed hooves to resolve gait abnormalities, and dewormed them.

Internal parasites are more of a problem for domestic horses than for their wild counterparts. Locals say the marsh grass diet serves as a natural wormer and is effective also for cattle. Most kinds of intestinal parasite are spread by manure. When horses are kept penned, they defecate in areas where others are likely to pick up worm eggs while grazing. Wild horses graze over a wider area, and manure is not encountered as frequently, although horses, especially foals, sometimes intentionally eat the droppings of other horses.

Chutes and pens were built to make veterinary care less of a rodeo event. Before the chutes were constructed, dewormer medication was given in a large trough mixed with food. The horses would compete over the offering. Often the dominant animals received too much, the subordinates not enough. The chutes allowed dewormer to be administered in precise doses via oral syringes.

With the dwindling of the herd, fertility declined. In one five-year span, no foals were born at all. The last remaining Banker stallion was genetically incompatible with three of his mares. These three would deliver healthy foals, but antibodies in their colostrum, or first milk, would attack and destroy the newborn's red blood cells, in a condition

Park Ranger Laura Michaels shares a quiet moment with Lawton Howard, a sociable pinto gelding.

called neonatal isoerythrolysis. At the time, the Park Service concluded that this reproductive failure was the result of inbreeding, but its assumption was later proven false. The hematological issue probably arose when outside horses were crossed into the herd, according to equine geneticist Gus Cothran. Blood type incompatibility is less likely in an inbred population because closely related horses tend to have similar blood types.

The Hennings saved three foals by bottle-feeding them, but something more had to be done. To save the herd from extinction, the Park Service brought in an Andalusian stallion named Cubanito. Modern Andalusians embody many of the same Spanish characteristics of the Banker horses and resemble the horses ridden by the Conquistadors. Cubanito was a handsome example of the breed.

Although bringing in outside blood plan resulted in live foals, Cubanito has since been criticized as a choice for this role. As it turns out, Cubanito carried both the genes necessary to perpetuate neonatal isoerythrolysis. When he was bred to the three problem mares, however, the resulting offspring were healthy and robust. The herd was on the increase again, but was no longer true to the original bloodlines.

According to Cothran, Andalusians, like Banker horses, are of Spanish bloodlines. But he writes, "the modern Andalusian is probably not directly related to the ancestors of the Ocracoke horses." The matings amounted to a crossbreeding, moving the genes of the Ocracoke herd away from the original lines. Several Ocracoke horses had been officially accepted by the Spanish Mustang registry, but Cubanito's foals were, as crossbreeds, ineligible for registration. The utilization of a Banker stallion from Currituck Banks or Shackleford would have kept the lines closer to those which their defenders sought to preserve.

They also tried to bring in a horse named Sailor, who was born on Ocracoke and removed to Hatteras by Dale Burrus when the Park Service was selling off Ocracoke stock. The mares wanted nothing to do with Sailor. He did manage to sire three or four foals, all males, but he was never fully accepted by the mares.

In addition to the problem with genetic incompatibility, some of the mares simply did not conceive. Hormone therapy was initiated in 1977, and subsequently three of the four problem mares foaled.

Also at this time a run of sheer bad luck befell the healthy foals. One died at birth. Three became sick and died from overeating. One punctured his foot, probably on a reed out in the marsh, as a newborn. His tendon contracted until he was walking on his fetlock rather than his hoof. He underwent surgery and was fitted with a cast, and he ultimately survived.

With veterinary care, the Banker herd began to recover. One mare reached the astonishing age of 40. That would be about 108 in human years. In her 40th year she gave birth to a foal probably sired by Sailor. (Unlike women, whose fertility is finite, a mare is never too old to conceive.) She was unable to rise after the birth, but she lived another six months, hand-fed by the Hennings, until she finally expired.

In 2015, there were 15 horses in the Ocracoke herd. Because of the infusion of outside bloodlines, members of the original strain stand larger than pure Banker horses, 14 and 15.2 hands at the withers. The pure Banker Shackleford and Corolla horses introduced to the herd are much smaller, standing between 12 and 13 hands.

Visitors who return to Ocracoke annually take pleasure in watching the foals mature into adults. The boardwalk and viewing platform allow even the least adventurous tourist to observe and appreciate these animals.

Ocracoke is a barrier island, surrounded by sea and sound. Consequently, sunrises over the Atlantic and sunsets over the Pamlico Sound can be spectacular.

Ocracoke Island lies directly east of the mouth of the Pamlico River, about 30 miles from the nearest point on the mainland. A link in the barrier island necklace, Ocracoke is separated from Hatteras Island by Hatteras Inlet to the northeast and from Portsmouth Island by Ocracoke Inlet to the southwest. The far northeast section of Ocracoke was once continuous with Hatteras Island.

Ocracoke remains an appealing Outer Banks village, all the more endearing for its inaccessibility. Most visitors arrive by ferry—the one from Hatteras is free. The National Park Service manages most of this island, and as a result it remains devoid of homes and businesses along the entire twelve-mile drive from the ferry to the village.

The handicapped-accessible Ocracoke Pony Pen allows virtually everyone a chance to get a close look at horses descended from herds that once roamed freely on the island. Year-round, the Pony Pen is a popular stopping point and picnic site for thousands of visitors. A brief synopsis of their supposed origins stands mounted on a plaque in front of the paddock. As with all Banker horses, legends, theories, and a few definite facts vie to explain their history. Misinformation appears in print so often that many take it as fact. Much is open to speculation.

Some point to the colony of Lucas Vásquez de Ayllón as a source for the Ocracoke horses, but this is extraordinarily unlikely. In 1526, Ayllón established a settlement at the mouth of what he called the "River Jordan," which is believed by many to be the Cape Fear River of North Carolina. (This is widely disputed, and various sources place it anywhere from the Chesapeake region to Georgia.). The NPS puts Rio Jordan in South Carolina or Georgia.

Ayllón was a judge in Santo Domingo. He'd shown interest in the North American mainland as early as 1521, when he sent an expedition as far as the vicinity of Myrtle Beach, SC, if the reported latitude is accurate (it probably isn't). In June, 1526, he set sail with three large ships (or four, or six), carrying "six hundred persons of both sexes"(or 300), including clergymen and physicians, and black slaves, goats, hogs, chickens, and one hundred (or 80, or 90) Spanish horses. His first stop was the "River Jordan," a body of water that flowed directly into the ocean. Both the Cape Fear River and Winyah Bay, SC, fit this description.

Soon after, his flagship ran aground in the entrance to the river and was destroyed. He explored upriver but did not find a suitable settlement site, so he headed down the coast 40–50 leagues. That measure could have been anywhere from 40 to 150 miles, because the length of a league varied, and the number of leagues was an estimate. Someplace south of his original destination, he founded the settlement of San Miguel in a marshy area on the River Canaan. The natives refused to feed them, then turned hostile. The starving colonists fell sick, and the slaves rebelled. Ayllón died of a fever in October 1526. The weather turned brutally cold, and the survivors fled. About 150 made it back to Hispaniola.

Some suggest that Ayllón's horses were left behind on North Carolina barrier islands after being released there to graze, safe from Indian theft. One argument was that their presence would be like living graffiti proclaiming "Spain was here" and that Spaniards were likely to return and reclaim the land. But even if they did leave horses on islands, the mouth of the Cape Fear River is about 150 miles from Ocracoke, and Ayllón's colony was undoubtedly well south of this. The mouths of the Pamlico or Neuse rivers would be somewhat convenient to Ocracoke, but records indicate that Ayllón's colony was located by a river or estuary that emptied

Three tall tales about Ocracoke (and one disturbing fact):

- Lucky Lindy's visit—Charles Lindbergh reportedly landed the *Spirit of St. Louis* on Ocracoke in 1927 and dined at Cedar Hummock Coast Guard Station. Everyone kept station cook Ben Gaskill in the dark until he finally told the guest, "You look like that Lindbergh fella." After returning from his historic solo trans-Atlantic flight, Lindbergh passed through North Carolina in October 1927 on a triumphal tour of the United States and Mexico. But his log puts him no closer than Greensboro. He retired his famous plane in April 1928 and skipped the dedication of the Wright Memorial in December to avoid upstaging Orville Wright. Whoever dropped by Ocracoke in 1927 wasn't Lindbergh and wasn't in the *Spirit*.

- *Kriegsmarine* shopping excursions—The Third Reich put 10 known saboteurs ashore in the United States—four on Long Island and four in Florida (Operation Pastorius, 1942), two in Maine (Operation Elster, 1944). Authorities caught them all quickly and rewarded six with unmarked graves. Contrary to persistent rumor, If the German submariners massacring Allied seamen just offshore had chugged into Silver Lake for groceries, the local populace would've reacted violently, joined by hundreds of Navy and Coast Guard personnel and civilian government employees.

- America's longest bridge—Bill Bryson evidently didn't visit the island, either, before he traced the leveling of its distinctive dialect back to "1957 when the federal government built Ocracoke a bridge to the mainland" (*I'm a Stranger Here Myself*, 2000).

- A new Bikini—Although the feds have never built a bridge to Ocracoke, in the '40s and '50s they seriously considered making the island part of a nuclear-weapons test range to replace two Pacific islands, Bikini and Enewetak. Evidently without much research, the one-man staff of Project Nutmeg declared the coast between Cape Hatteras and Cape Fear ideal for a 10,000-year sacrifice zone because was uninhabited (it wasn't), prevailing winds blow from the west (they don't), and fallout would hurt nothing important. Alarmed when the Soviet Union crashed the nuclear party and war erupted on the Korean Peninsula, the U.S. government decided to use land in Nevada that it already owned.

directly into the ocean, or a major arm of the ocean. The Pamlico and Neuse do not fit this description. There are no horses at Cape Fear. There are no wild island horses to the south until Cumberland Island and none to the north until Shackleford Banks. And clearly, starved, sick colonists would not have traveled hundreds of miles to place stock on Ocracoke.

It is likely that the horses were eaten by Ayllón's colonists. Other colonies were certainly not above eating their horses, and it is hard to believe that this one would starve rather than eat theirs. In Jamestown, Virginia, after all the cattle, hogs and horses had been consumed, a few planters even ate an Indian (or several) during the Starving Time—one man even ate his wife, according to John Smith in The *Generall Historie of Virginia, New England and the Summer Isles*. If Ayllón 's colony did not eat their livestock, then Native Americans, who lived on some barrier islands and seasonally hunted on others, surely would have. In the early 18th century, stockmen on the northern Banks complained about Indians' crossing Currituck Sound and poaching cattle.

None of the English settlers said a word about finding horses, goats, or any other livestock grazing in the marshes when they alighted. Thomas Harriot was the scientific advisor for the Lane colony of 1585. His *Briefe and True Report of the New Found Land of Virginia* was the first remotely scientific treatise on North America, and it influenced European thought and exploration for two centuries. In it he describes native animals and plants in detail, from the Carolina Parakeet to cacti, but he never mentions horses.

In 1585 Sir Richard Grenville set sail for Roanoke Island in command of a flotilla laden with colonists and the supplies that they needed to survive in the New World. On the way, he lost one ship and became separated from the rest. Upon stopping at Puerto Rico, he built a ship, reunited with one of his missing ships, and obtained horses, as illustrated in John White's watercolor of the fortified camp. Continuing to Hispaniola for more livestock, including additional horses, he captured two Spanish ships.

According to the log of Grenville's flagship *Tiger* reproduced in David Quinn's *Roanoke Voyages* (1955), while in Hispaniola he traded for "horses, mares, kyne [cattle], buls, goates, swine, sheepe . . . and such like commodities of the island." Spanish accounts add calves and dogs. Evidently this was not enough to adequately supply the expedition. On September 3, 1585, Ralph Lane wrote, "if Virginia had but Horses and Kyne in some reasonable proportion . . . no realme in Christendome

Santiago is a Banker stallion with pinto markings. He is no longer used for breeding within the Ocracoke herd because he is too closely related to many of the other horses.

were comparable to it."

Grenville himself sailed on the *Tiger*, , so he may have assigned the chore of transporting livestock that he didn't intend to eat *en route* to other vessels in the flotilla. Unfortunately, his ship ran aground in Wococon (probably Ocracoke Inlet or its predecessor), necessitating repairs. Some writers suggest that livestock thrown from the *Tiger* to lighten it escaped to run wild on the Banks. Documents do not mention livestock on the *Tiger*, however, and there is no other evidence to support this conclusion.

On Roanoke Island, under the leadership of Governor Ralph Lane, the 107 male colonists explored a lot of territory, inventoried a lot of natural resources, and antagonized a lot of Native Americans before the colony failed. The dense forests and malarial swamps of the interior were not very hospitable to horses, so the English did most of their exploring by boat or on foot. By late spring 1586, the colonists were hungry. Lane had to send half of them to the Banks to live off oysters and roots and whatever else was available. Before the men succumbed to starvation and hostile natives, Sir Francis Drake arrived and eventually gave the remaining colonists a ride back to England. As in Ayllón's case, we can conclude that the starving settlers consumed the horses before there was an opportunity to establish a free-roaming population.

John White and his colony of English families established a settlement on Roanoke Island in 1587, when they were unceremoniously dumped there instead of at their stated destination on the Chesapeake. The arrival of Virginia Dare, the first English child born in the New World, was a hopeful sign. But before long supplies ran short, and Governor John White returned to England to bring over a shipment of goods to sustain the colony. Unfortunately, English politics and the Spanish Armada delayed White's return. When he finally arrived, three years behind schedule, his colony was gone. The fate of the Lost Colony remains a mystery to this day.

By the end of the colonial period, the only two sizable settlements on the Outer Banks were Ocracoke and Portsmouth. At that time, Ocracoke Inlet was the most important passage to the local shipping trade, and these two towns stood on either side of it. Portsmouth was founded in 1753, and by 1770, it was the largest settlement on the Outer Banks. Livestock, including horses, roamed this island, too.

Like the rest of the Outer Banks, Ocracoke was long utilized for grazing livestock. 1706 records show that Ferdinand Green was permitted to "settle a stock" upon the banks at or near Ocracoke inlet. At various times, Cape Hatteras and Ocracoke were connected by land, and so Green's stock probably mingled with the stock of other farmers that ranged freely along the Banks north of present-day Hatteras Inlet, as well as any animals living on Ocracoke before this. Because horses and cattle roamed the rest of the Outer Banks from 1660s to the 1930s, it is likely that livestock was also established on Ocracoke long before records reflect their introduction.

In an 1810 letter to the editor of the Raleigh *Star*, an unknown writer describing Portsmouth, said, "Seven years ago an inhabitant of the Island of his own mark, Sheared 700 head of sheep—had between two hundred & fifty, & three hundred head of cattle & near as many horses . . . It is believed the Island at present is overstocked & much benefit would result from diminution of one third the present number." Forty-eight years later, Edmund Ruffin pointed out, "[T]he rearing of horses is a very profitable investment for the small amount of capital required for the business. There are some hundreds of horses, of the dwarfish native breed, on this part of the reef between Portsmouth and Beaufort harbor—ranging at large, and wild, (or untamed,) and continuing

The 75-foot Ocracoke Lighthouse was built in 1823. The shortest of the four lighthouses located on the Outer Banks, this iconic tower marked Ocracoke Inlet rather than some dangerous spot the coast. Photograph by Sedna10387 (public domain via Wikimedia Commons.)

the race without any care of their numerous proprietors." Portsmouth farmers would attend roundups on Ocracoke and vice versa to acquire new individuals for their herds.

The waters surrounding Ocracoke have long been a challenge to sailors. Aptly referred to the Graveyard of the Atlantic, the treacherous Diamond Shoals of Cape Hatteras extend up to ten miles into the sea. This is eastward enough to make land invisible to many mariners even in ideal conditions. Many a sailor thinking he was miles out to sea has run on the outer shoals without warning. The strong currents and extreme weather add to the difficulties. Southbound vessels were obligated to hug the coast in order to avoid fighting the Gulf Stream, and sometimes the passage between Gulf Stream and the shoals was only a mile or two, leaving little margin for error. All other things being equal, vessels carrying livestock from Puerto Rico to Massachusetts, which could travel well east of the shoals, would have been much less likely to run aground or sink near land than vessels carrying manufactured goods from Massachusetts to South Carolina.

In the past few hundred years, there have been over 600 recorded losses. The actual number is probably much higher. Before the 19th century, records are inconsistent and fragmentary. Wrecks were becoming commonplace, and people weren't always moved to write about them. Even the famous Union ironclad *Monitor* wrecked off Cape Hatteras in a storm.

Many ships carrying livestock passed by Cumberland, Assateague, and the Outer Banks in the 17th and 18th centuries, and there were probably undocumented wrecks of vessels containing horses. With many wrecks and poor recordkeeping, it is possible that equine shipwreck survivors contributed their genes to the Banker herds; but we have no proof. Wrecks alone do not explain why horses are where they are and not in other places equally hazardous to maritime traffic.

Furthermore, in the 19th century Edmund Ruffin commented that horses turned loose among the Bankers often succumbed to the harsh conditions and the poor-quality forage. In the 20th century, tough western mustangs introduced to Assateague died within the year. Even if shoaled ships did spill livestock, horses not acclimated to the Banks would likely have perished.

In 1794, lighthouses began to appear along the cape to minimize losses. The Ocracoke Light has been in continuous operation since 1823, the second-longest unbroken run in the country. After 1874, U.S. Lifesaving Service crews mounted on Banker horses or patrolling on foot monitored the beaches and struggled to rescue sailors from stormy seas. Stations were positioned a varying distance apart along the beach. Where they could, surfmen walked half the distance to the next station, turned a key in a clock or exchanged a token with another surfman, and then walked back, no matter whether Nature offered biting raw winds, blazing heat, or hurricane. The more horrendous the storm, the more likely their services would be needed.

Unflappable, loyal, sensible Banker horses worked in partnership with the men of the Lifesaving Service. They were caught from the free-roaming stock that had long existed on the island, and trained to haul lifeboats to and from the sea while nor'easters raged. They hauled equipment over the sand to shipwreck sites. The brave horses would stand in surging surf in the most violent tempest and wait while their riders rescued people from the waves.

Some legends hold that many early Outer Banks settlers made a living from stripping shipwrecks for lumber and goods, but there is little evidence that illicit wrecking occurred on a regular basis.

During the 1700s, however, pirates, including Edward Teach, the infamous Blackbeard, used these sparsely populated islands as hideouts, and Ocracoke Inlet provided plenty of cargo-laden ships to prey upon. ⊠The pirates fed upon the cattle and hogs that roamed the islands. Some believe that pirates brought horses to Ocracoke as a source of mounts or even food if necessary, but no evidence supports this belief. Besides, the herds were probably well established before pirates frequented the island. Contrary to popular lore, most pirates were not native to the Banks; the local population had little to do with piracy except complaining about it and opposing it.

Pirates were not the only ones who tried to sustain themselves on meat stolen from the barrier islands. Stock was abundant and largely unguarded. Passing mariners of all nationalities frequently availed themselves of this source of sustenance. During the Revolutionary War and the War of 1812, the British Navy frequently ran out of provisions. Militia units on the Outer Banks tried to prevent the British from taking livestock, but were not always successful.

Ocracoke Inlet was the major trade route to the interior of North Carolina, but it was fairly shallow and treacherous, and most ships could not pass through without a pilot. Some large or heavily-laden ships could not pass through it at all. Portsmouth became a major port for lightering (temporarily removing cargo onto shallow-draft boats so that they could ride over the bar and proceed through the inlet to ports like Bath and Beaufort) and transshipment (moving cargo by boat between ships on opposite sides of the inlet).

In 1846, the same storm that carved both Hatteras and Oregon inlets demolished much of the town of Portsmouth. The new inlet at Hatteras was deeper for a while, so the shipping business that kept

Ocracoke's unspoiled oceanfront is internationally renowned. In 2007, Dr. Beach proclaimed the lifeguarded section of its ocean beach the best beach in the country, and *Condé Nast Traveler* proclaimed all of Ocracoke's Atlantic frontage the fifth-best island beach in the world. But over the years, the island may have received more coverage for sunbathers' *lack* of coverage. Many miles of beach are deserted even in summer, so skinny-dipping without discovery or interference is possible. The Park Service prohibits nudity nonetheless.

Portsmouth prosperous shifted north. The population on Portsmouth Island declined from 685 in 1860 to 17 in 1956. In 1971 the last two residents moved to the mainland. Today Portsmouth stands as a ghost town, complete with houses, church, lifesaving station, school, and cemeteries. It is listed on the National Register of Historic Places and is maintained by the Cape Lookout National Seashore.

Barrier islands are always new, constantly shifted and rearranged by the elements, yet a feeling of timelessness awaits the visitor who hikes beyond the developed areas of Ocracoke. The island looks about the same as it did centuries ago, when there were hundreds of free-roaming horses and cows beyond the next dune. This changelessness is one of the reasons people keep coming back to Ocracoke. Time is less important here, and anyone who spends time on the island will gradu-ally subside into the ageless rhythm of tides, moons, and seasons.

Ocracoke is an endearing Outer Banks outpost, all the more so for its timelessness. It is a village of working watermen that has escaped the artificiality of resort communities. Most visitors arrive by ferry. The National Park Service manages most of the island, and as a result it remains devoid of homes and businesses along the entire twelve-mile drive from the ferry to the village.

The village is home to about 950 year-round residents. There are no high-rises, fun parks, or golf courses—just the authenticity of a work-ing fishing village. All the homes, restaurants, hotels, and shops are concentrated in Ocracoke Village, which is located on the sound side of the island around Silver Lake Harbor.

Although the pace is slow, there is always plenty to do. You can easi-ly walk or bicycle to all points within the village and explore quiet roads overhung by boughs of sprawling live oaks. You can charter or rent a boat at the marina, take a dolphin cruise or a kayak ecotour, parasail, swim, shell, or shop. There are nature trails, the British Cemetery his-toric site, and pirate history tours. The pristine beaches are ideal for walking, fishing, and swimming. You can drive your 4WD vehicle along the shore in certain designated areas.

A number of charter boats will take you to the ghost town on Portsmouth Island, where you can explore the old buildings, collect shells, and walk an empty beach. Portsmouth is maintained as a histor-ic site, but be forewarned that the mosquitoes are virulent. Vast num-bers of the insects lurk in the grass and rise in dark clouds to envelop visitors. There is a ranger station at Portsmouth Village, but otherwise there are no facilities except rest rooms available, so bring along eve-

The infamous pirate Blackbeard terrorized mariners traveling along the Atlantic coast in the early 1700s. Public domain photo from Wikimedia Commons.

rything you will need—sunscreen, powerful insect repellent, plenty of water, and food.

Shell collectors find myriad tideline treasures, particularly after a storm. Larger, unbroken shells are most abundant the hour before and after low tide. To collect large shells such as Knobbed Whelk, Lightning Whelk, and Channeled Whelk, stand in knee-deep water about 3 or 4 feet from the surfline and use a net to pull shells from the waves.

Ocracoke can be reached by any of three public ferries, private boat, or private plane. Small aircraft may land at the Ocracoke Island Airport, located slightly southeast of the village.

A free ferry carries vehicles south from Hatteras Village, where the paved two-lane road, NC 12, runs from the ferry dock at the northern tip of the island to Ocracoke Village at the southern end of the island. Try taking the Ocracoke Ferry just before dusk—it's typically less crowded, and the sight of the sun setting over the sound is unforgettable.

A second ferry dock, at the southern end of the island, offers toll connections to Swan Quarter, on the mainland, and Cedar Island, near the town of Atlantic. The Cedar Island Ferry runs on a limited schedule and is typically full. The ferry offers an air-conditioned lounge area. The fare is $15—reserve a spot by calling 1-800-BYFERRY or visiting www.ncdot.gov/ferry if you think you might want to take in Cedar Island or Swan Quarter. You MUST show up at least 30 minutes before departure to claim your boarding pass. If you are late, you will lose your reservation. If you cancel your reservation, staff will give your place to someone else and won't charge you. At this writing, the N.C. Department of Transportation is considering the addition of passenger-only ferry service between Hatteras Island and Ocracoke Village to spare day-trippers long waits to ride the vehicular ferries.

Aside from Ocracoke Village, the entire island is part of Cape Hatteras National Seashore. None of the lodging in Ocracoke is oceanfront—you will have to drive to the beach. The nearest beach access is 5–10 minutes away. If you drive a little farther, you can find a more secluded spot. The Variety Store sells groceries, hardware, bug spray, and other basic supplies for home, camping, or the beach.

Cape Hatteras National Seashore

1401 National Park Dr.
Manteo, NC 27954
252-473-2111
www.nps.gov/caha
https://www.facebook.com/CapeHatterasNS
https://twitter.com/CapeHatterasNPS
https://www.flickr.com/photos/capehatterasnps
https://instagram.com/capehatterasnps
Open year-round.

Ocracoke Island Visitor Center
49 Pilot Town Cir.
Ocracoke, NC 27960
252-928-4531
35.116291, -75.986193
Located near the Ocracoke ferry dock. Offers free programs on nature and history. Open 9 a.m.–5 p.m. daily except Christmas.

Ocracoke Pony Pen
NC 12
35.151101, -75.870210

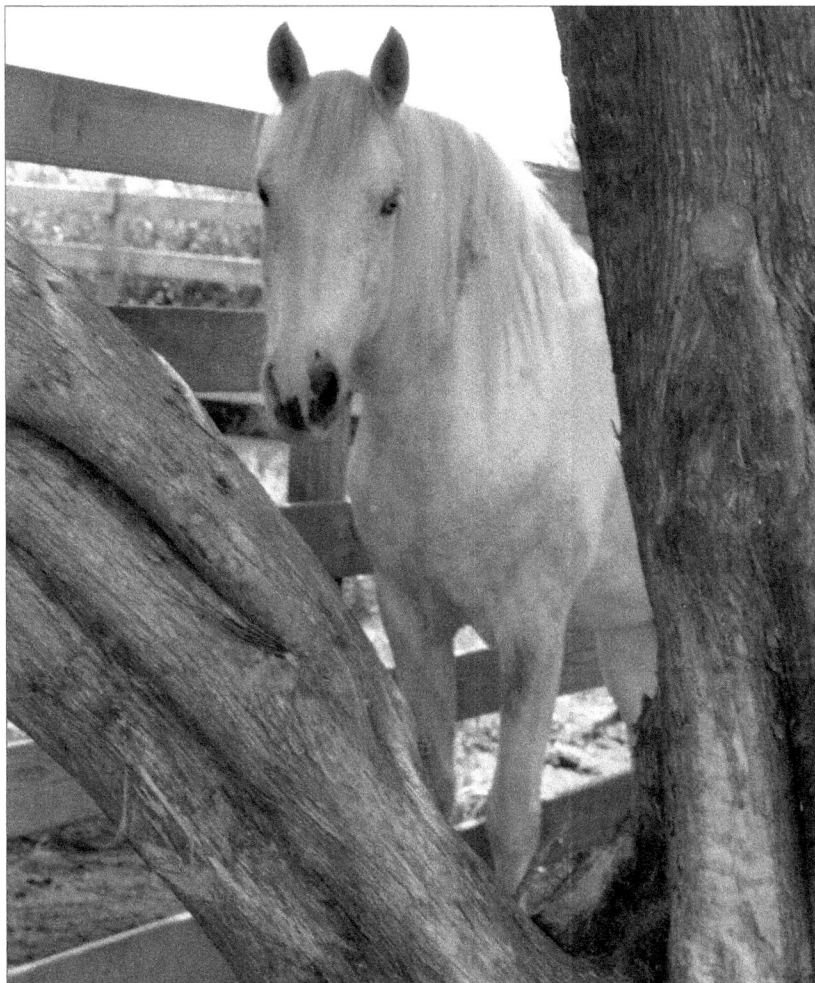

The GPS coordinates above are approximate; but all is not lost, and you won't be, either. There's only one highway, and you can't miss the pen unless you try. The 180-acre pasture to which the remaining Ocracoke horses are confined—despite the thousands of acres available—is on the north side of NC 12 about 7.9 mi. north of the Park Service visitor center in Ocracoke Village or 6.4 mi. south of the Hatteras Inlet ferry terminal. Park rangers present a free 30-minute program about the ponies at the site several times a week in summer, and you can visit anytime. Please note that entering the pen or feeding the horses through the fence is strictly forbidden.

Camping

Ocracoke Campground
35.125823, -75.922504
136 sites

The seashore runs the closest campground to the ponies, about 3.6 mi. south of their pen or 4.3 mi. north of the Park Service visitor center in Ocracoke Village. You can make reservations for the Ocracoke campground up to 6 months in advance at 1-877-444-6777 or on the Internet at www.recreation.gov.

Cape Hatteras NS has three other campgrounds not on Ocracoke Island: Oregon Inlet (120 sites), Frisco (127), and Cape Point (202). The last-named doesn't take reservations.

All four campgrounds allow tents, trailers, and motor homes up to 35 feet long. Each provides rest rooms, potable water, unheated showers, grills, and picnic tables, but no hookups (utility connections). Ocracoke, Oregon Inlet, and Frisco operate April–October; Cape Point, roughly Memorial Day–Labor Day. Check with the Park Service for exact opening and closing dates.

Adoptions
You can "adopt" a member of the Ocracoke herd in person at the Park Service visitor center. Or you can fill out the Adopt-a-Pony form at

http://www.nps.gov/caha/getinvolved/supportyourpark/ upload/Adopt-a-Pony-4-1-2015.pdf

Send the completed form with a check for $28 (payable to the National Park Service) to

**National Park Service
Ocracoke Ranger Station
PO Box 340
Ocracoke, NC 27960
Attn: Adopt-A-Pony**

Your donation (minus $3 for bureaucratic overhead) will go toward the horses' upkeep. In return, you'll receive "an 8"x10" photo and certificate of adoption with the pony's name, age, and description in a presentation folder." You'll also get the satisfaction of helping preserve a very old horse breed that came perilously close to extinction and still isn't in the clear.

Nearby Points of Interest

Ocracoke is a 775-acre village with roughly 950 permanent inhabitants located at the south end of Ocracoke island (and Cape Hatteras NS) about 30 miles by water from the mainland. In size and seclusion, it's more akin to Tangier Island, VA—about 700 people on 700 acres in the middle of Chesapeake Bay—than to wild-horse hot spots such as Ocean City, MD, Chincoteague, VA, and Corolla, NC. Ocracoke was once North Carolina's busiest port and a vacation retreat for wealthy mainland planters, but the Civil War began a century of decline and obscurity. World War II and its aftermath brought a hard-surface road, state-operated ferries, rediscovery by the traveling public, inevitable growth and change, and eventual reintegration into North Carolina, which for a while had seemingly forgotten the place. Mainlanders' attention had wandered before. In the 1760s, for example, the colonial government realized to its chagrin that Ocracoke, the commercial lifeline, and its taxpayers weren't in any county at all.

Now Ocracoke has a thriving community of artists and craftsmen, a nationally known musical group, an idiosyncratic community FM station, and a populace that's 20 percent Hispanic, up from 0 percent just a quarter-century ago. But Ocracoke still a long haul from anywhere else. It's still the last resort for many Northerners escaping down the coast. It still has the smallest K–12 school in the state—150 students, more or less. And it remains a quiet, informal, charmingly weathered settlement with limited lodging and dining options and not even a sidewalk to roll up at dusk.

All distances, in road miles from the Park Service visitor center (130 Pilot Town Cir. • Ocracoke, NC 27960 • 35.115942, -75.986788), are approximate, and most are probably superfluous. Aside from the Park Service campground (4.3 mi.), the pony pen (7.9 mi.) and the Hatteras Inlet ferry terminal (14.3 mi.), few attractions are much more than a mile from the center of Ocracoke Village or from one another.

Camping

Ocracoke Station/Beachcomber Campground
990 Irvin Garrish Hwy.
Ocracoke, NC 27960
252-928-4031

www.ocracokecamping.com
  29 sites, tenting, grills, picnic tables, full-service store. 0.9 mi.

Teeter's Campground
200 British Cemetery Rd.
Ocracoke, NC 27960
252-588-2030
www.teeterscampground.com
  A family-run campground with shady sites, hot water, and flush toilets. Like all other commercial establishments on Ocracoke, it's located in the village, so it's within walking distance of nearly everything. I felt very safe camping alone here as a young woman many years ago. RVs, campers, tents, hookups, Wi-fi. 0.4 mi.

Bed and Breakfasts

Anchorage Inn & Marina
205 Hwy. 12
Ocracoke, NC 27960
252-928-1101
www.theanchorageinn.com
  35 rooms, 2 suites, pet friendly.

The Castle at Silver Lake
155 Silver Lake Rd.
Ocracoke, NC 27960
Toll free 800-471-8848
252-928-3505
www.thecastlebb.com
innkeeper@thecastlebb.com
  11-rooms in an imposing three-story edifice built by Sam Jones; breakfast buffet. Also on the grounds is Castle Courtyard Villas, which consists of 27 1-, 2-, and 3-bedroom rental condos. 0.6 mi.

The Cove Bed and Breakfast
21 Loop Rd.
Ocracoke, NC 27960
252-928 4192
www.thecovebb.com

Sacajawea, a bay Banker mare, was born on Shackleford Banks in 2007 and joined the Ocracoke herd in 2010. In 2015 she foaled a filly named Hazelnut to the stallion Rayo, born of Ocracoke and Shackleford Banks bloodlines.

4 rooms and 3 suites, each with private bath and balcony; full breakfast. 1.1 mi.

Oscar's House Bed & Breakfast
660 Irvin Garrish Hwy.
Ocracoke, NC 27960
252-928-1311
http://thecovebb.com
info@thecovebb.com
    0.6 mi.

Hotels and Motels

Blackbeard's Lodge
111 Back Rd.
Ocracoke, NC 27960
http://blackbeardslodge.com

info@blackbeardslodge.com
Reservations toll free 800-892-5314
252-928-3421
$$$
Trip Advisor #7
    36 rooms and suites. Closed December–mid-March.

Captain's Landing Waterfront Hotel Suites
324 Hwy. 12
Ocracoke, NC 27960
252-928-1999
www.thecaptainslanding.com
$$
Trip Advisor #4, Virtual Tourist 5/5

Edwards of Ocracoke
216 Old Beach Rd.
Ocracoke, NC 27960
Toll free 855-646-8359
252-928-4801
www.edwardsofocracoke.com
$
Oyster 2.5 Pearls, Raveable #5, Trip Advisor #2, Virtual Tourist 4.5/5
    8 rooms, 3 efficiencies, 6 cottage apartments, 2 private cottages. Most have private screened porches or open porches and decks.

Harborside Motel
229 Irvin Garrish Hwy.
Ocracoke, NC 27960
252-928-3111
$$$
Raveable #6, Trip Advisor #9

Ocracoke Harbor Inn
144 Silver Lake Rd.
Ocracoke, NC 27960
252-928-5731
www.ocracokeharborinn.com
$

Oyster 2.5 Pearls, Raveable #4, Trip Advisor #1, Virtual Tourist 4.5/5

16 rooms and 7 suites. Continental breakfast in the lobby or on waterside deck.

Pony Island Motel
25 Lighthouse Rd.
Ocracoke, NC 27960
252-928-4351
www.ocracokeislandinn.com
$
Raveable #8, Trip Advisor #3, Virtual Tourist 4/5

Dining

Howard's Pub and Raw Bar
1175 Irvin Garrish Hwy.
Ocracoke, NC 27960
252-928-4441
www.howardspub.com
Lunch, dinner
$$
Dine.com 3.1/5, Menuism 4/5, Trip Advisor #8, Yelp 3.5/5, Zomato 3.7/5

Known for its sense of community and big-screen TVs. Howard's offers casual fun and occasional live music and dancing. Raw bar, burgers, pizza, sandwiches, wine, and more than 200 varieties of beer. 1.2 mi.

Back Porch Restaurant & Wine Bar
110 Back Rd.
Ocracoke, NC 27960
252-928-6401
http://backporchocracoke.com
Dinner
$$
Menuism 5/5, Trip Advisor #9, Yelp 4/5, Zomato 3.9/5

Quiet first-class dining, good service, and romantic atmosphere. 0.8 mi.

Back Porch Lunchbox
747 Irvin Garrish Hwy.
Ocracoke, NC 27960
252-928-3651
Bag lunches for the beach or the ferry or dining *al fresco*. Sandwiches, salads, smoothies, baked goods, fruit, ice cream, quick and easy. Next to the Pony Island Motel. 0.7 mi.

Flying Melon Café
181 Back Rd.
Ocracoke, NC 27960
252-928-2533
Brunch, dinner
$$
Trip Advisor #2, Yelp 4/5, Zomato 4.3/5

Ocracoke Fish & Seafood Company
416 Irvin Garrish Hwy.
Ocracoke, NC 27960
252-928-5601
$
Yelp 5/5
Not a restaurant, but a seafood market, in the last fish house on the island, run by the Ocracoke Working Watermen's Association. It's an option only if your rental allows cooking. 0.4 mi.

Ocracoke Pizza Company
659 Irvin Garrish Hwy.
Ocracoke, NC 27960
252-928-7777
https://www.facebook.com/OcracokePizzaCompany
Dinner
$
Yelp 4/5, Zomato 3.1/5
Handmade pizza, free delivery throughout village until late at night. Cash only. 0.7 mi.

Pony Island Restaurant
51 Ocean View Rd.
Ocracoke, NC 27960

The traditional clam chowder of the Outer Banks and the Delmarva Peninsula is, or was, very simple, usually consisting of little more than clams, potatoes, onions, and salt pork or bacon in clear broth. Some sources suggest that in very early days, even New England chowder was clear, and dairy products were served on the side if used at all. Milk or cream and eventually roux became integral to most New England chowder, though Block Island and other parts of Rhode Island held out a long while. Meanwhile, Portuguese settlers in Rhode Island and Italians in New York added tomatoes to clear chowder. Some versions of "Manhattan style" chowder gained enough ingredients that influential chef James Beard condemned them as "vegetable soup that accidentally had some clams dumped into it." In 1939 the Maine legislature debated a bill that forbade corrupting chowder with tomatoes. New England and Manhattan styles came to dominate restaurants, supermarkets, popular cookbooks, and eventually household kitchens far outside their original range, making other regional varieties harder to find. Some chowder served on the Eastern Shore, for example, has affinity with Manhattan style, and New England chowder turns up in restaurants nearly everywhere. Outer Banks or Hatteras style chowder is in retreat, but still obtainable. It usually consists of clams, potatoes, onions, rendered bacon or salt pork, and a generous amount of black pepper or even hot sauce. Of course, you can dig a tub of clams and make your own chowder if you have access to a kitchen and, ideally, a meat grinder for the clams.

Note: Most people find the small *Rangia* clams that inhabit low-salinity waters unpalatable. They may also be unwholesome. Because clamming isn't often an issue where they live, authorities that monitor water quality may not post contamination warnings.

252-928-5701
https://www.facebook.com/pages/Pony-Island-Restaurant/362195029755#_=_
Breakfast, lunch, dinner
$$$
Dine.com 3.7/5, Trip Advisor #10, Yelp 4/5, Zomato 3.4/5
The oldest eatery on the island, brimming with character. 0.9 mi.

Sweet Tooth & Fig Tree Bakery and Deli
1015 Irvin Garrish Hwy.
Ocracoke, NC 27960
252-928-3481
https://www.facebook.com/SweettoothFig-Tree-Deli-157763444383464
Breakfast, lunch
$$
Trip Advisor #14, Yelp 3.5/5
Full-service bakery and deli—freshly baked breads and desserts, salads, and vegetarian fare. Cappuccino, espresso, picnic lunches. 1.0 mi.

Horse-Related Activities

Charlie Horse Stables
Irvin Garrish Hwy.
Ocracoke, NC 27960
703-650-8007
www.charliehorsestablesnc.com
charliehorsestables@gmail.com
Summer only.

Morning Starr Beach Rides
1070 Irvin Garrish Hwy.
Ocracoke, NC 27960
252-921-0383
Guided trail rides and horseback weddings on the beaches of Ocracoke Island. 1.1 mi.

Other Attractions

Island Ragpicker
515 Irvin Garrish Hwy.
Ocracoke, NC 27960
252-928-7571
The Island Ragpicker is my absolute favorite of Ocracoke gift shops—and possibly, of all gift shops. The store draws you in from

"Oops" is a mare born after an unplanned romantic interlude between her parents, Charro and Feliz.

the heat and revives you with air conditioning as you explore the many rooms of unique products and craft items. As a person who generally dislikes shopping, it is out of character for me to spend much time in a store, but I never want to leave the Island Ragpicker. If you ever want to complete your Christmas shopping by mid-July, this is the place to do it. 0.5 mi.

Austin Boat Tours: Dolphin Cruises & Sunset Cruises
138 Loop Rd.
Ocracoke, NC 27960
252-928-4361

Trips to Portsmouth Island's unspoiled beaches. Great shelling, secluded beaches, ecotours, local history, Blackbeard's hideout! (Unfortunately, no buried treasure so far.) 1.0 mi.

Dare to Hyde Outdoor Adventures
PO Box 128
Fairfield, NC 27826
252-926-9453
www.daretohyde.com

This company offers customizable hunting, fishing, water sports, wildlife-watching, and photography experiences on the Outer Banks, the mainland, and the adjoining waters. It can provide accommodations at the Berkley Manor on Ocracoke, a former B&B 0.1 mi. from the ferry terminal once used by industrialist Sam Jones for entertaining guests. The Manor is also Ocracoke's largest rental house (sleeps 24) and an event site. The owners reportedly donate some part of their proceeds to Cross Trail Outfitters, a Christian hunting-and-fishing organization for boys with chapters in five states and headquarters in Plymouth, NC (toll free 866-543-4868 • http://teamcto.org).

Molasses Creek's Deepwater Theater and Music Hall
82 School Rd.
Ocracoke, NC 27960
252-921-0260
www.molassescreek.com
info@molassescreek.com
Molasses Creek, a folk group that won second place in the Talent from Towns Under 2000 Contest on the NPR series *A Prairie Home Companion*, plays here Thursday nights in summer. On Wednesdays the venue hosts the Ocrafolk Opry, a showcase of local musicians and raconteurs that may include Molasses Creek or its offshoot Coyote. Doors open at 7:30 p.m. and shows begin at 8. Tickets available online. Classes and other events are scheduled throughout the year. 0.7 mi.

Ocracoke Ghost & History Walk
170 Howard St.
Ocracoke, NC 27960
252-928-6300
Authentic spook tales and island history. Tours are offered on Tuesdays and Fridays at 7:30 p.m. Begins at Village Craftsmen on Howard Street. Call ahead for reservations. 0.6 mi.

Ocracoke Lighthouse
Lighthouse Rd.
Ocracoke, NC 27960
Toll free 888-493-3826
North Carolina's oldest operating lighthouse is 75 feet from focal

The Ocracoke Preservation Society offers exhibits and archives of historical documents. U.S. Navy photo by Chief Journalist John F. Williams (public domain via Wikimedia Commons).

plane to base. It's not open for climbing, but a small park surrounds it. 1.0 mi.

Ocracoke Preservation Society

49 Water Plant Rd.
Ocracoke, NC 27960
252-928-7375
www.ocracokepreservation.org

The Ocracoke Preservation Society is a nonprofit organization dedicated to preserving Ocracoke Island's rich historical and cultural heritage. The museum offers a collection of Ocracoke historical items, a research library, special exhibits, a gift shop, and events such as summer porch talks, a Wassail party, and art openings. The museum is open from Easter through Thanksgiving. 0.2 mi.

Portsmouth Island ATV Excursions

396 Irvin Garrish Hwy.
Ocracoke, NC 27960
252-928-4484

Two tours daily. from 8 a.m. to noon and 1 p.m. to 5 p.m. (weather permitting). 0.4 mi. See Side Trip 2, below.

Portsmouth Island Boat Tours
278 Irvin Garrish Hwy.
Community Square Docks
Ocracoke, NC 27960
252-928-4361

Tour takes you to enjoy secluded beaches, birdwatching, shelling, fishing and camping. The boat tours also include surrounding islands including Blackbeard's hideout, Fort Ocracoke, and dolphin watching. 0.3 mi.

Ride the Wind Surf & Kayak Shop
486 Irvin Garrish Hwy.
Ocracoke, NC 27960
252-928-6311

Surf camp, lessons, Kayak eco-tours. Rentals of surfboards, boogieboards, skimboards, wetsuits, and kayaks. Located on Highway 12 at Silver Lake. 0.5 mi.

Schooner *Windfall* Pirate Cruise
278 Irvin Garrish Hwy.
Community Square Docks
Ocracoke, NC 27960
252-928-7245

The schooner *Windfall* sails daily from the Community Store dock. 1-hour family pirate cruises with free loot for the kids. 0.3 mi.

Events

Blackbeard's Pirate Jamboree
Late October
http://piratejamboree.com
info@blackbeardslodge.com

This celebration, begun in 2013, is a smaller, more educational affair than the sprawling, brawling Pirate's Jamboree of the 1950s and 1960s, which helped the Outer Banks create a spring shoulder season. Still it involves a good part of the island in a bit of frivolity.

Ocracoke Island 10K/5K Run
Late April
www.ocracokeisland5krun.org
A fundraiser for WOVV-FM (see below), the Ocracoke School Athletic Boosters Club, and Ocracoke Community Park.

Ocracoke Working Watermen's Association Oyster Roast
Late December
416 Irvin Garrish Hwy.
Ocracoke, NC 27960
252-928-5601
www.ocracokewatermen.org
info@ocracokewatermen.org
Held at the Ocracoke Fish House on Silver Lake.

Ocrafolk Festival
Early June
252-921-0260
www.ocracokealive.org
info@ocrafolkfestival.org
A weekend of music, art, storytelling, crafts, food, and fun.

Outlying Destinations

Points of interest beyond Ocracoke Island. Distances, all approximate and rounded to the nearest whole number, are in road or water miles from the Ocracoke ferry terminal (130 Pilot Town Circle • Ocracoke, NC 27960 • 35.115942,-75.986788).

Camping

Camp Hatteras Resort and RV Park
24798 NC Hwy. 12
MP 40.5
Rodanthe, NC 27968
252 987-2777
www.Camphatteras.com
Tenting at Camp Hatteras was a summer tradition for our family for many years. The island is narrow here, and you can catch the

sunrise over the ocean and the sunset over the sound. There are several restaurants and shops within easy access, as well as an amusement water park. 58 mi.

Cape Hatteras KOA
25099 NC Hwy. 12
Rodanthe, NC 27968
Toll free 1-800-562-5268
252-987-2307

345 sites. Open all year. Partial handicap access. Accommodates big rigs. Tenting, laundry, groceries, wood, grills, Internet. 58 mi.

Cape Woods Campground
47649 Buxton Back Rd.
Buxton, NC 27920
252-995-5850
www.capewoods.com

34 mi.

Frisco Campground
53415 Billy Mitchell Rd.
Frisco, NC 27936

30 mi.

Frisco Woods Campground
53124 NC Hwy. 12
Frisco, NC 27936
Toll free 800-948-3942

30 mi.

Hatteras Sands Resort
57316 Eagle Pass Rd.
Hatteras, NC 27943
Toll free 888-987-2225
www.hatterassands.com

Near the Hatteras ferry terminal. 111 sites. Tenting, laundry, picnic tables, Internet. 24 mi.

Ocean Waves Campground
25313 NC Hwy. 12

Flocks of gulls fish in the wake of a ferry and coax tidbits from passengers. The North Carolina ferry system provides not only transportation, but also entertainment as you take in the sights from a sturdy boat. The ferry from Hatteras to Ocracoke is free. The ride takes 40 minutes to an hour or more, depending on weather and the location of the channel. Interruptions in service are common, especially in hurricane season..

Waves, NC 27982
252-987-2556
www.oceanwavescampground.com
68 sites. Tenting, laundry, cable TV, Internet friendly. $32–34 per family. Note: Contrary to events in the movie Nights In Rodanthe, wild horses do not roam this part of the Outer Banks and haven't since the 1930s! 57 mi.

Sands of Time Campground
40523 North End Rd.
Avon NC 27915
252-995-5596
http://sandsoftimecampground.com
sandsoftimecamping@embarqmail.com
Large Sites, full hookups, Free cable and Wi-fi, hot showers, laundry, and shady tent sites. One cottage for rent. Does not accept credit cards or personal checks. 42 mi.

Hotels and Motels

Cape Hatteras Motel
46556 NC Hwy. 12
Buxton, NC 27920
Toll free 800-995-0711
252-995-5611
www.capehatterasmotel.com
$$$
Trip Advisor #3 (on Hatteras Island)
  36 mi.

The Inn on Pamlico Sound
49684 NC Highway 12
Buxton, NC 27920
Toll free 866-995-7030
866-726-5426
252-995-7030
http://innonpamlicosound.com
$$$
Oyster 3 Pearls, Trip Advisor #1 (on Hatteras Island)
  A hybrid of B&B and hotel. It has just 12 rooms, but a highly regarded on-site restaurant, Café Pamlico, ranked #2 on Hatteras Island by TripAdvisor (Yelp 4/5). 33 mi.

Lighthouse View Motel
46677 NC Hwy. 12, Buxton, NC 27920
252-995-5680
$
AAA 2 Diamonds, Trip Advisor #4 (on Hatteras Island)
  The 73 oceanfront and oceanside units include efficiencies, duplexes, motel-style rooms, villas, and cottages. Amenities include oceanfront pool and hot tub, playground. 35 mi.

Dining

Bros Sandwich Shack
41934 NC Hwy, 12

Space #3, Avon
NC 27915
252-995-9595
www.brossandwichshack.com
Lunch, dinner
$
Trip Advisor #1 (on Hatteras Island), Yelp 5/5
   41 mi.

The Froggy Dog
40050 NC Hwy. 12
Avon, NC 27915
252-995-3337
www.froggydog.com
Info@froggydog.com
Breakfast, lunch, dinner, late
$$$
   Big breakfast, quick lunch. 42 mi.

Yaupon (*Ilex vomitoria*), an evergreen holly common on the coastal plain below Chesapeake Bay, is the only source of caffeine indigenous to North America. It's a close relative of maté (*I. paraguariensis*), which is consumed widely in Argentina and neighboring countries. Indians of the Southeast used large quantities of yaupon in social and medicinal beverages, and tribes as far away as the upper Midwest seem to have traded for it. As the scientific name implies, yaupon served occasionally as an emetic; but drunk unadulterated and in moderation, it's no more upsetting than coffee. In the early days of the Carolina colony, yaupon was briefly a more important export than tobacco. Poor residents of the coastal plain from the Outer Banks to the Gulf continued to brew it until the early 20th century.

To prepare yaupon, strip off the tender outer leaves and twigs; chop them fine with a hatchet or cleaver; and bake them on an ungreased cookie sheet at 400°F, turning often, until they're medium brown. Add 1 cup of leaves to 1 quart of boiling water; reduce heat and simmer until it turns dark amber; then strain. Yaupon tea is an acquired taste for many (sugar and lemon may help), but the raw material is free for the taking.

Orange Blossom Bakery & Cafe
47206 NC Hwy. 12
Buxton, NC 27920
252-995-4109
http://orangeblossombakery.com
Breakfast
$
Trip Advisor #3 (on Hatteras Island), Yelp 4.5/5
   35 mi.

Horse-Related Activities

Equine Adventures Beach Riding
52193 Piney Ridge Rd.
Buxton, NC 27920
252-995-4897

Riders must be at least 10 years old and 4'8" tall and weigh less than 200 lb. I rode here in the 1990s, and I am not sure whether it is currently run by the same people. My ride was wonderful. We left very early in the morning, just after sunrise, so the horses would not have to work in the heat of the day. Because I was an experienced rider, the guide mounted me on a tall bay Thoroughbred ex-racehorse named Zelda. The first part of the ride was through a maritime forest, then we traversed a swath of low dunes. When we reached the beach, the guide allowed us to canter. I had always wanted to canter on the beach, and I envisioned a slow, romantic rhythm. Instead, the guide flew by on his lively quarter horse and yelled "Race you!" The next thing I knew I was galloping at high speed down the empty beach neck and neck with the Quarter Horse. It was a tie. As it turned out, the guide had always wondered if his horse could beat Zelda, and he chose that moment to find out. I will remember that exhilarating ride always. 31 mi.

Other Attractions

Belhaven Memorial Museum
211 E. Main St.

Belhaven NC 27810
252-943-6817

A collection of random curiosities amassed by Eva Blount Way (1869–1962), including 30,000 buttons and an antique dental X-ray machine. The museum's second-floor location isn't handicapped-accessible, and some exhibits aren't for the young or squeamish; but admission is free. 58 mi. by way of the Swan Quarter ferry.

Burrus Flying Service
53252 Billy Mitchell Rd.
Frisco, NC 27936
252-986-2679
www.hatterasislandflightseeing.com

Flights leave from Billy Mitchell Airport, near the improvised airstrip that the pioneering general used in 1923 to prove the efficacy of high-altitude bombing by sinking two decommissioned battleships anchored off Cape Hatteras. 30 mi.

Cape Hatteras Lighthouse
Cape Point, off NC 12
Buxton, NC
252-995-4474
www.nps.gov/caha

The visitor center includes a museum, an audiovisual room, and a gift shop. From May through Columbus Day, hardy visitors may climb the 248 iron steps spiraling to the top, a feat that the Park Service equates to climbing a 12-story building There is a single handrail, a landing every 31 steps, and no air conditioning. The structure's height, 208 feet from foundation to top, makes it the tallest masonry lighthouse in the Western Hemisphere and the second tallest in the world. Natural westward migration of the island threatened to topple the lighthouse into the sea until 1999, when the Park Service spent $9.2 million to move it inland to a site less susceptible to erosion—for a while. 37 mi.

Chicamacomico Life-Saving Station
23645 NC Hwy. 12
Rodanthe, NC 27968
252-987-1552
www.chicamacomico.net

Museum of the U.S. Lifesaving Service housed in a restored 1874 station. Programs, reenactments, gift shop. Fee charged. 59 mi.

Frisco Native American Museum & Natural History Center
53536 NC Hwy. 12
Frisco, NC 27936
252-995-4440
www.nativeamericanmuseum.org

Open Tuesday–Sunday (weekends only in winter), 10:30 a.m.–5 p.m. 29 mi.

Graveyard of the Atlantic Museum
59200 Museum Dr.
Hatteras, NC27943
252-986-2995/986-2996
www.graveyardoftheatlantic.com

At the end of NC 12 beside the ferry terminal,. Maritime history exhibits with a focus on shipwrecks and lifesaving. 24 mi.

Historic Bath
207 Carteret St.
Bath, NC 27808
252-923-3971
www.nchistoricsites.org/bath
bath@ncdcr.gov

Bath, founded by Huguenots from Virginia in 1705, was Carolina's first town, first port of entry, first stationary capital, and home of John Lawson, the colony's first author. It may also have been the first town hereabouts to receive a formal curse. Denied permission to preach there in 1762, English evangelist George Whitefield shook the dust from his shoes (see Matthew 10:14) and declared that Bath would never be more than a village "forgotten by men and nations." For whatever reason, its population in 2010 was just 249, not much larger than in the 18th century. Bath was the last place where pirate Edward Teach, a.k.a. Blackbeard, resided intact and the first place his severed head visited as an ornament on Lieutenant Robert Maynard's bowsprit. In 1925, Edna Ferber caught up with the James Adams Floating Theater in Bath and began an association that led to her novel *Show Boat* and the Broadway musical and movies bearing the same title. Perhaps

The Cape Hatteras lighthouse in Buxton is open to the public for climbing.

prompted by Whitefield's ghost, she changed her novel's setting to the Mississippi River.

The Historic Bath State Historic Site includes St. Thomas Episcopal Church, the Bonner House, the Palmer-Marsh House, and the Van der Veer House. 73 mi. by way of the Swan Quarter ferry.

Mattamuskeet National Wildlife Refuge
85 Mattamuskeet Rd.
Swan Quarter, NC 27885
252-926-4021

A very low-key perserve that includes North Carolina's largest natural lake. Lake Mattamuskeet may have been formed by subsidence after a prehistoric forest fire had burned away the peat layer below. In any case, it's shallow, only 2-3 feet deep in most places. From 1911 to 1934, a public-private partnership drained the lake for farming and built the New Holland community within it. The lake refilled after investors sold out and the property became a wildlife refuge, but it's no longer entirely fresh. Drainage canals let brackish water enter from Pamlico Sound, and blue crabs in the lake can reach spectacular size. Opportunities for wildlife observation, photography, hiking, and fishing are numerous. The Swan Days festival in early December celebrates the annual return of tundra swans. 73 mi. by way of the Swan Quarter ferry.

Monitor Marine Sanctuary
35.0086, -75.4083
16 mi. SE of Cape Hatteras
Headquarters
Monitor National Marine Sanctuary
100 Museum Dr.
Newport News, VA 23606
757-599-3122
http://monitor.noaa.gov

The country's first national marine sanctuary, established in 1975 around the remains of the revolutionary ironclad USS *Monitor*, is a technical diver's dream. Several major components, including the engine, the propeller, and the turret, have been laboriously removed over the years for conservation at the Mariners' Museum in Newport News, VA; but the rest of the ship is still on the bottom, where it supports a dazzling variety of interesting sea life. The *Monitor* lies under 240 feet of water in a turbulent area on the inner edge of the Gulf Stream, so diving on it isn't for beginners. The sanctuary is both an archaeological site and a naval cemetery, and permission to dive is impossible to obtain on the spur of the moment. But the beauty of the site and the thrill of viewing close up the ship that changed naval history are worth the challenges. 33 mi. as the gull flies.

North Carolina Estuarium
203 E Water St.
Washington, NC 27889
252-948-0000
www.pfsestuarium.inapp.mobi

North Carolina has more estuarine waters than any state except Louisiana. The Albemarle-Pamlico estuary is the second-largest in the United States, after Chesapeake Bay. The Estuarium, the first facility of its kind in the world—part aquarium, part history museum, part art gallery—focuses on the astounding richness and diversity of the state's estuaries. Open Tuesday–Saturday, 10 a.m.–4 p.m., all year.

The Estuarium charges an admission fee ($5 for grownups, $3 for children ages 5-17 at this writing). But like the other educational facilities operated by the nonprofit Partnership for the Sounds, it also offers free riverboat tours April through October. Donations are accepted, and reservations are required. 85 mi. by way of the Ocracoke-Swan Quarter ferry.

Pea Island National Wildlife Refuge
Headquarters and visitor center
708 N US Hwy. 64
Manteo, NC 27954
252-473-1131

Located 10 miles south of Nags Head on NC 12, Pea Island National Wildlife Refuge includes 13 miles of undeveloped beach and thousands of acres of marsh. It was established in 1937 "as a refuge and breeding ground for migratory birds and other wildlife." Its species list includes more than 365 kinds of bird, 25 kinds of mammal, 24 kinds of reptile, and (despite the salty environment) 5 kinds of amphibian. 68 mi.

Events

Old Christmas
Early January
Rodanthe-Waves-Salvo Community Center
23186 Myrna Peters Rd.
Rodanthe NC 27968

The Bodie Island Light (correctly pronounced "body") was built in 1872 and stands 156 feet (48 m) tall. The name was probably derived from someone named Bodie/Body who lived or owned land in the vicinity. In 2010, the National Park Service gave it a facelift after first encasing it in scaffolding (right).

When the Calendar Act switched the British Empire from the Julian calendar the Gregorian in 1752, Christmas fell on what had been January 5. Outlying areas, such as the Outer Banks, didn't get the news quickly and didn't pay much attention when it arrived. Eventually local Christmas celebrations merged with Epiphany (January 6 on the Gregorian calendar) and may have incorporated elements of Jonkonnu, a year-end festival of African origin sometimes celebrated by slaves and even by whites in the Carolinas and Virginia.

In recent years, organizers have scheduled the Rodanthe observance on the first Saturday after New Year's Day in the interest of attendance and recuperation. It usually includes music, dancing, an oyster roast, and a traditional appearance by Old Buck, two guys in an unconvincing bull costume.

Local Contacts

Island Free Press
50244 Captain's Ct.
Frisco, NC 27943
252-995-5323
http://islandfreepress.org

Ocracoke Civic & Business Association, Inc.
PO Box 456
Ocracoke, NC 27960
252-928-6711
www.ocracokevillage.com
info@ocracokevillage.com

Ocracoke Preservation Society
49 Water Plant Rd.
Ocracoke, NC 27960
252-928-7375
http://site.ocracokepreservation.org

This nonprofit community organization is dedicated to the preservation of Ocracoke's rich historical and cultural heritage. Free-admission museum, research library.

WOVV-FM
252-928-9688
www.wovv.org
info@wovv.org
   A nonprofit community radio station (90.1 FM) operated by the
Ocracoke Foundation. Streaming audio available on the Web site.

More Information

Ballance, A. (1989). *Ocracokers*. Chapel Hill: University of North Caro-
     lina Press.
Gruenberg, B.U. (2015). *The wild horse dilemma: Conflicts and contro-
     versies of the Atlantic Coast herds*. Strasburg, PA: Quagga Press.
Henning, J. (1985). *Conquistadores' legacy: The horses of Ocracoke*.
     Ocracoke, NC: Author.
Kirkpatrick, J. (1994). *Into the wind: Wild horses of North America*.
     Minocqua, WI: Northword Press.
Mills, D.S., & McDonnell, S.M. (Eds.). (2005). *The domestic horse:
     The evolution, development and management of its behaviour*.
     Cambridge, United Kingdom: Cambridge University Press.

Sponenberg, D.P. (2011). *North American Colonial Spanish Horse update, July 2011*. Retrieved from www.centerforamericasfirsthorse. org/north-american-colonialspanish-horse.html

Stick, D. (1952). *Graveyard of the Atlantic: Shipwrecks of the North Carolina Coast*. Chapel Hill: University of North Carolina Press.

Stick, D. (1958). *The Outer Banks of North Carolina, 1584-1958*. Chapel Hill: University of North Carolina Press.

1 The One Thing (besides the horses) You Should Make Time For

Springer's Point Preserve, operated by the Coastal Land Trust, is a nature sanctuary comprising land where Blackbeard may have walked in the early 1700s. The beauty and biodiversity of this small tract are breathtaking. Few other nature trails will take you in such a short distance from the maritime forest to the sound beach; along salt marsh and grasslands; and past a natural rookery for wading birds such as white ibises, herons, and egrets. Industrialist Sam Jones and his beloved Ocracoke pony Ikie D. are buried here. Admission is free.

Getting to Ocracoke

Distances (all approximate) are in road miles to the Ocracoke ferry terminal (130 Pilot Town Circle • Ocracoke, NC 27960 • 35.115942,-75.986788).

Boston, MA, 740 mi.; New York, NY, 530 mi.; Philadelphia, PA, 440 mi.; Pittsburgh, PA, 600 mi.; Washington, DC, 370 mi.; Richmond, VA, 265 mi.; Raleigh, NC, 205 mi.; Columbia, SC, 370 mi.; Atlanta, GA, 680 mi.; Orlando, FL, 740 mi.

1. From Richmond, VA

I 295–I 64 interchange (37.522252, -77.270966); 262 mi.
- Exit onto I 64 E; go 63.3 mi.
- At exit 264 take I 664 S (Hampton Roads Beltway); go 20.1 mi, crossing the Monitor-Merrimack Bridge-Tunnel. (In certain conditions, the slightly longer route through the Hampton Roads Bridge-Tunnel may save time.)
- Take exit 15B and merge onto I 64 W toward Chesapeake/VA Beach. (Note: at this point, you'll actually be heading east.) Go 8.2 mi.
- Take exit 291B and merge onto I 464 S/VA 168 S toward US17 S ("Elizabeth City/Outer Banks"); go 0.4 mi. (Note: to take the next step, you'll need to shift quickly into the left lane.)
- Take VA 168 S 16.1 mi. (TOLL). Exit 8B (Hillcrest Parkway) is the last exit before the toll plaza. It leads to Battlefield Blvd. (VA 168 Business), which can be gridlocked on busy weekends.
- At the state line, VA 168 becomes NC 168 (Caratoke [sic] Highway). Continue south 18.3 mi.
- NC 168 ends at the junction with US 158 E. Keep straight and go another 28.7 mi., crossing the Wright Memorial Bridge over Currituck Sound.
- At the big intersection just beyond Home Depot, bear right on US 158 E, which turns south. In summer and on holidays, expect long delays approaching and leaving this waypoint. Go 19.2 mi.
- Turn left and take NC 12 toward Hatteras Island; go 58.9 mi.
- Take the ferry across Hatteras Inlet, about 5 mi.
- Follow NC 12 into Ocracoke Village, 13.8 mi.

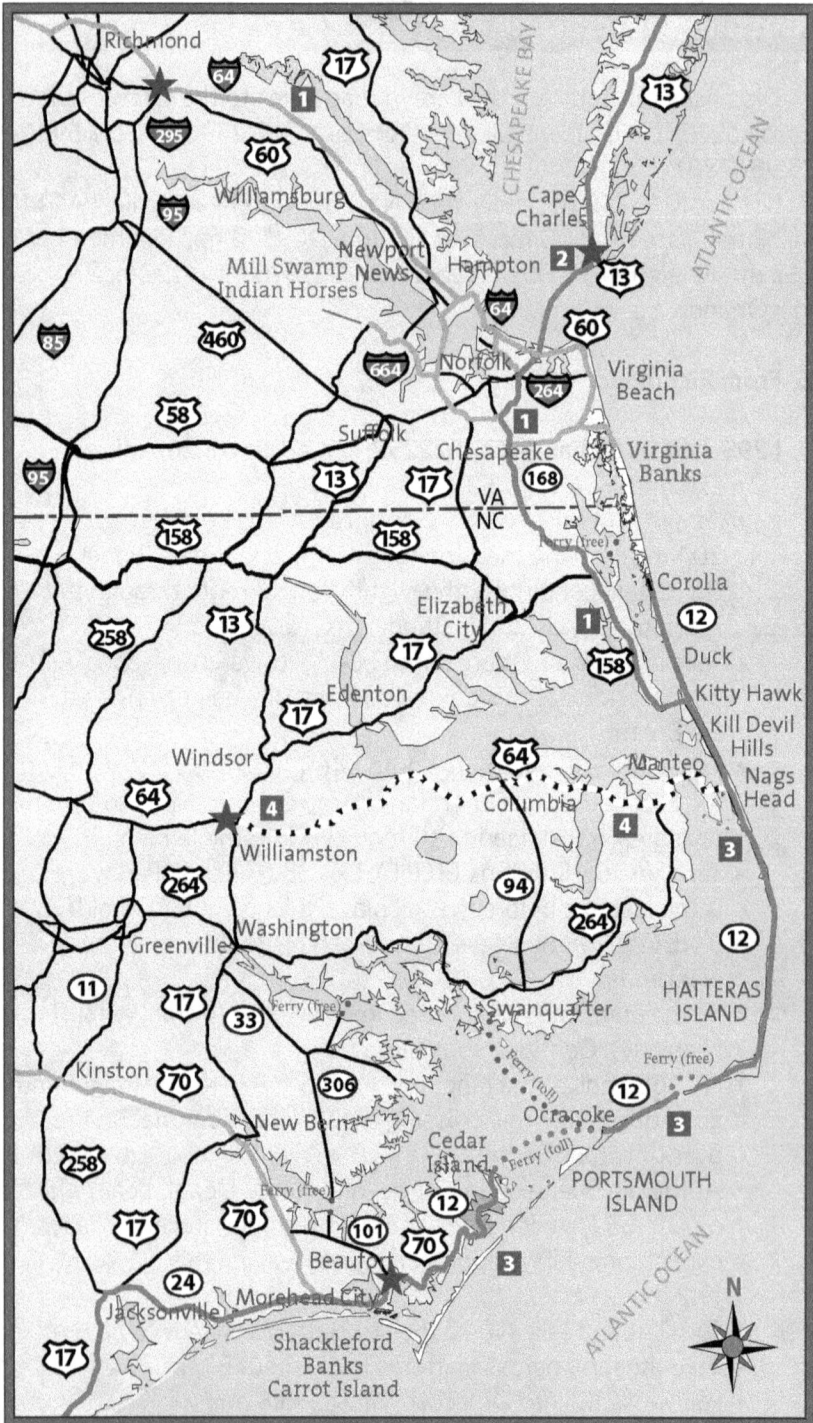

Taking I 95 to US 64 by way of Williamston (below) or Plymouth avoids the crowded stretch from Hampton Roads to Nags Head, but it adds 40–50 miles, much of it on two-lane roads.

2. **From the Eastern Shore of Virginia**
   North end of Chesapeake Bay Bridge-Tunnel (37.118173, -75.968801); 193 mi.
   - Take US 13 S, which becomes Northampton Blvd. in Virginia Beach; 23.2 mi.
   - Exit right onto I 64 E; go 10.2 mi.
   - Take exit 291B and merge onto I 464 S/VA 168 S toward US17 S ("Elizabeth City/Outer Banks"); go 0.4 mi. (Note: for the next step you'll need to maneuver quickly into the left lane.)
   - Take VA 168 S 16.1 mi., including the Chesapeake Expressway (TOLL; see below). Exit 8B (Hillcrest Pkwy.), the last exit before the toll plaza, leads to Battlefield Blvd. (VA 168 Business), which can be very crowded on busy weekends. Taking Battlefield Blvd. farther north may entail risk of delay at the Great Bridge draw span, which opens hourly 6 a.m. to 7 p.m. and on demand at other times.
   - At the state line, VA 168 becomes NC 168 (Caratoke [sic] Highway). Continue south 18.3 mi.
   - NC 168 ends at the junction with US 158 E. Keep straight and go another 28.7 mi., crossing the Wright Memorial Bridge over Currituck Sound.
   - At the big intersection just beyond Home Depot, bear right (south) on US 158 E. This intersection handles 80–90 percent of the vehicular traffic for the Banks from the Virginia line to Ocracoke, so it's one of the worst chokepoints along the route. On summer weekends, backups often begin miles north of the bridge. Once you make the turn toward Ocracoke, congestion will decrease, but not much. Go 19.2 mi.
   - Turn left and take NC 12 toward Hatteras Island. From here on, you will encounter only two-lane roads that are frequently clogged even in the off season. Go 58.9 mi.
   - Take the ferry across Hatteras Inlet, about 5 mi.
   - Follow NC 12 into Ocracoke Village, 13.8 mi.

   CBBT tolls are based on 16 vehicle classes. Most personal cars, trucks, and vans are Class 1. Only E-ZPass holders are eligible for discounts, such as for a round trip within 24 hours. For current information, call 757-331-2960, visit www.cbbt.com/, or subscribe to @FollowTheGulls on Twitter.

Weekend tolls on the Chesapeake Expressway (VA 168) increase by 100 percent or more right before Memorial Day and don't return to normal until a week after Labor Day. Taking US 17 S and US 158 E through Elizabeth City lets you circumvent the toll and some of the congestion in South Hampton Roads. It's longer, though, and the last 50 miles of the trip are the same as above.

3. **From Beaufort, NC**
   US 70, intersection of Cedar and Live Oak streets (34.717558, -76.656933); 58 mi. including a 20-mi. ferry ride.)
   - Take US 70 E (Live Oak St.) 5.2 mi.
   - Turn right to stay on US 70 E; go 6.4 mi., crossing the North River.
   - At the intersection with Marshallberg Rd. in Smyrna, turn left to stay on US 70 E; go 6.2 mi., crossing Williston Creek and Jarrett Bay.
   - Just past the Davis Volunteer Fire Dept., turn left to stay on US 70 E; go 8.2 mi., crossing Oyster Creek and passing the community of Stacy.
   - About 1,000 ft. beyond the bridge over Salter Creek, turn left on NC 12 N (Cedar Island Rd); go 12.0 mi.
   - Take the ferry to Ocracoke, about 20 mi.

When the Cedar Island ferry isn't running, you'll have to take an alternate route. The shortest, which adds about 80 miles, can take the most time. It entails taking the free state ferries across the Neuse and Pamlico rivers to reach the toll ferry from Swan Quarter. Driving to Swan Quarter by way of New Bern and Washington adds another 20 miles, but can save an hour. The northern route through Manteo is about as fast though it's about 100 miles longer.

4. **From Williamston, NC**
   US 64-US 17-US 13 interchange (35.839247, -77.053127); 125 mi.
   - Take US 64 E; go 88.8 mi. through Plymouth, Columbia, and Manteo to Nags Head.
   - Turn right on NC 12 toward Hatteras Island; go 58.9 mi.
   - Take the ferry across Hatteras Inlet, about 5 mi.
   - Follow NC 12 into Ocracoke Village, 13.8 mi.

Ferries

For the latest information, visit the NCDOT Ferry Division site at www.ncdot.gov/ferry

Cedar Island-Ocracoke
3619 Cedar Island Rd.
Cedar Island, NC 28520
35.0167324, -76.3162224
252-225-7411
Reservations toll free 800-293-3779

Fares range from $1 for a pedestrian to $45 for a vehicle or combination up to 65 ft. long. Late October–mid-March: leaves Cedar Is. at 7 a.m., 10:30 a.m., and 4:30 p.m.; leaves Ocracoke at 7:30 a.m., 1 p.m., and 4 p.m. Mid-March–mid-May and late September–late October: adds a 1 p.m. departure from Cedar Is. and a 10 a.m. departure from Ocracoke. Mid-May–late September: leaves Cedar Is. at 7, 10, 11:30, 1, 4, and 5:30; leaves Ocracoke at 7:30, 10, 1, 3, 4:30, and 8. About 2 hr., 15 min.

Swan Quarter-Ocracoke
748 Oyster Creek Rd.
Swan Quarter, NC 27885
35.3947740, -76.3258870
252-926-6021
Reservations toll free 800-293-3779

Fares are the same as on the Cedar Island run. Late September–mid-May: leaves Swan Quarter at 10 a.m. and 4:30 p.m.; leaves Ocracoke at 7:00 a.m. and 1:30 p.m. Mid-May–late September: leaves Cedar Is. at 7, 10, 1, and 4:30; leaves Ocracoke at 6:30, 9:30, 1, 3, 12:45, and 4. About 2 hr., 30 min.

Hatteras-Ocracoke
59063 N.C. Hwy. 12 S.
Hatteras, NC 27943
35.2118843, -75.6985022
Toll free 800-368-8949
252-986-2353

January 1–March 31: Leaves Hatteras hourly from 5 a.m. to midnight, skipping every third hour; leaves Ocracoke hourly from

4:30 a.m. to 12:30 a.m., skipping 5:30 a.m. and every third hour thereafter. April 1 through mid-May and early October through December 31: leaves both terminals hourly from 5 a.m. to midnight. Mid-May through early October: leaves Hatteras hourly 5–7 a.m. and 8 p.m.–midnight, half-hourly 7:30 a.m.–7 p.m. Leaves Ocracoke hourly 5–8 a.m. and 8 p.m.–midnight, half-hourly 8:30 a.m.–7:30 p.m. About 55 min.

Bayview-Aurora
229 NC 306 N.
Bath, NC 27808
NC 306
Aurora, NC 27806
35.377136,-76.748407
252-964-4521

Leaves Bayview, on the north side of the Pamlico River, year-round every 90 min. from 5:30 a.m. to 11 p.m. except at 12:15, 3:15, and 9:15 p.m. Leaves Aurora, on the south side, every 90 minutes from 6:15 a.m. to 12:30 a.m. except at 9:45 a.m. and 12:50 and 10 p.m. About 30 min.

Cherry Branch-Minnesott Beach
2300 Ferry Rd. (NC 306)
Havelock, NC 28532
34.937435,-76.810913
12254 NC 306
Arapahoe, NC 28510
34.968072,-76.805205
Toll free 800-339-9156
252-447-1055

Leaves Cherry Branch, on the south side of the Neuse River, 27 times a day from 5 a.m. to midnight at intervals from 30 to 120 min. Leaves Minnesott Beach, on the north side, on a comparable schedule from 5:25 to 12:30 a.m. About 20 min.

Side Trip 2

Portsmouth Island

The Theodore and Annie Salter House and Visitor Center on Portsmouth Island. The restored historic village has exhibits here and in the school, the post office and general store, and the lifesaving station. Photograph courtesy of the U.S. National Park Service.

For 200 years, Ocracoke Inlet was the busiest conduit of waterborne commerce between Chesapeake Bay and Charleston, SC. Well into the 19th century, the inlet carried two thirds of North Carolina's exports. In 1842 alone, more than 1,400 merchant vessels, almost four a day, passed through the inlet or anchored outside the bar to exchange cargo with small short-range vessels (lighters). Portsmouth, established as a pilot town in 1753 and augmented with a long-vanished fort in response to Spanish raids, became the largest settlement on the Outer Banks. Although the population grew until the Civil War, economic decline began in 1846, when a hurricane opened two alternative inlets, Oregon and Hatteras, just as shoaling made Ocracoke Inlet harder to negotiate. The Rebellion cut off trade from 1861 to 1865 and forced many islanders to emigrate. After the war, canals, railroads, and highways prevented a return to prosperity by gradually eliminating commercial traffic through all the local inlets. Diehard inhabitants survived mostly on fishing, but by the 1950s fewer than 20 remained. In 1966, most of Portsmouth Island became part of Cape Lookout NS, which the Park Service took another decade to organize. Henry Piggott, descendant of slaves who had done the heavy lifting in Portsmouth's lightering operation, died in 1971. The other two permanent residents soon moved away, leaving only weathered structures on the landscape and a puzzling dot on state road maps.

Portsmouth isn't quite the ghost town celebrated in the popular press, however. Park Service employees and volunteers, holders of Park Service leases, and owners of small parcels not absorbed by the seashore live in the 250-acre historic district at various times. (Private property and occupied public buildings alike are off-limits to visitors.) Hundreds of fishermen, birdwatchers, shell collectors, history buffs, curiosity seekers, and descendants of former Portsmouth residents visit every year. Portsmouth gets an unexpectedly high volume of wheeled traffic because the Park Service lets an Ocracoke company conduct ATV tours, and a concessionaire operates a tiny vehicular ferry to the Long Point Cabin Area on Core Banks, 17 mi. south; see below.

Comforts are few. The Park Service provides rest rooms at the Salter House Visitor Center and composting toilets near the lifesaving station; but the island has no restaurant, store, motel, lifeguard, emergency room, concession stand, bait shop, vending machine, pay phone, or public source of potable water. You'll have to bring everything you need—food, water, clothing, suitable footwear, sun screen, insect repellent, etc.—for the length of stay you plan. Camping is allowed, but only outside the relatively sheltered historic district. Except in mid-winter—sometimes, maybe—the legendary mosquitoes present a challenge to health and sanity.

On the other hand, beauty and privacy are abundant. Fishing, shelling, birdwatching, swimming, and sunbathing are almost unmatched. Exhibits are open all year in the Salter House—which Theodore Salter moved from Middle Community, about a mile south, so he and his wife, Annie, the postmistress, would have a shorter walk—and in Salter's store, the school, and the Life Saving Station. (The Methodist Church, whose predecessor was destroyed by a hurricane in 1913, is closed at this writing for repair of damage done by Hurricane Sandy in 2012.) Resident interpreters offer programs April to November. Strolling through the eerie quiet, you can visit the ruins of the 1827 mariners' hospital; the grave of Sam Tolson, arrested by Union soldiers in Elizabeth City for his resemblance to John Wilkes Booth; and Henry Piggott's house, painted pink because of a mail-order mixup. In even-numbered years, the Portsmouth Homecoming, usually held at the Methodist Church, brings locals, caretakers, and visitors (who sometimes make up about half the crowd) together in April for a day of fellowship; for more information, visit the Friends of Portsmouth Island Web site, http://friendsofportsmouthisland.org

Rudy Austin's Portsmouth Island Boat Tours
278 Irvin Garrish Hwy.
Ocracoke, NC 27960
252-928-4361 / 928-5431
www.portsmouthislandboattours.com

Passengers only. Leaves Ocracoke twice a day "in season"; call for reservations beginning in April.

Portsmouth Island ATV Excursions
P.O. Box 790
Ocracoke, NC 27960
252-928-4484
www.portsmouthislandatvs.com

Passengers only. Leaves Ocracoke at 8 a.m. and 1 p.m. daily, April 1–November 30. The usual maximum is six people per trip ($85 each), but larger groups can be accommodated with advance notice.

Morris Marina Kabin Kamps & Ferry Service
1000 Morris Marina Rd.
Atlantic, NC 28511
252-225-4261
www.portsmouthislandfishing.com/cabins.aspx
info@portsmouthislandfishing.com

Passengers and vehicles. Runs on demand to the Long Point Cabin Area (open March–November; reservations: http://recreation.gov or toll free 877-444-6777). Round-trip rates range from $35 for an ATV to $400 for a vehicle or equipment that takes up the entire deck. Passengers over the age of 6: $14 each. Extra gear: $2/ square foot. Guided tour of Portsmouth Village: $50 a person (groups of 4–10); must be booked two weeks ahead.

Note: beach driving is chancy anywhere and more so in Cape Lookout NS. Whereas the Park Service will cite you for speeding or other misdeeds, it won't help if you break down or get stuck. Using private-sector resources to remove your truck from the intertidal zone may cost a great deal more than the ferry ride out.

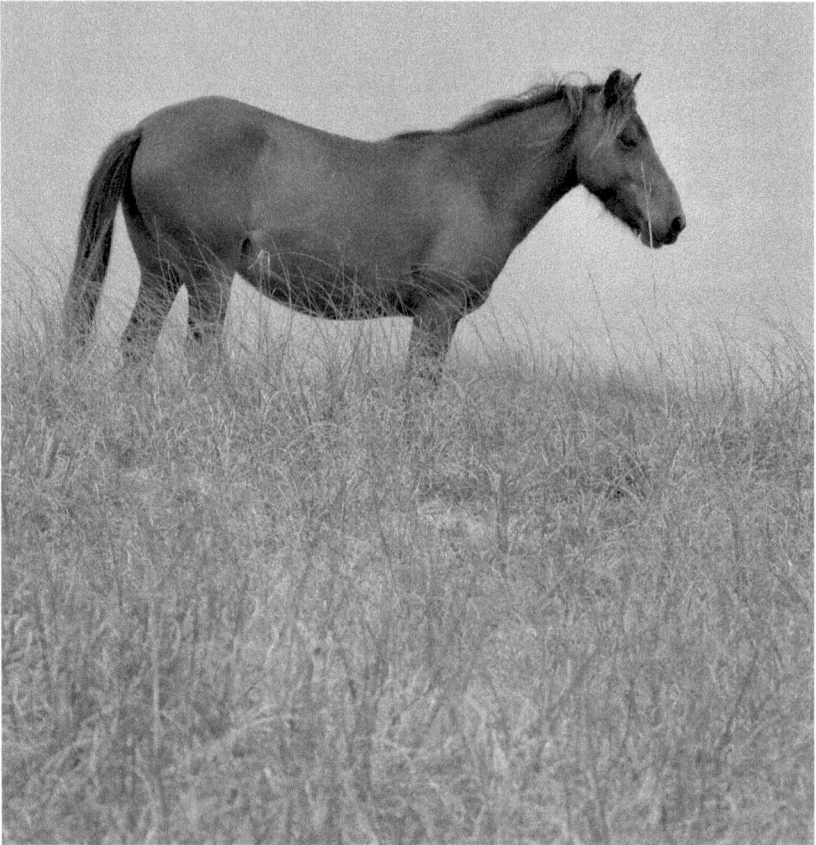

Side Trip 3

Mill Swamp Indian Horses

Tangier • Onancock

17

13

CHESAPEAKE BAY

64

ATLANTIC OCEAN

60

Cape
Charles

Williamsburg

10

64

Newport
News

Hampton

Chesapeake Bay Bridge-Tunnel

13

Mill Swamp
Indian Horses

Smithfield

Norfolk

460

258

664

Virginia
Beach

Suffolk

264

Chesapeake

165

Sandbridge
Virginia
Banks

58

13

17

168

615

VA

158

158

Knotts
Island

NC

158

Corolla

Elizabeth City

12

Duck
Southern Shores

17

158

Kitty Hawk

13

Edenton

ALBEMARLE SOUND

64

Kill Devil Hills

Mill Swamp Indian Horses is a program of Gwaltney Frontier Farms, Inc., a nonprofit that works to prevent the extinction of the Corolla Spanish Mustang [sic]. Its offsite breeding program produces foals from formerly wild Corolla and Shackleford horses and seeks to place them in satellite breeding stations. Located outside Smithfield, VA, the program also teaches the taming and gentle training of wild horses using natural horsemanship. To learn more about the breeding program or to schedule a visit to Mill Swamp Indian Horses, e-mail Steve Edwards at msindianhorses@aol.com

Mill Swamp Indian Horses
13644 Bethany Church Rd.
Smithfield, VA 23430
37.015977, -76.684163
www.msindianhorses.com
http://msindianhorses.blogspot.com
msindianhorses@aol.com

Steve Edwards and his student Lydia Barr work together to saddle train a formerly wild Corolla stallion named Edward Teach (a.k.a. Blackbeard). The horse was removed from his Outer Banks island to treat a large infected neck wound. Because he was unable to return to the wild, Steve and his students successfully gentled and trained him, introducing him humanely to his satisfying new life as a riding horse.

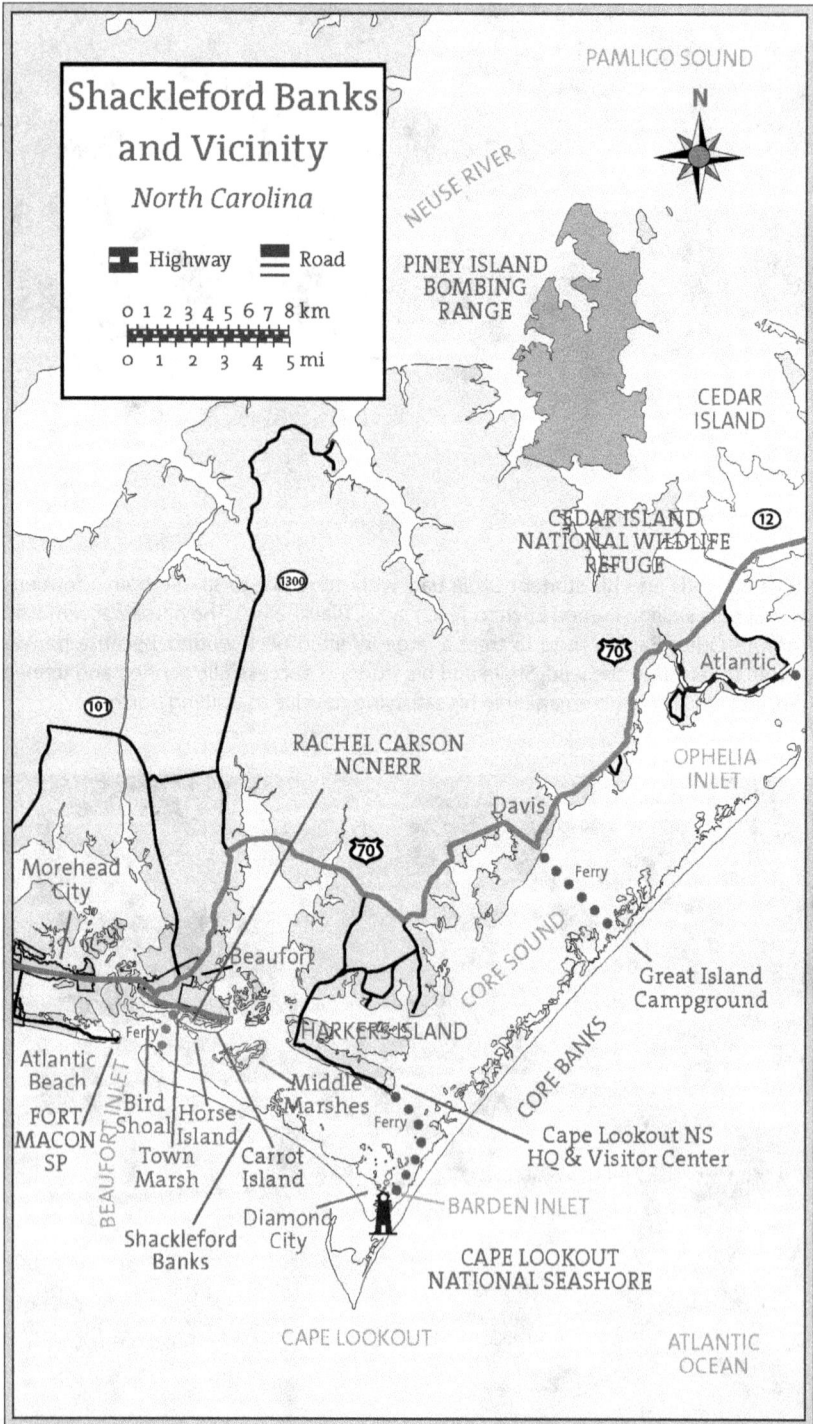

Shackleford Banks and Vicinity

North Carolina

Highway   **Road**

0 1 2 3 4 5 6 7 8 km

0   1   2   3   4   5 mi

PAMLICO SOUND

N

NEUSE RIVER

PINEY ISLAND BOMBING RANGE

CEDAR ISLAND

CEDAR ISLAND NATIONAL WILDLIFE REFUGE

12

1300

70

Atlantic

101

OPHELIA INLET

RACHEL CARSON NCNERR

Davis

70

Ferry

Morehead City

CORE SOUND

Beaufort

Great Island Campground

HARKERS ISLAND

CORE BANKS

Atlantic Beach

Ferry

Middle Marshes

Ferry

FORT MACON SP

Bird Shoal

Horse Island

BEAUFORT INLET

Town Marsh

Carrot Island

Cape Lookout NS HQ & Visitor Center

Shackleford Banks

Diamond City

BARDEN INLET

CAPE LOOKOUT NATIONAL SEASHORE

CAPE LOOKOUT

ATLANTIC OCEAN

Chapter 3

Shackleford Banks

Carrot Island, and Cedar Island

North Carolina

For centuries, free-roaming horses lived and died on the 60-odd miles of North Carolina barrier islands that now constitute Cape Lookout National Seashore. Today, they remain only on Shackleford Banks, a narrow ribbon of sand roughly 9 miles long perpendicular to the south end of Core Banks.

North and South Core Banks extend 44 miles from southwest to northeast, a long, slender stretch of low dunes, grasses, shrub thickets, maritime forest, and spreading salt marshes. The landscape changes from wide tidal sand flats at Portsmouth Island to continuous dunes

A mare unofficially known as Hermione gallops though a grassy flat on Shackleford Banks.

At the west end of Shackleford Banks, natural sand dunes rise as high as 35 feet.

and small freshwater marshes at Cape Lookout. Compared to Core Banks, Shackleford displays more environmental diversity, with dunes as high as 35 feet at the western end, a dense maritime forest, marshes, and grassland. About 3½ miles east of Beaufort Inlet, the island's profile shifts abruptly from high dunes to low overwash flats.

Here again, locals believe that the original Shackleford horses swam to shore from Spanish shipwrecks long before the English colonized the New World. The shoals off Cape Lookout and along the banks are certainly treacherous, and ships often carried horses and other livestock. To add to the confusion, several credible sources have written that shipwrecks probably brought horses to Shackleford as early as 1565, but in each case reference a source of debatable significance.

Dr. Sue Stuska, the Park Service wildlife biologist who manages the Shackleford herd, points out that any shipwrecked horses that reached the island would have been the same type of horses that the colonists raised on the mainland—chiefly Spanish-blooded horses acquired from breeding ranches in the Caribbean. Few records exist, and the horses have been there for so long many generations grew up believing that they were native to the islands. Through the 1800s, locals frequently informed island visitors that the horses were a native species.

The eastern end of Shackleford Banks is lower and flatter.

But because human settlements were successful here for many decades, it is more probable that most, if not all these horses, descended from the livestock turned loose by mainlanders or left behind when the owners left to resettle on the mainland, repelled by a series of severe storms.

The island horse herds have managed to survive violent storms for more than 300 years. Most large hurricanes bring individual losses, however. Every East Coast barrier island that supports a population of wild horses has seen drownings occur in large storms. Ida swept five Carrot Island horses into the water and drowned them. Their bodies surfaced some time later on Harker's island 3 miles away. Three others were carried off alive and deposited on Shackleford Banks, about a mile south, where they stood in an anxious knot, trying to rejoin their fellows.

The geographical features of Shackleford Banks, Carrot Island, and Cedar Island place the horses residing on them at greater risk. From northern Florida to Cape Hatteras, the shoreline is oriented from southwest to northeast, then abruptly, as it reaches the Beaufort area, it turns a corner to run very nearly east-west. Consequently, a broad expanse of ocean lies to the south and southwest of Shackleford Banks and Cape Lookout, which allows hurricanes following the coast to strengthen over warm seas before slamming into the Outer Banks full force. These storms rotate counterclockwise, exposing Core Banks to the unmitigated onslaught of storm-frenzied wind and waves, especially if the eye passes to the west. (Winds are strongest in the northeastern quadrant.) Shackleford is partially protected from the brunt of many storms in the lee of the longer island. Likewise, Cedar Island lies protected behind Core Banks.

Inlet/outlet systems function as self-adjusting safety valves. They are created during storms or floods when storm surge washes a corridor through the sand. Hurricane storm surge is created by the forces of low atmospheric pressure, winds, and surface currents circling around the eye and by the piling of water pushed from the deep ocean to the shallows. The mounded water carries sand and whatever else it can pick up across the island toward the mainland.

As the storm moves away and the wind reverses direction, the water rushes back to the sea. This swollen, unruly tide escapes by smashing through the barrier island into the ocean, producing an inlet by finding an outlet. If the water had no outlet, the barrier islands would function as dams, holding the excess water in the sound and increasing mainland storm damage due to flooding. Between storms, sand fills in the defect, reducing inlets to shallow, narrow channels.

With every storm the Foundation for Shackleford Horses is inundated by e-mail from concerned people who want to know whether the wild horses will be removed from the islands. If the horses are to live as wildlife, they must be left to take their chances with the forces of nature as their ancestors did for centuries before them. To round up the horses would be to rob them of their liberty and to risk injury as they are confined in close quarters, loaded onto barges, and transported in trailers. In fact, a wild horse roundup places them at greater risk than would a hurricane, and some years bring a number of hurricanes and strong nor'easters. Federal law mandates that any horses removed from the island not return.

Hurricane Irene made landfall at Cape Lookout August 27, 2011, as a Category 1. When Carolyn Mason, president of the Foundation for Shackleford Horses, returned to the island to count heads, she found not a single horse was lost, and in fact, the census had increased. Shortly after the 90 mph winds slammed into Shackleford Banks, a mare named Anastasia foaled a leggy bay colt. The name of Shackleford

A Shackleford mare and stallion negotiate a maze of sand dunes *en route* to the marsh.

horses always begin with the same letter as that of their mothers. In this case the choice was obvious—they named him Aftermath.

The first known residents of the area were the Coree Indians, who had lived on and around the islands since prehistoric times. In fact, the name *Core Banks* may be a diminutive of *Coree*. John Shackleford purchased Shackleford Banks in 1714, giving it its current name. English colonists inhabited the island in the 1760s, and by the mid-1800s, Shackleford Banks was home to more than 600 people in several communities.

After the American Revolution, shipping increased along the Atlantic seaboard, and consequently, so did shipwrecks. A 95-foot-tall light station was built at Cape Lookout in 1812, but the structure was too low and too dim to warn ships of the perilous shoals that extended 10 miles into the ocean. In 1859, the station was replaced by the present 163-foot lighthouse, which was outfitted with a Fresnel lens that directed its beam far across the water. In 1873 the lighthouse was painted with a bold pattern of black and white diamonds to enhance visibility. Even so, shipwrecks remained commonplace on the treacherous shoals.

With 500 residents, Diamond City was the largest village on Shackleford Banks, situated on the east end of the island near the Cape Lookout Light. At the time, Shackleford was connected to Core

The Cape Lookout lighthouse stands on Core Banks, which is separated from Shackleford Banks by Barden Inlet. Until the Hurricane of 1933 the two islands were connected. These horses are grazing on the site where Diamond City once flourished.

Banks by a marshy neck known as The Drain. The settlement apparently took its name from the distinctive diamond pattern of the adjacent lighthouse. Shackleford Banks supported an oyster house, a factory that extracted oil from porpoises, a crab-packing plant, schoolhouses, businesses, and churches. By the mid-1700s, Banker watermen were hunting migrating pods of right whales as they migrated north from their calving grounds. It appears that these shore-based whaling operations operated successfully for more than 150 years. The residents' sheep, goats, cattle, and horses freely roamed the island, often wandering north to Core Banks.

Shackleford is generally higher than Core Banks and has a more varied landscape, including 35-foot dunes at the western end. By some accounts, Shackleford supported a dense maritime forest before loggers harvested a majority of the old-growth trees. Other authorities claim that most timber cutting met the immediate needs of the inhabitants.

Around 1840, timber cutting and livestock grazing took the blame for destabilizing the dunes, which began to engulf the woods on the eastern end of the island. A photograph from 1917 shows live dunes engulfing the remaining forest, with leafless "ghost" trees thrusting

Ferries carry visitors to Core Banks to tour the Cape Lookout Lighthouse. Core Banks is an excellent place to collect shells and to spend the day at a secluded beach.

up through the sand. Eventually, geologists came to realize that it is a natural characteristic for some dune systems to spontaneously mobilize and swallow everything in their path, independent of the activities of man or beast.

In the late 1800s, a series of serious storms tested the mettle of the island residents. Then on August 17, 1899, the great San Ciriaco hurricane flattened Shackleford. Named for the saint on whose feast day the storm made landing in Puerto Rico, it struck San Juan as a category 4, flogging the island with estimated sustained winds of 135–140 mph and killing 3,369 people. After flanking the Dominican Republic and Haiti, the mighty storm grazed Florida, then strengthened and hit the North Carolina banks as a category 3 hurricane.

On Shackleford, seven ships were wrecked. Houses were washed off their foundations, and crops and gardens were decimated. Carcasses of dead horses and sheep lodged in trees. Families watched in horror as the waves unearthed buried family members and scattered their bones. On Ocracoke, about 100 horses and cattle were drowned. Two porpoises, caught in the storm surge, swam across the island and lodged in an oak tree.

After this devastating hit, most Cape Lookout residents moved to the more stable ground of the mainland. Many settled in the Promised

Land section of Morehead City or on Harkers Island. Until the 1990s, two telephone poles stood in the surf at the site of the old settlement; now, even these are gone.

Because Barden's Inlet did not separate Shackleford from Core Banks until the Hurricane of 1933, horses and other animals were free to wander the length of both islands. Edmund Ruffin, an agricultural authority from Virginia, visited the area about 1858. He noted in his 1861 book *Agricultural, Geological, and Descriptive Sketches of Lower North Carolina and the Similar Adjacent Lands* that the horses were "all of small size, with rough and shaggy coats, and long manes. They are generally ugly. Their hoofs, in many cases, grow to unusual lengths. They are capable of great endurance of labor and hardship, and live so roughly, that others from abroad seldom live a year on such food and under such exposure."

Mainland residents in Atlantic and other surrounding communities often visited Core Banks to slaughter hogs and cattle when they needed meat. Some mainland residents spent the summer in cottages on Core Banks, and cabins were used for seasonal hunting and fishing.

At one time, developers considered building a bridge to Shackleford and developing the island as a tourist destination, but ultimately it was designated a wilderness. Cape Lookout National Seashore was established in March 1966, extending about 55 miles from Ocracoke Inlet south to Beaufort Inlet. Because of federal protection, Cape Lookout escaped the commercialism and population growth of the Cape Hatteras area. The only access is by private boat or by ferry, and

---

The U.S. Coast Guard Beach Patrol was an important part of coastal defense during World War II, but not without its foibles. Most of the personnel assigned to the Outer Banks were from other states, and some found the local dialect unintelligible. On one occasion, Coasties detained two suspicious-acting men in a rowboat who responded to interrogation in "broken English." You guessed it—they were natives. Suspicions ran both ways. Regular worshipers at Duck Methodist Church, on the northern Banks, were convinced that the Norwegian construction workers from the Poyners Hill Beach Patrol barracks who attended services one Sunday were the vanguard of a German invasion.

In the mid-1990s, a lone telephone pole stood in Barden Inlet, a memento of the village that once flourished on Shackleford Banks.

there are no roads and few facilities. The Park Service rents rustic cabins on Core Banks, and the Cape Lookout Lighthouse complex has restrooms and drinking water.

Situated on the Atlantic flyway, Cape Lookout NS is frequented by least 275 species of birds, both residents and seasonal visitors, including the bald eagle, peregrine falcon, and piping plover. Wildlife is everywhere. Raccoons hunt for invertebrates in the shallows, probing the tidal creek with sensitive fingers as if reading Braille. Non-poisonous snakes coiled like pretzels bake on sunny logs. In the summer months, newborn loggerhead turtles emerge on moonlit nights and flipper their way to the sea, while four other sea turtle species forage in the adjacent waters. Feeding black skimmers unzip the glassy water with their wakes. The island also supports terns, mergansers, herons, egrets, snapping turtles, rabbits, nutria, river otter, and many other varieties of wildlife.

The bands of wild horses vary widely in size, six to sixteen individuals being typical. Just as there is no "typical" human family, scientists disagree on what constitute normal horse behavior, and the horses themselves sometimes disagree with the scientists! Behavior and social norms may vary widely from herd to herd and from band to band.

Dominic, freeze-branded "14R," herds his mares away from the watering hole with a lowered head in a driving posture.

The band generally adheres to a set pattern of activity, moving along well-worn trails to locations within the home range that provide food, water, and relief from insects. The alpha mare will usually lead the herd in daily activities with the stallion bringing up the rear, but he will move to the front if there is danger ahead. When the herd runs from a threat, the stallion will snort an alarm and the herd will mobilize, foals towards the center, the stallion placing himself between his band and the menace.

Stallions gather the band using a driving posture—head low, ears flat, menacing look in the eye. Moving the lowered head from side to side, "snaking," implies extreme threat, which, if unheeded, will be followed by a nasty bite. Rank has privileges. The most dominant horse is the first to drink and has first choice of the available food, followed by the beta, and then the subordinates in descending order of status.

A dominant stallion generally will not permit another male to remain past puberty, but occasionally one makes exceptions. Some harem stallions let a subordinate male remain with the herd as long as he remembers his place and does not attempt to mate with the mature mares. Two-male harems were rare on Shackleford in the early 1980s, when the sex ratio was typically two females to every male. During the late 1990s, the ratio was closer to one to one, and two-stallion herds were more common.

Horses do not usually defend territories, but instead maintain a sphere of in tolerance. If another stallion comes too close, battle may ensue. Here Dominic (right) ran into Bilbo's (center) personal space while in pursuit of his wayward mare, Hermione (far left). The alpha males began to fight, and ultimately Bilbo drove Dominic away.

A mid-rank mare warns two younger mares away from the watering hole by flattening her ears, warning them that they must wait for her to drink her fill before accessing the well. Horses dig these water holes with their hooves—when they reach the water table, mostly fresh water seeps into the depression.

Horses have a complicated social structure, and they communicate with one another continually using postures, gestures, and expressions.

Ordinarily, wild horses don't defend a territory. Instead they maintain a "sphere of intolerance." The stallion grazes his band of mares within a preferred range, attacking any rival males that violate his invisible boundaries. Shackleford Banks has the distinction of being one of the few places in the world where biologists have observed horses defending territories rather than simply guarding harems. This territoriality is due in part to the narrowness of the island and the low dunes and grassland that allow the stallions to detect intruders from a distance. (A single Assateague stallion, Comma, was observed displaying similar territorial behaviors on a similarly narrow, treeless stretch of island.)

Horses communicate among themselves almost constantly, but the majority of their messages are nonverbal. Contrary to the almost continuous chorus of inappropriate whinnies and snorts dubbed into most Western movies, horses don't use their voices very often. Horses evolved to live on grasslands, and herd members usually remain in sight of one another at all times. The flattened ears and head toss of an irate mare is as effective as any vocalization and is less likely to draw the attention of predators.

Pecking order is crucial to the social structure of the herd. When a new horse enters the band, fights ensue until the newcomer establishes a position in the hierarchy. After this initial trial, he or she generally

Wild horses often preferentially eat the tips of saltmarsh cord grass as they emerge above the water line. Shorebirds often follow at the horses's hooves to eat invertibrates disturbed by their foraging.

maintains status by nonviolent displays such as pinning back the ears whenever another horse intrudes. These threats are well heeded by lower-ranking individuals, so actual kicking and biting is usually unnecessary. The purpose of a dominance system is to reduce overall aggression in the group, and as long as a horse's position is well defined, he or she feels secure, even if very low in rank.

Social dynamics are usually more complicated than simple rank, however. Horse number one may be dominant over horse number two, who is dominant over horse number three, while horse number three is dominant over horse number one. As confusing as these relationships can be to human researchers, every horse knows his or her status.

Horses have personalities as unique and varied as those of dogs or people. Each forms friendships within the herd and displays unique preferences and quirks. Like people, horses have personality conflicts. A stallion may be affectionate with one mare and bicker constantly with another. Even mothering skills differ from mare to mare. Foals from previous years, especially fillies, may remain close to their mothers. Understanding a horse's basic need for companionship, a role or status within the herd, and physical contact with other horses, it can

Lactation takes a tremendous toll on a mare's health. If her energy intake does not match the calories she uses to make milk for her foal, she will lose weight. Immunocontraception can give her a break between foals to regain her health. In unmanaged wild herds, mares move from pregnancy to lactation to pregnancy without the opportunity to regain a healthy weight.

make one uncomfortable to realize just how artificial and sterile are the lives of many domestic horses, kept solitary in a box stall or paddock much of the time.

The Shackleford Banks horses make their own water holes by digging in the sand with their hooves until they reach the water table. Fresh water seeps slowly into the depression. A lens of fairly fresh water floats atop the heavier saline layer, and the sand serves to filter out some of the salt. Sometimes they dig so deep that only their rumps are visible as they imbibe from the pool. Pony herds often spend hours near the watering spot to ensure that each herd member gets enough. They also drink from pools of rainwater that form during the wet season.

Some Shackleford horses are ribby, with lean hips and large, round abdomens, presumably from eating large quantities of low-nutritive fodder. Most of the horses that appear excessively thin are very old, and, like elderly people, often have trouble maintaining weight due to

In the mid-1990s, many of the lactating mares of Shackleford Banks were excessively thin, probably because of the pressure of overcrowding and repeated reproduction.

worn teeth and other factors. Lactating mares can also appear thin because of the difficulty of meeting the caloric needs of themselves and their foals. Stallions drop weight during the breeding season, when patrolling for rivals and driving a band take priority over grazing. Young mares maintained on PZP contraception and nursing foals are usually round and well-fleshed.

Body-fat reserves are used as an energy stash in case the animal needs to burn it for fuel in times of physical stress. If a horse does not have these reserves and energy is needed, the animal will break down muscles and burn protein for fuel.

Horses once grazed not only on Core Banks, but also on other islands in the area, including Hog Island, Browns Island, Harbor Island, Chain Shot Island, and Cedar Island. For generations, Banker people and Banker horses worked as partners. The horses provided transportation, muscle, and recreation. Children grew up bareback and barefooted, running the beaches and swimming the sounds mounted on the rugged little horses. Horses were removed to Harkers Island or the mainland for riding, sometimes just for the summer. Come September, the horses were regretfully returned to the island to resume their wild lives, while the children would resume their domesticated ones.

Shackleford horses are rugged and hardy, curious and smart. Carolyn Mason of the Foundation for Shackleford Horses commented, "When most horses who haven't been handled see something unusual, they often will spook and run away. A Shackleford will walk right up and investigate."

The national seashore's goal for Shackleford Banks was to let it revert to a natural wilderness state. Sheep, goats, and cattle were removed from all the barrier islands, but local residents petitioned for the Banker horses to be left roaming free on Shackleford. Ultimately, in 1987, the National Park Service allowed a representative herd of feral horses to remain on Shackleford "because of their potentially historic origin."

Without sheep, goats, or cattle to compete with them for resources, the horses multiplied rapidly, from 108 individuals in 1982 to a 1996 estimated high of more than 240. The equine population overgrazed the island and strained the ecosystem.

A management crisis had developed. Nature's way of keeping the balance is to allow surplus animals to die of starvation when food sources are depleted. If the Park Service did not intervene, large numbers of horses would suffer preventable deaths, and in the process certain native plants could also be grazed out of existence.

This had already recently happened on Carrot Island, a small sand spit lying to the north of Shackleford. Carrot, along with Town Marsh, Bird Shoal, and Horse Island, is part of the Rachel Carson component of the North Carolina National Estuarine Research Reserve. Carrot Island appears on maps as early as 1777, and it was the site of a fishery in the early 1800s. In the 1920s, the U.S. Army Corps of engineers dredged Taylors Creek and deposited the sand on Carrot, building it higher and increasing its stability.

Feral horses have lived on Carrot since the late 1940s (which, coincidentally, was around the time Rachel Carson did her research in that area). Apparently a local doctor named Luther Fulcher, who also owned horses on Shackleford Banks, ran six of his horses on Carrot Island. After Fulcher died, the horses lived as wild, sustaining themselves with no human assistance. Their descendants thrived and multiplied, living across the creek from the Beaufort waterfront.

Beaufort, NC (founded 1713), and Beaufort, SC (1711), are both named for Henry Somerset, the 2nd Duke of Beaufort (1684-1719). But the first gets the French pronunciation, BOH•furt. The second is properly pronounced in the English manner, BEW•furt.

When a population outgrows its food resources, the result is often a die-off. On Carrot Island, NC, 29 horses died of starvation in the winter of 1986–1987. By the mid-1990s (below), the Carrot Island herd contained healthy animals that were for the most part in balance with their environment.

With nothing to curb their fertility, the horses proliferated and overgrazed the marsh grasses. By 1986, the horse population on this small island had reached 68. There simply was not enough food for all of them.

Mother Nature handled the overpopulation problem in her own way during the winter of 1986–1987. Famine and parasites killed 29 individuals within a few months. Once concerned locals realized what was happening, they brought in hay as supplementary feed; but the starving horses, accustomed to native grasses, often refused to eat it.

Spring brought numerous foals, and by August 1988, the herd numbered 51. The N.C. Division of Marine Fisheries had helped them through the 1987–1988 winter by providing twenty bales of hay each week. A point well ensured fresh water. But clearly this level of human assistance could not continue. If the horses were to remain living in the wild, their numbers would have to be kept in balance with their environment.

Horses remain on the Rachel Carson Reserve due to the strong public sentiment attached to them. In 1988 the State removed 33 of 52 horses. Nine of the 33 removed tested positive for equine infectious anemia and were euthanized. Private individuals adopted the remainder. In 1996 the population was up to 30, and a dart-gun birth control plan was initiated. The program was effective, and in 2008 the census was 42 healthy horses. The birth control program is the only regular intervention in their lives—otherwise they are managed as wild animals.

By the late1990s, Park Service personnel feared that the Shackleford Banks herd would suffer a die-off similar to that which occurred on Carrot Island if they did not take action to decrease the population. To better understand the relationship of the horses to the native wildlife and vegetation, the Park Service used research by Dr. Gene Wood and Dr. Daniel Rubenstein. Data in hand, the Park Service pondered how best to handle the equine population dilemma.

Although horses were entitled to protection under the 1980 general management plan, Park Service policy was to intervene when exotic animals or plants "threaten to alter park resources or public health." Should Shackleford Banks support many horses, few horses, or none at all? Local communities argued that these animals were cultural resources. The Park Service could neither deport them nor keep them without ignoring part of its mission.

While many of the horses on Shackleford Banks were in poor condition, others were strong and robust, like Dionysus, an alpha stallion with a large band of mares on the west end.

Many ecologists saw horses as uninvited guests to a dinner table set to nourish native wildlife. One strategy was to remove the horses once and for all. The public was opposed to this; the majority of locals wanted them to remain. Many locals grew up on the backs of Banker horses and considered them an important part of their cultural heritage.

The Park Service also considered taking a number of horses off the island and "managing" the rest. They felt that a herd of roughly 60 horses could be self-sustaining. Fewer horses would leave less genetic diversity, necessitating an infusion of outside genes periodically to revitalize the gene pool.

Many locals favored controlling the population through annual roundups, in keeping with local tradition. Horse pennings had been commonplace on these islands for centuries, and it seemed fitting to hold with historical tradition. As on Chincoteague to the north, an annual roundup could stimulate tourism, and proceeds from the sales of young stock could support horse management on the island. The Park Service opposed this plan, asserting that the potential for injury to both horses and humans was too great. Furthermore, removal of foals alters the social and reproductive dynamics of natural horse behavior, and horse penning would trample the vegetation and disrupt the environment.

In 1994 officials from Cape Lookout NS held a series of public meetings and discussed these options with other interested groups at the North Carolina Maritime Museum in Beaufort. Surprisingly, more than half of those present seemed to feel that the horses should be removed or, if allowed to remain, prevented from breeding and simply left to live out their natural lifespans. After 20 or 25 years, the horses would be gone.

Ultimately the Park Service decided to gather all the horses, test them for equine infectious anemia, destroy any positive reactors, and put a large number up for adoption. Mares returned to the island would receive annual contraceptive vaccines to limit fertility. With the birth rate in check, the population would never again exceed that which the island could comfortably sustain. Both the horses and their environment would be healthier.

As these plans began to take shape, local residents petitioned to block Park Service interference with the island herds. Their protests did not deter the Park Service. In November 1996, the agency herded all 184 horses (considerably fewer than the its original estimate), into

The Shackleford Herd was tested for EIA and the healthy horses were released back to the island. The Park Service freeze-branded their rumps with large white numerals for identification.

pens. Veterinarians Coggins-tested every horse, checking for the presence of EIA antibodies in its blood.

EIA, also known as swamp fever, a disease that only affects equids, is caused by a retrovirus similar to HIV, the one that causes AIDS in humans. It occurs worldwide, but predominantly in warmer climates, and there is no vaccine or cure. It is spread by horseflies, which transfer the blood from infected hosts into healthy animals, who may then develop the disease. After an incubation period of two to four weeks, infected horses may show symptoms such as fever, weakness, weight loss, jaundice, lack of coordination, and swelling of the legs and underbelly. Some will die. Once infected with EIA virus, equids remain infected for life. Some positive testers are highly infectious; others are less so. Most positive horses have a chronic form, show no obvious symptoms, and are only weakly contagious.

Horse advocates vociferously opposed EIA testing of the Shackleford Banks herd. If EIA existed on Shackleford, it had been there for a very long time, and the herd had adapted to the disease, as many wild cat populations have adapted to feline immunodeficiency virus, caused by another virus similar to HIV. Clearly, if over-population was an issue, the presence of the disease was not limiting herd growth, and most of the horses appeared to be in good flesh and lived long lives. Many believed that the push for EIA testing was a ploy to justify destroying the animals, ridding the agency of the wild horse problem.

Seventy-six horses tested positive for EIA, including 16 of the 18 dominant herd stallions on Shackleford Banks. The Park Service re-leased the 108 negative-testers after freeze-branding large letters and numerals on their rumps to make identification easier.

The Park Service made plans to euthanize the diseased individuals. Horse advocates were horrified. Many positive testers showed no out-ward sign of illness and appeared in robust good health. The Founda-tion for Shackleford Horses, a nonprofit organization founded by local residents, proposed quarantine sites for the infected horses to live out their lives, which were rejected by the officials.

No other practicable options surfaced, and The N.C. Department of Agriculture and the Park Service abruptly decided to euthanize 76 horses. Their bodies were buried in a landfill.

A second roundup in March 1997 captured 103 horses. Five of these were positive for EIA. The Foundation for Shackleford Horses was ready this time and had obtained prior approval for a quarantine site. The Park Service gave these animals to the Foundation, sparing them from destruction.

In 1998, President Clinton signed a bill ensuring that 100 to 110 wild horses will be permitted to remain on Shackleford Banks, a num-ber that should maintain enough genetic diversity for a healthy herd. The welfare of the Shackleford horses is now managed jointly by the Foundation and the Park Service, incorporating the expertise of veteri-narians, biologists, scientists, politicians, and local citizens. The Park Service is responsible for ensuring that the horses have enough food and water and that they remain free from EIA and other diseases. A roundup in 1999 confirmed that there are no more positive reactors on Shackleford Banks, so it is unlikely that these horses should ever contract the disease again.

When officials shifted their focus to testing the Cedar Island wild horses for EIA, they nearly wiped out that herd, too. Cedar Island is perhaps best known as the place where the state ferry docks after its journey southwest from Ocracoke. The island, mostly brackish marsh, was named by early settlers for its stands of juniper (Atlantic white

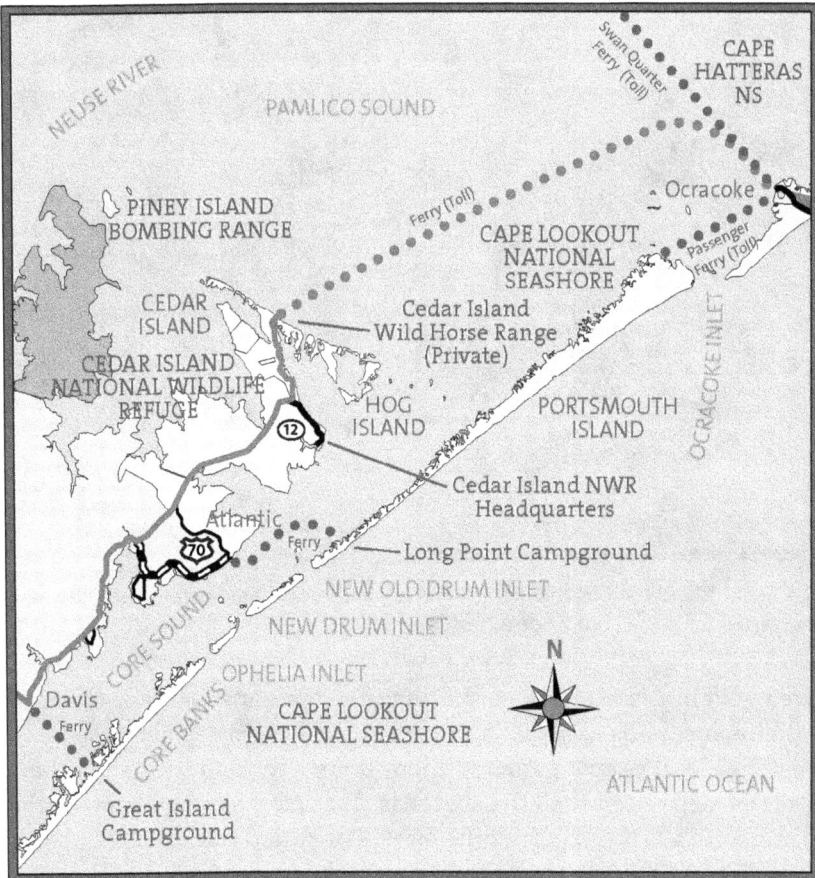

In the era of free range, Cedar Island, Core Banks, and the nearby mainland supported countless head of livestock. Now only a few horses and cattle remain on a small private preserve near the Cedar Island ferry terminal.

cedar). Today it's home to a traditional fishing community with a population around 300, connected to the mainland by a bridge. The main road, NC Highway 12, stops at the ferry dock and picks up again in Ocracoke, 22 miles away. More than half of the island belongs to the Cedar Island National Wildlife Refuge.

A series of low islands and marshes privately owned by longtime residents functions as an unofficial wild horse sanctuary. The range lies east of the ferry dock and extends for about 8 miles, in a swath about 2 miles wide. For more than a century—and quite possibly much longer—herds of 100–200 bays, pintos, buckskins, and blacks

The Cedar Island herd of wild Banker Horses was almost eradicated when the herd was tested for EIA. All but 2 horses tested positive and were euthanized.

lived wild in these marshes, sharing the abundant forage with other wildlife, including cagey wild cattle that charged when surprised.

When local people gathered them every 4th of July, many others came to help or to watch the spectacle. The free-roaming horses of the island were a beloved part of the local history and culture.

In June 1997 the Cedar Island horses were gathered and tested for equine infectious anemia. Of the 15, 13 were positive for EIA and were euthanized. Only two mares remained from the old lines. All the horses at the nearby White Sands riding stable were also infected and were destroyed.

The island residents were determined to save the herd and worked to reestablish it on its historic range land with the approval of the property owners. A Shackleford stallion with bloodlines similar to those of the euthanized horses was relocated to run with the Cedar Island mares, and over the next couple of years, a few Shackleford mares joined the herd.

By 2010, there were 39 horses in the Cedar Island marshes, 6 of them gelded, most between the ages of 8 and 12. Thirty to forty wild cattle also roam these marshes, as they have for over a century. The horses are on private land that is generally not open to visiting, but boaters often spot them along the beaches southeast of the ferry dock.

Bucky, the last remaining horse from the original bloodlines, has produced several fine foals, including Gay, a look-alike filly named for an elderly Cedar Island resident.

New foals are named for elderly or deceased Cedar island residents—Becky, Kassie, Ronald, Ulva, Ina May. Bucky, the lone buckskin mare, is the sole survivor of the original herd. She has produced a number of foals, and in 2010, she delivered Gay, a lovely buckskin filly who looks very much like her.

On Shackleford Banks, wild horses are managed by the Foundation for Shackleford Horses and Dr. Sue Stuska, the Park Service wildlife biologist in charge of their welfare. The Park Service now makes an effort to integrate public input into management plans. From a distance, Stuska delivers contraception via dart gun, documents new foals, and evaluates the health of each individual, but does not feed, touch, or interact with the horses except in extraordinary circumstances. The Park Service treats them as wildlife and grants them the space in which they can be wild horses. The agency does not provide veterinary care, farrier care, or vaccines. If a horse is suffering from a terminal condition, seashore staff decides whether to euthanize on a case by case basis.

Cape Lookout National Seashore encourages the breeding of horses with rare lineages, and limits the reproduction of horses with bloodlines that are well-represented on the island. Dr. Stuska sometimes removes horses from the island if they are injured, or if there is a surplus of juveniles from well-represented bloodlines. Rather than conducting a roundup, she quietly sedates the animal and takes it away without disturbing the band.

The Foundation for Shackleford Horses periodically offers horses for adoption to approved homes for a $600 adoption fee. They are highly intelligent and quickly learn to enjoy the company of people. Pony-sized, most are between 12 and 13 hands in height, but can easily carry adults.

Banker Horses are astonishingly rugged, durable, and unflappable. Their endurance is legendary. Steve Edwards of Mill Swamp Indian Horses (see Side Trip 3) describes an informal race between Holland, his 14-hand (56-in./1.42-m) Shackleford, and a Spanish Mustang stallion descended from the legendary Choctaw Sundance. Carrying a 160-lb/73-kg rider, Holland was allowed to choose his own speed and gait. He ran 5 mi/8 km in 20:54, finishing a half mile (0.8 km) ahead of the well-bred stallion (Edwards, 2009, July 16). On a 50-mi/80-km long-distance ride, Edwards (2009, September 14) described Holland as "absolutely impeccable. He carried 220 lbs forty miles with about 35–38 of those miles at a trot and averaged 5.5 mph. I have no idea how many more miles he could have done." In a blog post Edwards wrote of Holland:

> When I ask him to go, he goes. Where I ask him to go, he goes. When we get to the briers, he goes. When we reach deep water, he goes. As far as I ask him to go, he goes. As smoothly as I asked him to go, he goes. With the ground frozen rock hard, he goes. With the ground parched and baked rock hard, he goes. With the sun glaring down on us, he goes and in the pitch darkness of the night, he goes.

The same can be said for the once-wild Corolla horses Steve uses in his program. Banker horses are tough. While horse breeders select horses to pass along traits like beauty, athletic ability, and temperament, wild horses reproduce if they survive to adulthood in good health and have the social skills to find and keep a mate. After hundreds of years of clinging to life in an often-inhospitable environment, Banker horses have become survivors, small horses with strong hooves, great intelligence and curiosity, efficient gaits, and the ability to thrive on poor forage.

To adopt a horse or to make a contribution to help defray expenses, contact

The Cedar Island herd is healthy and thriving on private land donated by local residents. They share their range with 30–40 moody wild cattle.

Foundation for Shackleford Horses
306 Golden Farm Rd.
Beaufort, NC 28516
252-728-6308
Info@shacklefordhorses.org

Most who visit the wild horses in this region of North Carolina stay in Beaufort, the third-oldest town in the state. The picturesque waterfront is low-key and slow-paced, featuring a marina, boardwalk, shops, restaurants, and music at night. There are historic walks and ghost tours. If you stand at the edge of Taylor's Creek, you may see wild horses grazing across the water on Carrot Island.

Accessible from Beaufort Harbor, the Rachel Carson Component of the North Carolina National Estuarine Research Reserve comprises a chain of small islands that lie across Taylor's Creek from the Beaufort waterfront, near the mouth of the Newport River in southern Carteret County. The islands are continually shaped by the push and pull of wind, weather, and tides. The Rachel Carson site includes tidal flats, flooded salt marshes, sandy beach, subtidal soft bottoms, dredge spoil areas, sand dunes, shrub thicket, and maritime forest. The waters of the Rachel Carson Reserve are ideal for kayaking, bird watching, and nature photography.

An estuary is a transition zone between fresh and salt water habitats. The Newport River enters from the west and the North River flows in from the east. Beaufort Inlet contributes salty Atlantic waters into Back Sound, which defines the southern border of the reserve. The melding of the fresh and saline waters brings high concentrations of nutrients to the waters and sediments of the estuary.

Rachel Carson is a nursery for many marine species, a nesting site for waterfowl, and a stopover for migrants traveling the Atlantic Flyway between their winter habitat in Central and South America and breeding grounds in the far north. The Atlantic Flyway brings more than 200 species of migrating birds to the islands in the spring and fall, including 23 rare or endangered species. Middle Marsh is the site of an egret and heron rookery. The waters surrounding the islands are home to bottlenose dolphins, 52 species of fish, and a multitude of invertebrates such as whelks and clams.

Banker horses can be seen on Carrot Island, which is located across from the Beaufort waterfront. In general, if you are short on time and want to see wild horses, look for them on Carrot Island, which is an easy 5-minute boat ride from the Beaufort waterfront. The horses are usually easy to find, but on one visit I had to hike through a half mile of marsh to reach them. A half-mile self-guided nature trail is marked with numbered posts, winding through the estuary and crossing mudflats, pine woods, sandy meadows, and salt marshes. Wildlife native to Carrot include loggerhead sea turtles, river otters, gray foxes, raccoons and marsh rabbits.

Sand Dollar Island, a small sandbar about the size of a football field that emerges at low tide, is famous among shell collectors for its abundance of sand dollars. Wear goggles and search the shallow bay waters, and you can collect hundreds of sand dollars in a single afternoon. Bring collecting containers and bags or paper to cushion them—sand dollars are exceptionally fragile. You can pack them in layers in your bucket separated by layers of padding. Take only dead white sand dollars. Sand Dollar Island is about 15 minutes from shore by boat.

Bird Shoal has is an important roosting and feeding site for waterfowl, although few birds nest on this sand spit. Species includes ruddy turnstone, willet, short-billed dowitcher, and sanderling. Hundreds

I had the pleasure of riding Holland on an extended trail ride when I visited Mill Swamp Indian Horses. Standing at 14 hands, Holland is tall for a Shackleford. He has an excellent work ethic, moving out with energy as if he can't wait to see what is beyond the next bend of the trail. Moving at speed over exposed roots, mud, and uneven ground, he never made a misstep, and never spooked.

of Black Skimmers visit the shoal during fall migration. The Audubon Society's Christmas bird counts suggest that more endangered Piping Plovers winter here than any other site along the east coast.

Hikers can explore Horse Island and the Middle Marshes with a special permit. If a permit isn't forthcoming, a boardwalk across from the North Carolina Wildlife Resources Commission boat ramp on Lennoxville Road leads from the edge of Taylor's Creek to a platform overlooking a large lagoon.

Cape Lookout National Seashore

131 Charles St.
Harkers Island, NC 28531
252-728-2250
Visitor center open daily 9 a.m.–5 p.m.
Light Station visitor center located on Core Banks open April–November, 9 a.m.–5 p.m.

Cape Lookout NS comprises about 28,500 acres of unspoiled barrier islands. The seashore is 55 miles in length and includes North Core Banks (Portsmouth Island), Middle Core Banks; South Core Banks (including Cape Lookout); and Shackleford Banks. Access is by boat charter. The Cape Lookout Lighthouse is open for climbing on designated days, May through September.

Wild horses can be easily found on Shackleford Banks, a ribbon of sand 9 miles long, but only a mile wide. Colorful shells are easily collected along the beaches, and horse bones are often found in the marsh.

Core Banks offers solitude; miles of unspoiled, primitive beach; a magnificent lighthouse; camping; primitive cabins; beach driving; and shell collecting. The dunes and the sandy hook to the south of the lighthouse are important nesting areas for beach-breeding birds. Birders may see white ibises, American oystercatchers, long-billed curlews, Wilson's and piping plovers, terns, northern gannets, and black skimmers.

Island Express Ferry Service

600 Front St.
Beaufort, NC 28516
1800 Island Rd.
Harkers Island, NC 28531
252-728-7433
www.islandexpressferryservices.com
info@IslandExpressFerryServices.com

Island Express Ferry Service has been the Cape Lookout National Seashore concessionaire since 2013. Ferries depart year-round from the town of Beaufort and Harkers Island and transport visitors to

A green Heron scarfs a minnow on a Beaufort dock. These clever birds often use twigs or insects as bait to attract fish.

Core Banks, including the Cape Lookout Lighthouse, which is open for climbing May through September. Ferries from Harkers Island access Core Banks and the East end of Shackleford Banks. Ferries from Beaufort access the west end of Shackleford banks and the Lighthouse area of Core Banks. You can specify the pickup time—later in the day, the next day, the next week, or longer. Reserve your boat 7 days a week at the ticket booth, by telephone, or online. The ferry schedule is accessible online. All reservations require payment in full at time of booking—cash and major credit cards accepted. Reservations may be made no more than one (1) year in advance.

Camping

Cabin rentals available on Core Banks from March through December.

Twenty-four rustic cabins are available on Cape Lookout NS. These cabins are arranged to accommodate 4, 6, 8, or 12 people and are rented on a per-night basis. The cabins are rustic, but each includes several beds with mattresses, a gas stove with an oven, potable water, sinks, toilets and hot showers. Some cabins have screened porches. There are hookups for generators, if you bring your own. Bring everything else you'll need, including cookware and linens. Access to the island is by boat. Charter ferries are available at Harkers Island and elsewhere.

Primitive camping is allowed free of charge at the seashore, including Shackleford Banks and Bear Island, and in the Croatan National Forest. You may pitch your tent almost anywhere along the 55 miles of North and South Core Banks and Shackleford Banks. Driftwood fires are permitted below the high-water line. Bear Island has private campsites. Croatan National Forest offers public campgrounds and primitive camping.

Reservations
Great Island cabins 252 728 0942
Long Point Cabins 252 728-0958
Rates range from $54 to $168 per night, depending on season and size of cabin.

Campers, choose your tenting sites carefully. The flats behind the dunes may be dry at low tide and appear to be protected high ground, but they can unexpectedly flood as the tide comes in. If the grass under your tent is the type that grows in moist areas, odds are the tide will inundate the site. Cell phone reception can be patchy. There are no trash cans on Cape Lookout NS—bring all your trash back to the mainland for disposal. On Shackleford Banks, stay well away from the wild horses. Bring binoculars or a telephoto lens so you can "get close" while keeping your distance.

Rachel Carson Component of the NCNERR

135 Duke Marine Lab Rd.
Beaufort, NC 28516
252-728-2170
http://portal.ncdenr.org/web/crp/rachel-carson

Rachel Carson National Estuarine Research Reserve is a treasure of a wildlife sanctuary, accessible only by boat. Numerous boat operators on the Beaufort waterfront stand ready to ferry your group to explore the wetlands. Horses are usually easy to find on Carrot Island, but getting within photographic range may take a bit of walking. The islands—Carrot Island, Town Marsh, Bird Shoal, Horse Island, Sand

A band of wild horses congregates on an island in the Rachel Carson Reserve. The Beaufort waterfront is visible in the background.

Dollar Island and the Middle Marshes—cover about 2,025 acres and stretch for more than three miles.Distances, all approximate, are in road miles from the Island Express Ferry Service dock (600 Front St. | Beaufort, NC 28516 | 34.715694, -76.663747).

Nearby Points of Interest

Camping

Arrowhead Campground
1550 Salter Path Rd.
Atlantic Beach, NC 28512
  171 sites, swimming pool, laundry, recreation hall, pets allowed. 15.4 mi.

Coastal Riverside Campground
216 Clark Ln.
Beaufort, NC 28516

252-728-5155

Pier, boat ramp, bathhouse, shady sites, dump station, RVs allowed. 11.4 mi.

Salter Path Family Campground
1620 Salter Path Rd.
Atlantic Beach, NC 28512
252-247-3525
www.salterpathcamping.com

Oceanside and soundside campsites, boat ramp, hot showers, planned activities. 15.5 mi.

Whispering Pines Campground
2791 NC Hwy. 24
Newport, NC 28570
252-726-4902
www.wprvpark.com
info@wprvpark.com

100 hookups, boat ramp and pier. Fire pits. Pets okay. Open year-round. 16.2 mi.

Bed and Breakfasts

County Home Bed & Breakfast
299 NC Hwy. 101
Beaufort, NC 28516
252-728-4611

Beaufort's only bed and breakfast listed on the National Register of Historic Places. Dating from 1914, this building once housed the local "old folks' home." Each room is a studio apartment including a kitchenette with refrigerator stocked with fruit juice and yogurt. Complimentary wine, gas grills, croquet, and use of bicycles. For breakfast, the hostess brings you a basket of warm muffins and bagels. 10 rooms. 2.0 mi.

Anchorage House Bed and Breakfast
211 Turner St.
Beaufort, NC 28516

Toll free 800-934-9968
252-728-9908/342-9030
www.anchoragehouse.net
   Charming 1866 Gothic Revival cottage with heart pine floors and doors, archways and mantels made of mahogany. Wireless internet access, private bathrooms, cable TV. 4 rooms. 0.3 mi.

Ann Street Inn
707 Ann St.
Beaufort, NC 28516
Toll free 877-266-7814
252-728-5400
www.annstreetinn.com
Located in Olde Beaufort, a block from the waterfront, this historical 1832 home is decorated with heirlooms, art, and antiques. Two rooms have whirlpool tubs. 0.2 mi.

Captain's Quarters Bed & Biscuit
315 Ann St.
Beaufort, NC 28516
Toll free 800-659-7111
252-728-7711
www.captainsquarters.us
0.3 mi.

Cousin Martha's B&B, Spices and Gifts
305 Turner St.
Beaufort NC 28516
Toll free 877 464-7487
252-728-3917
www.satansbreath.com/Martha/marthas1.htm
   Expect to feel welcome—online reviewers invariably remark on the warm hospitality of the innkeepers. Eclectically decorated. Try Chef Elmo's trademarked Satan's Breath seasoning and sausage spices. Gift shop sells 18 different sausages plus art, antiques, and hand-painted furniture. 0.4 mi.

Langdon House Bed and Breakfast
135 Craven St.
Beaufort, NC 28516

252 728-5499

Built in 1733, Langdon House is the oldest B&B house in Beaufort. Porches, parlor, landscaped gardens. Breakfast options. 0.2 mi.

Old Seaport Inn Bed & Breakfast (formerly Delamar)
217 Turner St.
Beaufort, NC 28516
Toll free 800-349 5823
252-728-4300

Four rooms. Built in 1866 and considered by many to be Beaufort's most authentic historic bed and breakfast. Antique guestrooms, three common sitting areas, upper and lower porch, English courtyard garden, complimentary continental breakfast. 0.4 mi.

Otway House Bed & Breakfast
368 US Hwy. 70
Beaufort, NC 28516
252-728-5636
www.otwayhouse.com

Situated on 6 acres certified as a National Wildlife Federation habitat. 4 guest rooms furnished with antiques, equipped with full private baths, air conditioning, ceiling fans, and cable TV. Pet friendly—offers a fenced-in area for dogs to unwind. 9.8 mi.

Pecan Tree Inn
116 Queen St.
Beaufort, NC 28516
Toll free 800-728-7871
252-728-6733

Housed in an 1866 Masonic lodge schoolhouse, Pecan Tree has three porches, a 5,000-square-foot flower and herb garden, and a generous continental breakfast. 7 rooms. 350 ft.

The Red Dog Inn
113 Pollock St.
Beaufort, NC 28516
252-728-5954

Half a block from the waterfront. 3 rooms, dog-friendly accommodations (dogs get their own bed filled with treats and toys), and a bottomless candy jar. 0.2 mi.

Hotels and Motels

Bask at Big Rock Landing
814 Shepard St.
Morehead City, NC 28557
252-499-9200
$
AAA 3 Diamonds, Trip Advisor #2 (in Morehead City)

High-speed Internet, continental breakfast, business center, fitness center. Like many other chain motels, it has a Web site whose URL is too long to reproduce here and likely to change anyway. Just look it up in your favorite search engine. 3.5 mi.

Beaufort Inn & Suites
101 Ann St.
Beaufort, NC 28516
Reservations toll free 800-726-0321
252-728-2600
www.beaufort-inn.com
$$
AAA 3 Diamonds, Trip Advisor #1 (in Beaufort), Virtual Tourist 4/5

Exercise room, outdoor hot tub, complimentary breakfast. All rooms have a balcony, refrigerator, coffee maker, and hair dryer; all suites include a microwave. 0.5 mi.

Caribbe Inn
309 E Fort Macon Rd.
Atlantic Beach, NC 28512
252-726-0051
http://caribbe-inn.com
$
Oyster 2 Pearls, Raveable #2, Trip Advisor #1 (in Atlantic Beach), Virtual Tourist 5/5

Microwave and refrigerator in every room, boat slips with floating docks, picnic area. No smoking, no pets. The kid-friendly tropical color scheme and murals of sea life may not be to everyone's taste, but the Caribbe won the Trip Advisor Travelers' Choice Award in 2014 and 2015. 6.4 mi.

DoubleTree by Hilton Hotel
2717 W Fort Macon Rd.
Atlantic Beach, NC 28512
252-240-1155
$$
AAA 3 Diamonds, Trip Advisor #3 (in Atlantic Beach)
    Oceanfront, 200 rooms, 16 suites, onsite pier, two restaurants, WiFi, business center, pool, exercise room. Pet-friendly; no smoking. The Web site, which is easy enough to look up, is another with a crazy-long URL. 8.5 mi.

Hampton Inn Morehead City
4035 Arendell St.
Morehead City, NC 28557-9900
252-240-2300
$$
AAA 3 Diamonds, Frommer's Recommended, Raveable #1, Trip Advisor #1 (in Morehead City)
    118 smoke-free rooms, hot breakfast (included), outdoor pool, fitness center, business center, free WiFi. Yet another Web site URL omitted for brevity. 6.4 mi.

Inlet Inn
601 Front St.
Beaufort NC 28516
Toll free 800-554-5466
252-728-3600
www.inlet-inn.com
$$$
Trip Advisor #2 (in Beaufort), Virtual Tourist 4.5/5
    Offers "the privacy of a hotel but with the amenities, charm and service of a bed and breakfast." Waterfront view—you may see wild horses on Carrot Island across the creek. 36 large modern rooms, some with private porches or fireplaces. Continental breakfast, free WiFi, refrigerators in every room. No pets, no smoking. 100 ft.

Island Inn of Atlantic Beach
215 W Fort Macon Rd.
Atlantic Beach, NC, 28512

252-726-3780
www.islandinnrentals.com
reservations@islandinnrentals.com
$$
Oyster 2.5 Pearls, Trip Advisor #2 (in Atlantic Beach)
38 rooms, suites, and apartments, some pet-friendly. 6.2 mi.

Outer Banks Houseboats
324 Front St.
Beaufort NC 28516
252 728-4129
www.outerbankshouseboats.com
$$$
Rent a houseboat for a week and live on the water! The boat will be dropped off at your desired location, and you can come and go by way of a 21' Carolina skiff. 0.2 mi.

Dining

Boardwalk Café
510 Front St.
Beaufort, NC 28516
252-728-0933
http://beaufortncrestaurants.com/Boardwalk-Cafe.php
Breakfast on weekends, dinner Wed.–Sat.
$$$
A laid-back restaurant with a waterfront view and outdoor seating, Boardwalk Café offers a breakfast buffet and menu, beef, fresh local fish, pastas, homemade soups, and salads. Catch the weekend breakfast buffet Saturday and Sunday from 7 to 11 a.m. 50 ft.

Clawson's 1905 Restaurant & Pub
429 Front St.
Beaufort, NC 28516
252-728-2133
www.clawsonsrestaurant.com
Lunch, dinner; closed Sun.
$

A Beaufort landmark, Clawson's 1905 has been recommended by Frommer's, Fodor's, and *Traveler Magazine*. Dine in an atmospheric building, which was once Clawson's General Store around the turn of the 20th century. Local seafood, steaks, ribs, pasta, and craft brews. Specialties include shrimp & grits, Core Banks shrimp & crab saute, shrimp tempura, and slow-cooked baby back pork ribs. 0.1 mi.

Front Street Grill at Stillwater
300 Front St.
Beaufort, NC 28516
252-728-4956/6978
http://frontstreetgrillatstillwater.com
Lunch, dinner; closed Mon.
$

Waterfront location offers spectacular views; crisp, white linen napkins and tablecloths. Local seafood and prime beef—crab spring rolls with plum sauce Down East clam chowder, baked oysters, goat cheese salad, and Key lime pie. Reservations are highly recommended for dinner. 0.2 mi.

No Name Pizza and Subs
408 Live Oak St.
Beaufort, NC 28516
252-728-4978/4982
also
5218 US 70 W., Suite B
Morehead City, NC 28557
252-773-0654/773-0655
www.nonamepizzaandsubs.com
Lunch, dinner
$

Where the locals go for dinner. Excellent pizza, a wide variety of subs, hamburgers, pasta, chicken— even authentic baklava! Greek salad, laden with feta cheese and accompanied by garlic bread, is a must-have. Dine-in or drive-through service, open seven days. 0.6 and 9.4 mi.

Aqua Restaurant
114 Middle Lane
Beaufort, NC 28516

In the Low Country of South Carolina and Georgia, shrimp burgers often consist of chopped shrimp formed into patties. This is necessarily the kind sold in grocery stores. (Notable among them is Chef Big Shakes Original Shrimp Burger, which became a crowdfunding sensation after failing to get a nibble in season 2 of *Shark Tank*.) Anything else would be just shrimp on a bun.

That's exactly what a North Carolina shrimp burger is—a heap of individually fried breaded shrimp presented as a sandwich. Wherever this variety originated, two drive-ins on the Crystal Coast are generally recognized as its twin peaks. Of course, there's spirited debate over which is Everest and which is K-2.

El's Drive-In, founded in 1959, is in the heart of the state's second-busiest port. It still doesn't take plastic, though it has added an ATM. Big Oak Drive-In (1976) occupies a converted beach house in an unincorporated part of Bogue Banks where residents, many of them descended from squatters in the fish-camp era, didn't get a hard-surface road until 1953 or clear titles to their property until 1979. Sometimes it offers banana pudding to top off its regular fare. Prudent visitors will do their own research.

El's Drive-In
www.elsdrivein.com
theoriginalsuperburger@gmail.com
Lunch, dinner, late
$
Roadtrippers 4.5/5, Trip Advisor #8 (in Morehead City), Yelp 3.5/5, Zomato 3.9/5
6.3 mi.

Big Oak Drive-In & BBQ
1167 Salter Path Rd.
Salter Path, NC
252-247-2588
Lunch, dinner
$$
Roadtrippers 4.5/5, Trip Advisor #1 (in Salter Path), Yelp 4/5, Zomato 3.9/5)
14.5 mi.

252-728-7777
www.aquaexperience.com
Dinner, late; closed Sun.–Mon.
$
Menuism 4/5, Roadtrippers 4.5/5, Trip Advisor #1, Yelp 4.5/5, Zomato 3.7/5

"Small plates, big plates, great wines." The Aqua Restaurant supports local farmers and fishermen by offering fresh local products prepared with a creative touch. Aqua's small plates hold small portions to pass around the table; the big plates hold full-sized dinners. 0.2 mi.

The Beaufort Grocery Co.
17 Queen St.
Beaufort, NC
252-728-3899
www.beaufortgrocery.com
Lunch, dinner; closed Tues.
$$
Roadtrippers 4.5/5, Trip Advisor #3, Yelp 4/5, Zomato 4/5

Fresh local seafood, choice steaks, chicken, veal and lamb, with fresh vegetables, freshly baked breads and homemade desserts. Beaufort Grocery Co. serves a Sunday Brunch and also has a delicatessen with meats, cheeses, homemade salads and breads. 50 ft.

Blue Moon Bistro
119 Queen St.
Beaufort, NC 28516
252-728-5800
www.bluemoonbistro.biz
Dinner, late; closed Sun.
$$
Roadtrippers 4.4/5, Trip Advisor #8, Yelp 4.5/5, Zomato 3.7/5

Blue Moon offers fine dining worthy of an upscale restaurant in a laid-back, friendly, historic setting. 0.1 mi.

Captain's Choice Restaurant
977 Island Rd.
Harkers Island, NC 28531

252-728-7122
www.captainschoicerestaurant.com
Breakfast (Fri.–Sun.); lunch, dinner (Tues.–Sun.)
$$

Captain's Choice serves Down East cuisine including beef, chicken, vegetables, chowders, and salads. Substantial seafood buffet. 17.4 mi.

Cru Wine Bar & The Wine Store/Beaufort Coffee Shop
120 Turner St.
Beaufort, NC 28516
252-728-3066
www.thecruwinebar.com
Breakfast, lunch, dinner, late
$$$
Zomato 3.5/5

Located in a restored historic building near the waterfront, the Cru Wine Bar operates as a combined wine store, wine bar, and coffee shop. You can enjoy live music, free Internet, Escazú artisan chocolates (made in Raleigh), specialty cocktails, pizzas, quesadillas, soups, sandwiches, and more. 0.2 mi.

Fish Tales at Town Creek Marina
232-A W Beaufort Rd.
Beaufort, NC 28516
252-504-7263
www.fishtalesattowncreek.com
Lunch, dinner, late; closed Mon.

Casual waterfront family restaurant serving fresh local seafood, chicken, and specialty dishes. 1.1 mi.

Ribeyes Steakhouse
509 Front St.
Beaufort, NC 28516
252-728-6105
www.ribeyessteakhouse.com
Lunch (Sun.–Fri.); dinner, late
$$
Trip Advisor #12, Yelp 4/5, Zomato 3.3/5

Highly rated for a chain restaurant. Serving choice Omaha grain-fed steaks, boneless chicken breasts, seafood, and pork chops—all grilled and accompanied by unlimited salad. 250 ft.

Royal James Cafe
117 Turner St.
Beaufort, NC 28516
252-728-4573
$$
Roadtrippers 4/5, Zomato 3.6/5

Terms such as *pool hall* and *dive* turn up frequently in online reviews. Early 1950s Formica, wood, and neon décor. Shrimp burgers (see p. 149), hot dogs, Down East clam chowder. Antique Brunswick pool tables, jukebox, video games, flat-screen TV. 0.2 mi.

Ruddy Duck Tavern
509 Evans St.
Morehead City, NC 28557-4218
252-726-7500
www.ruddyducktavern.com
Lunch, dinner; closed Mon.
$
Trip Advisor #1 (in Morehead City) , Yelp 4/5, Zomato 4.1/5

Emphasizes pub grub and seafood. 3.2 mi.

Sanitary Fish Market and Restaurant
601 Evans St.
Morehead City, NC 28557
http://sanitaryfishmarket.com
Breakfast, lunch, dinner
$$
Menuism 4/5, Roadtrippers 3/5

The first restaurant on the Morehead City waterfront, founded in 1938. 3.2 mi.

Sea Side Galley
311 Island Rd.
Harkers Island, NC 28531
252-728-6171
$
Yelp 5/5, Zomato 3.1/5

How do you tell a male green frog from a female? The tympanum is the external structure that we think of as the frog's ear. In the female, the tympanum is about the size of the eye. In the male, the tympanum is about twice that size. This frog is a male.

Attached to a filling station and gift shop. Seafood, burgers, subs, pizza and more; easy on the wallet. 15.8 mi.

The Spouter Inn
218 Front St.
Beaufort, NC 28516
252-728-5190
http://thespouterinn.com
Dinner (hours vary seasonally)
$
Menuism 3/5, Roadtrippers 4.5/5, Trip Advisor #2, Yelp 4/5, Zomato 3.7/5
Fresh local fish, scallops parmesan, bouillabaisse, soft-shell crabs, prime rib, and unique medleys of pasta and seafood. In-house bakery. 0.3 mi.

Horse-Related Activities

Eterna Riverview Stables
1006 Lake N Shore Dr.

Morehead City, NC 28557
252-726-8313
    8.0 mi.

Trade-Win IV Farm
400 Laurel Rd.
Beaufort, NC 28516 252728-2666
252-728-0030
tradewinfarm@gmail.com
    Horse riding lessons on 44 acres. English and Western riding for all ages and ability levels. 9.0 mi.

Other Attractions

Fort Macon State Park
2300 E. Fort Macon Rd.
Atlantic Beach, NC 28512
252-726-3775
www.ncsparks.net/foma.html
fort.macon@ncmail.net
    Fort Macon, first garrisoned in 1834, was used in the Civil War and episodically until the end of WWII. General Robert E. Lee was stationed there as a young officer and influenced its design. The visitor center runs a 20-minute orientation film in the auditorium every half hour and exhibits period artifacts and uniforms. The history is often brought to life through reenactments and demonstrations, such as musket firing.
    The volunteer tour guides are well-versed in the fort's history. Recorded narrations describe the Commandant's Quarters, the World War II barracks and mess hall, and the gunpowder magazine at the touch of a button. The site also includes a nature trail and a large sandy beach, but swimming is prohibited because of the dangerous currents. 9.5 mi.

North Carolina Maritime Museum
315 Front St.
Beaufort, NC 28516
252-728-7317
www.ncmaritimemuseum.org

A wealth of educational exhibits, programs and field trips with a focus on North Carolina's maritime history and coastal natural history. Watch the boat builders at work and see artifacts from the Queen Anne's Revenge, Blackbeard's ill-fated vessel which sank in Beaufort Harbor. 0.2 mi.

Beaufort Historic Site
100 Block of Turner St.
Beaufort , NC 28516
Toll free 800-575-SITE
252-728-5225

Beaufort Historic Site, managed by the Beaufort Historical Association, hosts nearly 60,000 visitors annually to the heritage tourism site. Attractions include tours of restored buildings from the 1700s, classes, workshops, special events and historical re-enactments. 0.2 mi.

Core Sound Waterfowl Museum and Heritage Center
1785 Island Rd.
Harkers Island, NC 28531
252-728-1500

Open Mon.-Sat. 10 a.m.-5 p.m., Sun 2-5 p.m. Experience Down East through exhibits and traditional cultural gatherings. In December, Waterfowl Weekend features music, storytelling, boat building, decoy carving, artwork, and local seafood. A number of educational programs are geared to students of all ages. 19.4 mi.

Crystal Coast Air Tours
150 Airport Rd.
Beaufort , NC 28516
252-728-2323

Operating out of the Michael J. Smith Airport in Beaufort. Several tours offered, rates include seating for up to 3 passengers. Reservations required, open year-round. 2.3 mi.

Good Fortune Sail Charters
Beaufort Town Docks
Front St.
Beaufort, NC 28516
252-247-3860

252-241-6866 cell
www.goodfortunesails.com
rwhite010@ec.rr.com

Guided coastal tours and led by a marine biologist aboard the 42-foot custom-built sailboat *Good Fortune*. Boat accommodates six people for full-day and two-hour tours, educational trips, group and corporate charters, ecology outings, turtle, dolphin, and wild-horse watching, snorkeling, sunset sailing, birding, shelling and kayaking.

Island Express Ferry Service
600 Front St.
Beaufort, NC 28516
252-728-7433
www.islandexpressferryservices.com

National Park Service concessionaire. Ferry Trips to Cape Lookout National Seashore (Shackleford Banks and Cape Lookout Lighthouse) Departing daily from Town of Beaufort Ferry Gateway and Harkers Island Visitor Center. 0.0 mi.

Lookout Cruises
600 Front St.
Beaufort, NC 28516
252-504-SAIL
www.lookoutcruises.com

Tours aboard a 45-foot catamaran for up to 42 passengers, April 1 through November 30. Two-hour dolphin watch. Six-hour trip to Cape Lookout with catered lunch, snacks, fresh fruit, shell bags, and complimentary beverages. 90-minute sunset cruise. Reservations recommended. 0.0 mi.

North Carolina Aquarium at Pine Knoll Shores
Roosevelt Drive
Pine Knoll Shores, NC 28512
Toll free 1-800-832-FISH
252-247-4003;
www.ncaquariums.com/pine-knoll-shores
pksmail@ncaquariums.com

The aquarium offers a variety of programs, mostly in summer. These include surfing lessons with all the required equipment for $15/person. 9.1 mi.

Horses dig for water on Shackleford Banks. When the hole reaches the water table, fresh water seeps into the depression, and the horse can drink. The territories of many bands often overlap at these watering holes, and horses take turns using them throughout the day and night.

Old Burying Ground
400 Ann St.
Beaufort, NC 28516
PDF brochure and map at http://www.beauforthistoricsite.org/wp-content/uploads/2014/04/BHA-Old-Burying-Ground-Brochure.pdf

The Old Burying Ground holds the graves of many of Beaufort's early residents, ancestors of many present-day inhabitants. A map of the gravesites and guided tours are available through the Beaufort Historical Association. More than 200 stones date from before the Civil War. The earliest readable date on a marker is 1765, but many of the smooth, illegible stones are thought to be older. Older still are graves marked with shells or wooden slabs. Ancient live oaks—ironically topped with resurrection ferns—spread their knobby arms over the disarray of markers.

Some of the graves hold historical figures, such as Captain Otway Burns, a privateer and boat-builder who became a hero of the war of 1812. Others are remarkable for the tales that surround them. One grave contains the victims of a shipwreck. Another holds a girl who died of yellow fever and was buried in a glass-topped case. One grave holds a young girl who died at sea returning from England. Her grief-stricken father promised her mother that he would bring her back home to Beaufort for a proper burial. He preserved her body in a keg of rum for the voyage—and later buried her in the same keg. Visitors pay their respects by leaving seashells and small toys at her gravesite. 0.2 mi.

Theodore Roosevelt Natural Area
Roosevelt Dr.
MP 7
Pine Knoll Shores, NC
252-726-3775
www.ncaquariums.com/pine-knoll-shores/plan-your-visit/helpful-hints/theodore-roosevelt-natural-area-nature-trails

300 acres of maritime forests and freshwater ponds donated to the state by the family of President Theodore Roosevelt. Adjacent to the aquarium. 9.1 mi.

TourBeaufort.Com
Front St.
Beaufort, NC 28516
252-515-0356
www.TourBeaufort.com

This company offers a variety of tours including the historic Beaufort Ghost Walk, ecology and sunset sailing, kayak tours and boat tours to Carrot Island and Cape Lookout Lighthouse. Reservations required.

Events

Bald Is Beautiful Convention
September
Bald Headed Men of America
3819 Bridges St.
Morehead City, NC 28557

As founder John Capps says, "Morehead is less hair." Evidently Bald Head Island, at the mouth of the Cape Fear River is too remote. 6.2 mi.

Beaufort Pirate Invasion

August
Various locations
Beaufort, NC 28516
252-728-5225
beaufortpirateinvasion.com

A piratical celebration that has nothing to do with Blackbeard. Instead, this edutainment extravaganza commemorates Spanish attacks on Beaufort during the War of the Austrian Succession (1740–1748).

Core Sound Decoy Festival

First full weekend in December
Core Sound Decoy Carvers Guild
P.O. Box 89
Harkers Island, NC 28531
252-838-8818
http://decoyguild.com
info@decoyguild.com

A major gathering for decoy carvers and collectors. Includes several competitions for new decoys plus antique decoy exhibits, retriever demonstrations, duck- and loon-calling contests, raffles, and food. Held at the Harkers Island Elementary School. 17.9 mi.

North Carolina Seafood Festival

Early October
Various locations
Morehead City, NC
http://ncseafoodfestival.org

The biggest scheduled gathering in the state east of I 95; average attendance is nearly 200,000.

Loon Day

Second Saturday in May
Core Sound Decoy Carvers Guild
1574 Harkers Island Rd.
Beaufort, NC 28516
252-504-3520
http://decoyguild.com
info@decoyguild.com

A celebration of "Harkers Island turkey," once a staple Down East, that includes a decoy judging and auction. Held at the Guild headquarters (the H. Curt Salter Building) in the unincorporated mainland village of Straits. 14.4 mi.

Wooden Boat Show
Early May
North Carolina Maritime Museum
315 Front St.
Beaufort, NC 28516
252-728-7317
www.ncmaritimemuseum.org

Wooden-boat exhibits, sailboat races, sailboat rides, demonstrations of traditional skills, and a boatbuilding contest are among the edifying offerings. 0.2 mi.

Outlying Destinations

Points of interest more than 20 road miles from the Island Express Ferry Service dock (600 Front St. | Beaufort, NC 28516 | 34.715694, -76.663747). Distances, all approximate, are rounded to the nearest whole number.

Camping

Cedar Creek Campground & Marina
111 Canal Dr.
Sea Level, NC 28577
252-225-9571
www.cedarcreekcampgroundandmarina.com

Open April–November. 60 Sites, tenting allowed. 14 mi. from the Cedar Island ferry terminal. 28 mi.

Hotels and Motels

Driftwood Motel
3575 Cedar Island Rd.

Cedar Island, NC 28520
252-225-4861
www.clis.com/deg/drift2.htm

The Driftwood is a 37-room motel on the waterfront, adjacent to the ferry dock. . Run by friendly, interesting local people. This motel has character and its own humble charm, but don't expect modern rooms, new furniture, or immaculate upkeep. Dogs are allowed. Cable television with HBO included, no phones in room. Prices vary, usually in the neighborhood of $90. 38 mi.

Driftwood Campground

Guests need not make reservations to stay at this campground, which has tent and RV sites with full or partial hookups. Driftwood Campground is adjacent to the Driftwood Motel and Restaurant and the ferry terminal. The site offers access to Core Sound and Cedar Island Bay. The sparsely populated Cedar Island contains miles of open beach to explore; with sea kayaking, windsurfing, kiteboarding, and swimming just a few of the many outdoor activities. Cedar Island National Wildlife Refuge is five miles from the campground, and Cape Lookout National Seashore is across the bay. The marshlands of the refuge are a good place to spot waterbirds, songbirds, and raptors.

Dining

Pirate's Chest Restaurant
3575 Cedar Island Rd.
Cedar Island, NC 28520
252-225-4861
$

Weekend prime rib special. Local seafood, pasta, fresh-made clam chowder, and desserts. 38 mi.

Chef and the Farmer
120 W. Gordon St.
Kinston, NC 28501
252-208-2433
http://chefandthefarmer.com
Dinner; closed Sun.-Mon.
$$$

AAA 4 Diamonds, Yelp 4.5/5, Zomato 4.5/5

Opened in 2006 by a local couple who had moved back from Manhattan, C&F is more than a welcome relief from the national chains and greasy spoons lining US 70. It's a magnet that attracts discriminating diners from all over eastern North Carolina.

If you drop in at the right time, you may become an extra in *A Chef's Life* on PBS. The Peabody Award-winning documentary series and cooking show, entering its fourth season as this book goes to press, focuses on the challenges of running a first-class farm-to-fork restaurant in a recovering agricultural town. Nearby attractions include Mother Earth Brewing (the first LEED Gold-certified brewery in the United States), which is open the same days of the week, and the historic CSS *Neuse*. 77 mi.

The evergreen wax myrtle (*Myrica cerifera*) provided medicine, insect repellent, and seasoning for Native Americans living as far north as Delaware. European settlers used its waxy berries to make scented, smokeless candles and sometimes in soap. The shrub's medicinal properties are debatable, but its leaves, placed under or around sleeping bags and ground cloths or crushed and rubbed over clothing and exposed skin, do fend off mosquitoes. (On the other hand, rubbing yourself or your belongings with any wild vegetation is an efficient way to meet other pests.) Wax myrtle isn't as powerful a repellent as DEET or even beautyberry, but the price is right. The leaves are also an agreeable substitute for, or addition to, bay leaves in soups and in water for boiling or steaming seafood. The leaves and wood, both of which will burn green, are excellent for cooking or smoking food, especially bluefish (*Pomatomus saltatrix*). Note: wax myrtle was used in folk medicine to induce labor, so pregnant women should avoid it. Northern wax myrtle or bayberry (*Myrica pensylvanica*—note the spelling) overlaps the range of wax myrtle as far south as the northern Outer Banks and has similar uses. Wax myrtle is so common on the wild-horse islands that most visitors don't notice it. Although it's a moderately popular landscaping plant, government agencies and private citizens often obliterate it by the acre. If you ask, someone will probably give you enough to experiment with.

Horse-Related Activities

Country Carriage Stables & Tours
4526 NC Hwy. 24
Newport, NC 28516
252-808-7314

Horseback riding, riding lessons, general store and much more! Also able to provide carriage services at a location of your choice. 22.8 mi.

Outer Banks Riding Stable
120 Driftwood Dr.
Cedar Island, NC 28520
252-225-1185
http://horsebackridingonthebeach.com

All guided tours—no experience necessary. Come enjoy beach riding through the waves, island-hopping, the beautiful scenery, and wildlife. On route 12 beside the Cedar Island ferry dock. 38.4 mi.

Other Attractions

Cedar Island Ferry
3619 Cedar Island Rd.
Cedar Island, NC 28520
1-800-BY-FERRY
Terminal 252-225-7411

The Cedar Island ferry is not just a means of transportation. It's also the closest thing to a cruise ship you're likely to find hereabouts—pleasant, relaxing, and restorative. On a good day, the dock is about an hour's drive from Beaufort over twisty two-lane roads. When tourists or school buses are out, allow more time. The auto ferry voyage to Ocracoke usually takes 2.25 hours. Rest rooms and an air conditioned lounge area with vending machines are available to passengers. Ferry reservations are highly recommended. Drivers without reservations can park in the stand-by lane and wait for a vacancy. Check in at least a half hour before your departure time, or your reservation will be given to someone else. 38 mi.

Cedar Island National Wildlife Refuge
879 Lola Rd.
Cedar Island, NC 28520
252-225-2511/926-4021
www.fws.gov/cedarisland

This wildlife refuge on the southern end of Cedar Island consists of approximately 11,000 acres of irregularly-flooded, brackish marsh and 3,480 acres of pocosin and woodland habitat. The refuge offers opportunities for hiking, bird-watching, boat launching, wild-horse watching, picnicking, and duck hunting. 36 mi. (to headquarters)

The Pepsi Store
256 Middle St.
New Bern, NC 28560
252-636-5898
www.pepsistore.com

In 1893 pharmacist Caleb Bradham made history by tinkering with an unauthorized, possibly incomplete copy of the Coca Cola recipe. He changed the name of his concoction from Brad's Drink to Pepsi-Cola in 1898 and founded what eventually became the multinational conglomerate Pepsico in 1902. The birthplace of "The Taste Born in the Carolinas" is now a shop specializing in Pepsi products. Every May 27 it celebrates Bradham's birthday by rolling back the price of a Pepsi to the original 5 cents. ("Twice as much for a nickel too. /Pepsi-Cola is the drink for you.") 41 mi.

Tryon Palace
529 S. Front St.
New Bern, NC 28562
252-639-3500
www.tryonpalace.org

The premier historic site in North Carolina includes the restored 1770 governor's palace, several outlying historic buildings, and the high-tech North Carolina History Center. 42 mi.

Local Contacts

Crystal Coast Tourism Authority
3409 Arendell St.

Morehead City, NC 28557
Toll free 800-786-6962
252-726-8148
www.crystalcoastnc.org

Carteret County Chamber of Commerce
801 Arendell St., Suite 1
Morehead City, NC 28557
Toll free 800-622-6278
252-726-6350
www.nccoastchamber.com
cart.coc@nccoastchamber.com

More Information

Fear, J., et al. (2008, August). *A comprehensive site profile for the North Carolina National Estuarine Research Reserve.* Retrieved from www.nerrs.noaa.gov/Doc/PDF/

Gruenberg, B.U. (2015). *The wild horse dilemma: Conflicts and controversies of the Atlantic Coast herds.* Strasburg, PA: Quagga Press.

Ives, V. (2007). *Corolla and Shackleford Horse of the Americas inspections—February 23–25, 2007.* Retrieved from www.corollawildhorses.com/wp-content/uploads/2012/08/HOA-report.pdf

Kirkpatrick, J. (1994). *Into the wind: Wild horses of North America.* Minocqua, WI: Northword Press.

Mills, D.S., & McDonnell, S.M. (Eds.). (2005). *The domestic horse: The evolution, development and management of its behaviour.* Cambridge, United Kingdom: Cambridge University Press.

Prioli, C. (2007). *The wild horses of Shackleford Banks.* Winston-Salem, NC: John F. Blair.

Stick, D. (1952). *Graveyard of the Atlantic: Shipwrecks of the North Carolina Coast.* Chapel Hill: University of North Carolina Press.

Stick, D. (1958). *The Outer Banks of North Carolina, 1584–1958.* Chapel Hill: University of North Carolina Press.

1 The One Thing You'll Talk About for Years

Take a walk on the wild side! Your best opportunity to understand and appreciate the wild horses of Shackleford Banks lies with the Horse Sense and Survival tours offed by the Cape Lookout National Seashore. Led by rangers or the park biologist, these four-hour hikes reveal secrets about the horses, their relationships, and the way they live. You will walk through mud and deep sand, climb dunes, and wade though marsh to gain intimate views of these inspiring horses.

? Getting to Shackleford

Distances (all approximate) are in road miles from the Island Express Ferry Service dock (600 Front St. | Beaufort, NC 28516 | 34.715694, -76.663747).

Boston, MA, 770 mi.; New York, NY, 560 mi.; Philadelphia, PA, 470 mi.; Pittsburgh, PA, 600 mi.; Washington, DC, 360 mi.; Columbia, SC,

295 mi.; Atlanta, GA, 505 mi.; Orlando, FL, 665 mi.

1. From Richmond, VA

I 295–I 64 interchange (37.522252, -77.270966); *262 mi.*

- Take I 295 S; go 29.2 mi.
- At Petersburg, VA, bear left at the fork and merge onto I 95; go 90 mi.
- At Rocky Mount, NC, take Exit 138 B, US 64 E; go 31.5 mi., through Tarboro
- At exit 496, take US 13 S/NC 11 S toward Greenville; go 12.5 mi.
- Turn right onto US 264 E (Greenville Blvd.); go 3.6 mi.
- Turn left on US 264 E toward Washington; go 16.9 mi.
- Turn right onto US 17 S; go 16.9 mi.
- Outside Vanceboro, bear left onto US 17 S Bypass; go 19.3 mi, crossing the Neuse River into New Bern.
- Exit onto US 70 E toward Havelock; go 17.5 mi.
- At Havelock, turn left on NC 101 E (Fontana Blvd.); go 22.2 mi
- Turn left on US 70 W (Live Oak St.).

Taking US 70 E all the way from New Bern avoids the two-lane NC 101 and saves about a mile, but involves going through downtown Morehead City.

2. From the Eastern Shore of Virginia

North end of Chesapeake Bay Bridge-Tunnel (37.118173, -75.968801); *226 mi.*

- Take US 13 S, which becomes Northampton Blvd. in Virginia Beach; 23.2 mi.
- Exit right onto I 64 E; go 10.2 mi.
- Take exit 291B and merge onto I 464 S/VA 168 S toward US17 S ("Elizabeth City/Outer Banks"); go 0.4 mi.
- Bear right and take exit 15B; merge onto Dominion Blvd. (US 17 S); go 29.8 mi., entering North Carolina.
- Bear left onto US 17 S Bypass around Elizabeth City; go 68.7 mi., past Edenton, and Windsor.
- At Williamston take Exit 514, then turn right onto US 17 S; go 35.4 mi., past Washington.
- Outside Vanceboro, bear left onto US 17 S Bypass; go 19.3 mi, crossing the Neuse River into New Bern.
- Exit onto US 70 E toward Havelock; go 17.5 mi.

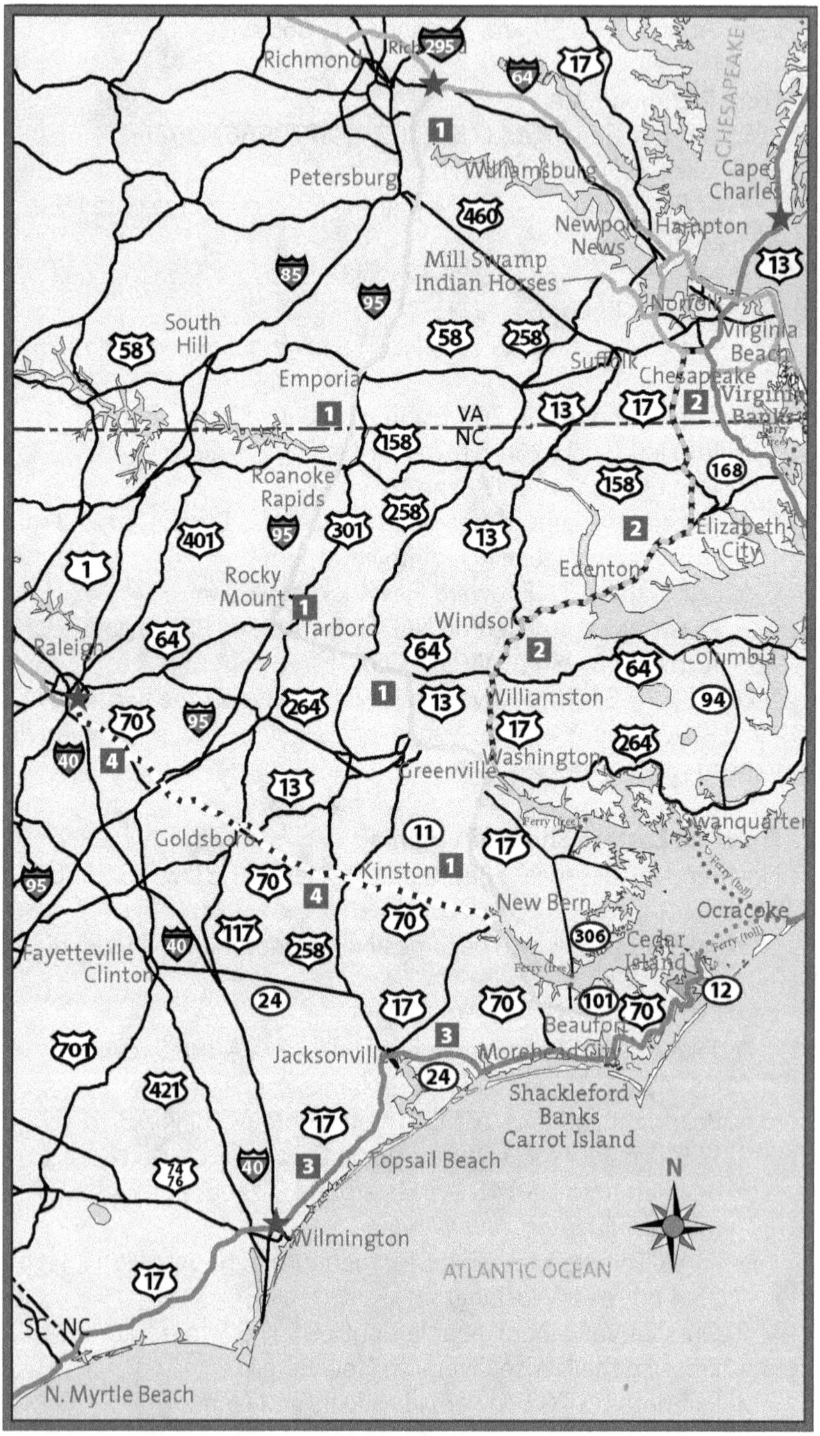
Richmond
Petersburg
Williamsburg
Newport News
Hampton
Cape Charles
CHESAPEAKE
Mill Swamp Indian Horses
Norfolk
Virginia Beach
South Hill
Emporia
Suffolk
Chesapeake
Virginia Banks
VA
NC
Roanoke Rapids
Elizabeth City
Edenton
Rocky Mount
Tarboro
Windsor
Raleigh
Columbia
Williamston
Washington
Greenville
Swanquarter
Goldsboro
Kinston
New Bern
Ocracoke
Cedar Island
Fayetteville
Clinton
Beaufort
Morehead City
Jacksonville
Shackleford Banks
Carrot Island
Topsail Beach
N
Wilmington
ATLANTIC OCEAN
SC
NC
N. Myrtle Beach

- At Havelock, turn left on NC 101 E (Fontana Blvd.); go 22.2 mi
- Turn left on US 70 W (Live Oak St.).

CBBT tolls are based on 16 vehicle classes. Most personal cars, trucks, and vans are Class 1 ($13 one way, $15 Fri.–Sun., May 15–Sept. 15). Discounts, such as for return within 24 hours, apply only to E-ZPass holders. For current information, call 757-331-2960, visit www.cbbt. com/, or subscribe to @FollowTheGulls on Twitter. NC 101 is two lanes. Taking US 70 E all the way from New Bern saves about a mile, but involves going through downtown Morehead City.

3. From Wilmington, NC

I 40/I 140/US 17 interchange (34.319621,-77.872467); *92mi.)*

- Take US 17 N; go 43.3 mi.
- At Jacksonville, exit onto US 17 N-NC 24 E toward Camp Lejeune, Morehead City, and New Bern; go 3.6 mi.
- Bear right on NC 24 toward Camp Lejeune and Morehead City; go 37.4 mi.
- Bear right on US 70 E (Arendell St.); go 8.2 mi., passing through Morehead City and crossing the Newport River into Beaufort.

4. From Raleigh, NC

I 40/I 440 interchange (35.755428,-78.60014); *149 mi.*

- Take I 40 E; go 8.1 mi.
- Take Exit 309 to US 70 E; go 39 mi.
- At Goldsboro, merge onto US 70 E-US 13 N-US 117 ALT N; stay on US 70 E as the other routes branch off; go 25.2 mi.
- At Kinston, bear right on US 70 E (New Bern Rd.); go 53.8 mi., passing through New Bern.
- At Havelock, turn left on NC 101 E (Fontana Blvd.); go 22.2 mi
- Turn left on US 70 W (Live Oak St.).

US 70 is a four-lane surface road from Raleigh to Morehead City. Routes that take advantage of limited-access highways (I 40 and US 264) are longer and not entirely free two-lane driving.

Side Trip 4
Mt. Rogers

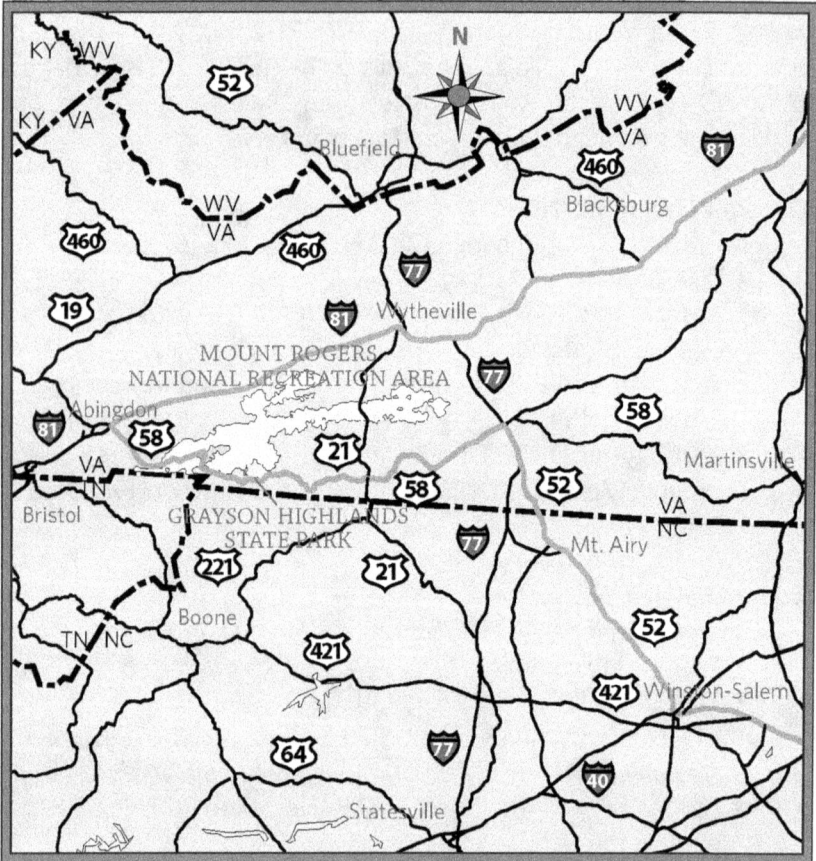

Though Mt. Rogers is a day's drive (370–510 mi.) from any of the wild horse islands, it bears mention because it's home to a herd of ponies that have lived unfettered since 1974. The scenery is breathtaking, and the Appalachian Trail traverses the parks. Mt. Rogers National Recreation Area, an offshoot of George Washington and Jefferson National Forests, and the adjacent Grayson Highlands State Park encompass the highest point in Virginia (Mt. Rogers, 5,728 ft.) and every other spot in the state above 5,000 feet in elevation. Logging in the 19th century left the mountains denuded, and brush eventually

Horses have run free in the Virginia highlands since they were introduced in 1974.

began overrunning the new grassland. The U.S. Forest Service decided to reclaim the open areas, preserve their panoramic vistas and wildlife habitat, and reduce fire hazards by letting livestock graze there. Sheep and cattle fared badly, so in 1974 the agency released a small herd of ponies, mostly Shetlands. They've kept brush under control ever since and become popular with visitors. About 150 ponies roam the area today, foraging at higher altitudes mainly in summer and descending as cold weather sets in. The Wilburn Ridge Pony Association's annual auction, established to keep the population in check, is a highlight of the Grayson Highlands Fall Festival in late September.

Although the ponies have been around only 41 years at this writing, and their introduction is copiously documented, popular lore has already begun to weave a romantic web around them. One Internet site says that they "have lived up on this area of Wilburn Ridge for longer than most folks can remember." Another: "There are many theories of their origin, but no one really knows. The ponies were there long before the park was established in 1965." The herd is 9 years younger than Mt. Rogers NRA and only 7 years older than MTV, it's mysterious only to the uninformed, and it's not entirely wild yet. But it's fun to watch, and it inhabits a gorgeous place that affords many opportunities for hiking and other outdoor activities. The ponies are usually easy to find, and

Two mares initiate mutual grooming in a meadow near the Appalachian Trail. The herd at Mt. Rogers and Grayson Highlands consists of small, colorful horses of pinto, roan, bay, chestnut, and silver dapple. The Wilburn Ridge Pony Association sells the year's foals at auction each fall.

even a cell-phone camera can capture striking images of them against the moody mountainous backdrop.

Mount Rogers National Recreation Area
3714 Highway 16
Marion, VA 24354-4097
Toll free 800-628-7202
276-783-5196
Usual office hours are 8:00 a.m.-4:30 p.m. Monday through Friday. From mid-May until mid-October, it's also open 9:00 a.m.-5:00 p.m. Saturday.

Grayson Highlands State Park
829 Grayson Highland Lane
Mouth of Wilson, VA 24363
276-579-7092
GraysonHighlands@dcr.virginia.gov
Visitor center hours are typically 10:00 a.m.-6:00 p.m. daily, Memorial Day through Labor Day.

Two mares initiate mutual grooming in a meadow near the Appalachian Trail. The herd at Mt. Rogers and Grayson Highlands consists of small, colorful horses of pinto, roan, bay, chestnut, and silver dapple. The Wilburn Ridge Pony Association sells the year's foals at auction each fall.

Rugby Volunteer Rescue Squad and Fire Department
RR 2
Mouth of Wilson, VA 24363
276-579-2261
RR 2 Mouth of Wilson, VA 24363
http://ghfallfestival.50megs.com

This organization joins the state park to sponsor the Grayson Highlands Fall Festival in late September.

If you pass through North Carolina's Piedmont Triangle in your travels, stop by the James Hunt Horse complex, a 30-acre enclave within the North Carolina State Fairgrounds in Raleigh. It has an 81,000-square-foot main show arena that seats nearly 5,000 spectators, and something of interest goes on there nearly every week. You can view the schedule at www.ncstatefair.org/events/calendar.htm

Gov. James B. Hunt Jr. Horse Complex
1025 Blue Ridge Rd.
Raleigh NC 27607
919-839-4701

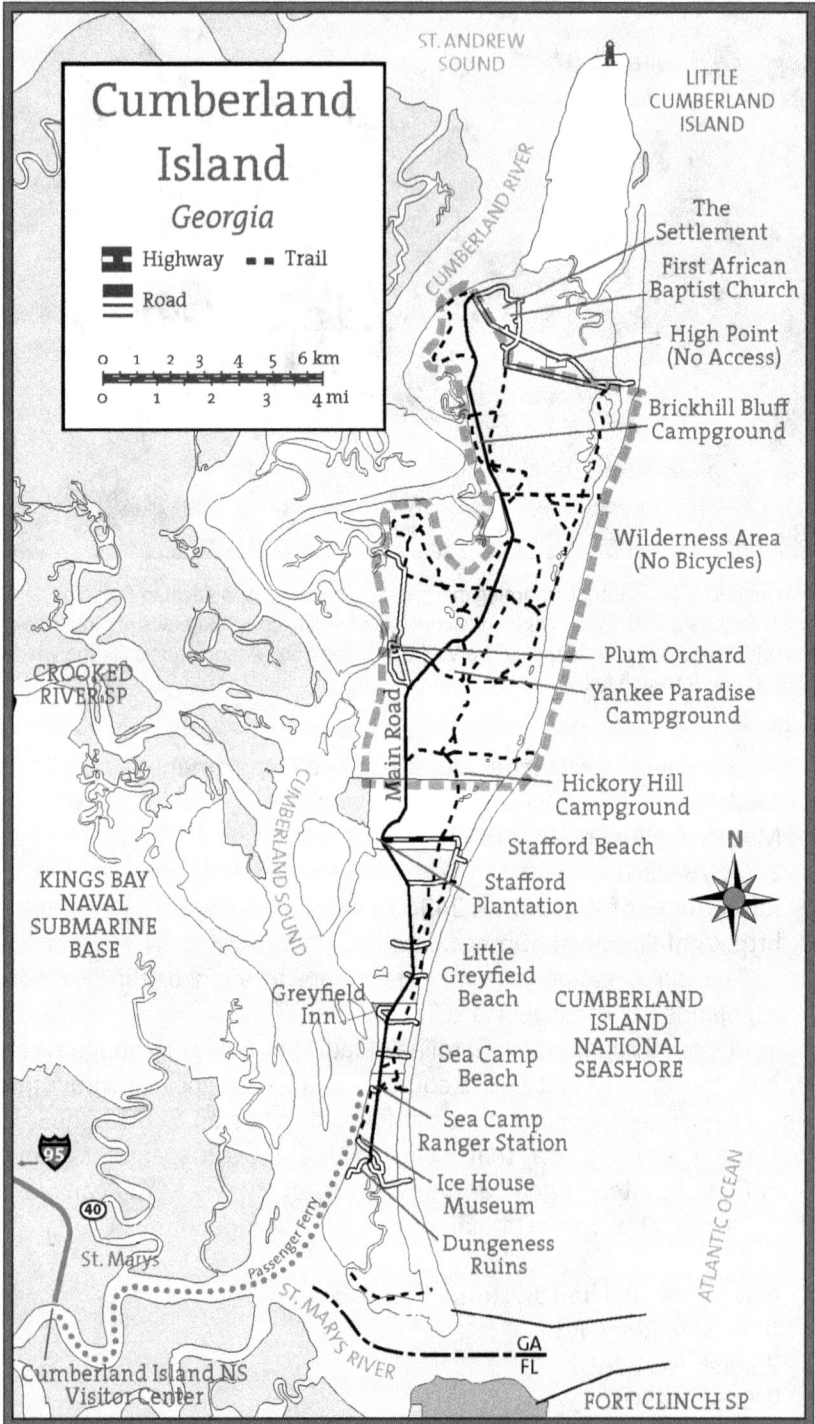

Cumberland
Island
Georgia

Highway　　　Trail
Road

0　1　2　3　4　5　6 km
0　1　2　3　4 mi

ST. ANDREW
SOUND

LITTLE
CUMBERLAND
ISLAND

CUMBERLAND RIVER

The
Settlement

First African
Baptist Church

High Point
(No Access)

Brickhill Bluff
Campground

Wilderness Area
(No Bicycles)

Plum Orchard

Yankee Paradise
Campground

Hickory Hill
Campground

CROOKED
RIVER SP

CUMBERLAND SOUND

Main Road

Stafford Beach

Stafford
Plantation

N

KINGS BAY
NAVAL
SUBMARINE
BASE

Little
Greyfield
Beach

CUMBERLAND
ISLAND
NATIONAL
SEASHORE

Greyfield
Inn

Sea Camp
Beach

Sea Camp
Ranger Station

Ice House
Museum

Dungeness
Ruins

ATLANTIC OCEAN

95

40

St. Marys

Passenger Ferry

ST. MARY'S RIVER

Cumberland Island NS
Visitor Center

GA
FL

FORT CLINCH SP

Chapter 4

Cumberland Island

Georgia

One of the largest undeveloped barrier islands in the world, Cumberland is almost three miles wide at its broadest point and nearly 18 miles in length. The island is a mosaic of diverse ecosystems including primary and secondary dunes, interdune meadows, wax myrtle thickets, mowed lawns, fresh and salt marshes, and pristine beach, as well as one of the largest maritime forests in the United States. Over 20,000 acres are designated wilderness.

Unlike the other American coastal islands roamed by wild horses, Cumberland Island is mostly lush, dense subtropical forest of saw palmetto, magnolia, cedar, holly, pine, and myrtle. Majestic 300-year-old live oaks stand like wizened sentries along the pathways, Spanish moss trailing wispily from their limbs. Broad swaths of light filter through the dense forest canopy to stumble over the confusion of saw palmettos below.

Popular legend holds that the wild horses of Cumberland Island descend from Jennets maintained there between 1566 and 1675, when Spain established a fort and missions on the island. While this origin is possible, there is no evidence. Horses were probably brought to Cumberland Island by the late summer of 1739, but the current population has been heavily influenced by the many horses brought by the Carnegies from the mid-1800s.

Over the last 500 years, Cumberland Island has been repeatedly developed and exploited, then abandoned to reclaim its primitive character. Native Americans made minimal impact, but the Spanish, English, and American residents transformed the island with forts, missions, logging, cotton plantations, estates, a hotel complex, and numerous other projects. Between waves of human habitation, mansions crumbled and native vegetation and wildlife encroached. Since the Cumberland Island National Seashore was established, the island's wilderness persona has been encouraged to reassert itself on most of the island.

A bay mare and her foal eye my intrusion nervously, poised for flight though the palmettos if I should approach too closely. While the horses at the south end of Cumberland Island are tolerant of human presence, those to the north are shy and standoffish.

People have been foraging on Cumberland Island for over 4,000 years, and it is the site of one of the earliest known ceramic assemblages found in the New World. Many of the trails on the island today are remnants of the pathways of the ancient Timucuan natives. They subsisted largely on seafood and wild game, and left behind ceramic shards and numerous shell middens throughout the island.

After Europeans discovered Cumberland in 1562, the Spanish governor of Florida established the missions of San Pedro de Mocama and San Pedro y San Pablo de Puritiba to convert the natives to Christianity. Researchers believe that missionaries brought livestock to the island sometime after this. The mission was abandoned sometime after 1675.

In 1736, General James Oglethorpe, founder of the English colony of Georgia, established two English forts on the island—Fort St Andrew at the north end, and fort Prince William to the south. Cumberland's present name came about through the suggestion of an Indian boy named Toonahowie, who visited London with his Uncle Chief Tomochichi and General Oglethorpe. Toonahowie struck up a friendship with the 13-year-old son of King George II, Prince William Augustus, Duke of Cumberland. To seal the friendship, upon parting William gave Too-

Many brick and stone chimneys remain in the vicinity of the Stafford Mansion. Most were once part of slave cabins.

A wild stallion grazes beside a large pergola, part of the Dungeness ruins.

nahowie a gold watch. Toonahowie, in turn, asked General Oglethorpe to name this island after the Duke of Cumberland. Fort Prince William, built on the southern end of the island, also honored the young duke, and Dungeness, originally constructed as Oglethorpe's hunting lodge, was named for the royal county seat in Kent.

Spanish forces clashed unsuccessfully with English colonists at the southern fort in 1742, and their defeat ended Spanish incursions into the area of English Georgia. Before the American Revolution, there were few settlers on Cumberland, but thereafter planters moved in to grow rice, indigo and corn and raise horses, cattle and

A wild horse grazes beneath the wing of an airplane on the Stafford Plantation. Sea Island cotton was once grown in this expansive field.

hogs. Colonists harvested Cumberland's live oak trees for ships timber, lumber and shingles.

After the war, General Nathanael Greene bought extensive property on Cumberland Island, intending to harvest live oak to sell for shipbuilding, and to build a home for his family on the site where Oglethorpe had maintained his hunting lodge, Dungeness. Unfortunately, Greene died before he could begin to build or turn a profit. Greene wrote that in 1785, shortly after the war, at least 200 horses and mules roamed the island. In 1796, Green's widow Catherine married Phineas Miller, the general's secretary and her children's tutor. They built a palatial four-story mansion also named Dungeness, which rose to four stories and was surrounded by terraced gardens that grew many exotic foods. The Millers frequently held elegant parties, and Cumberland became a social hub for the affluent. Phineas Miller also died, leaving Catherine once again alone.

Georgia was founded as a free colony, but its prohibition of slavery lasted barely a decade. At the outbreak of the Civil War, black residents of Cumberland Island, most of them slaves, outnumbered whites 7:1.

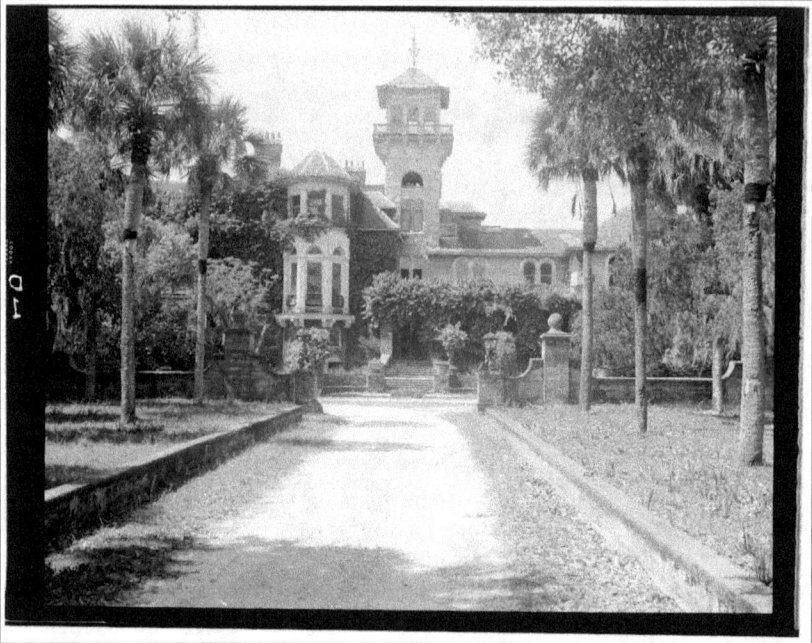

The 50-room mansion Dungeness was once a social center for the rich and famous guests of the Carnegies. Photograph courtesy of the National Park Service.

From the end of the Revolution to the Civil War, Sea Island cotton was the major cash crop of Cumberland Island. More than half of the island was cleared for farming. Slaves lived in small cabins—today a cluster of stone chimneys marks the spot. Horses were necessary for working these plantations and for traversing the 18-mile length of the island. When the Civil War began, the planters of Cumberland retreated to the mainland for safety. The families returned to find Dungeness burned to the ground except its stone walls and chimneys.

Robert Stafford, Jr., son of Thomas and nephew of Robert Stafford, acquired land over time until his holdings around the present-day Sea Camp area totaled 8,125 acres. Census reports show Stafford kept 30–40 horses on his plantation between 1850 and 1870, and sold "marsh tackies" captured from free-roaming stock.

During the 1850s Stafford owned up to 348 slaves, who were emancipated when he was in his 70s. The profitable island plantations owed their success to slave labor, and after the Civil War, agriculture was no longer sustainable. Before the Civil War, there were

The home ranges of several bands overlap at the lawns of the Dungeness ruins, causing overgrazing. Dungeness is one of the best places on the island to watch wild horses. The ruins are a short walk from the Dungeness dock, and most of the time horses can be found grazing on or near the grounds. The horses at the southern end of the island are more likely to wear colorful roan or appaloosa coats, in contrast to the chestnuts and bays most commonly found elsewhere.

10–12 large, productive plantations on Cumberland, but by 1876, all had folded.

By 1878, two hotels were operating on the northern end of Cumberland Island. They reached a peak in popularity in the 1890s and 1900s and shut down by 1920. In 1928, the Candler family, made wealthy by the Coca-Cola Company, purchased the land.

Thomas Morrison Carnegie, brother and partner of steel magnate Andrew Carnegie, bought the plantation at Dungeness in 1881 for his wife Lucy and their family. They erected another Dungeness mansion on the site of the first, graced by verandahs, turrets, and gables and boasting 50 rooms.

Like the earlier Dungeness, this great house soon became a social center for the wealthy. Thomas and his wife Lucy welcomed guests and entertained them with activities such as hunting, fishing, golfing, and cruising aboard the Carnegie yacht, also named Dungeness.

Thomas Carnegie died in 1886 at the age of 43, leaving Lucy with 9 children and a large inheritance. Lucy went on to acquire 90 percent of Cumberland Island, turning it into a vast, self-sufficient family pre-

Many breeds have contributed to the Cumberland Island wild horse herd. In the mid-1990s, I photographed a white mare who had the clear lines of a purebred Arabian running with a wild band.

serve staffed by about 200 employees. Lucy set about expanding the Dungeness complex to include more than 20 buildings, as well as walls, decorations, and a pergola (colonnaded walkway). A recreation and guest house east of the mansion included a heated pool, a steam room, a recreation room, a squash court, and guest bedrooms. Other houses, docks and structures were built all over the island. Seven of Lucy's nine children married, and she presented four of these with mansions on Cumberland Island.

Lucy gave the Stafford mansion to her eldest son William along with cash for renovations, but in 1900 the old homestead burned. On the site, William built a second Stafford house which was similar to the previous structure, but with a fire-resistant stucco exterior.

Lucy's wedding gift to her son Thomas Carnegie II was a 29-room home known as The Cottage, built on the grounds of Dungeness. It burned in the 1940s. Lucy's daughter Margaret (nicknamed Rhetta) used her husband's wealth to build "Greyfield," a two-story home two miles to the north of Dungeness. Greyfield now operates as an elite and expensive inn.

The wild horses of Cumberland Island are often taller and longer-legged than those of the other East Coast herds. A two-year-old roan colt champs at a bay mare with Thoroughbred conformation by pulling back the corners of his mouth and making exaggerated nursing motions. This gesture means "Don't hurt me, I'm only a baby."

Lucy Carnegie built Plum Orchard for her son George when he married Margaret Thaw in 1898. Eight years later, Margaret expanded the mansion to include 30 major rooms, 12 bathrooms and lavatories, and many smaller rooms.

When Lucy died in 1916, Andrew II, Thomas II, and Margaret remained trustees of the estate. Initially, the Carnegies maintained their affluent lifestyle, but finances grew tight in the mid-1920s, and plummeted with the stock market crash of 1929. While the Carnegies valued the primitive nature of the island, financial difficulties forced the family to generate income by closing Dungeness and capitalizing on Cumberland's resources. Cumberland narrowly escaped being transformed into a major development similar to Coral Gables, FL, and it was nearly strip-mined for titanium-bearing ilmenite. At one point, the island was almost commandeered by the federal government for a NASA base, and at another it was nearly converted into a residential retreat for the affluent, complete with natural areas, golf courses, and other recreational facilities.

In the 1950s, Cumberland Island was subject to poaching and vandalism, and Lucy Ferguson and the other land owners resorted to "hunting" the poachers. Shortly after a group of Florida poachers escaped a volley of their gunfire, Dungeness was destroyed by a fire that could be seen for miles along the mainland coast. Nobody was ever arrested for the crime. The ruins of Dungeness remain a popular

The wilds of Cumberland Island are filled with incredible biological diversity. Golden orb spiders weave huge webs in the saw palmettos (top), and nocturnal green tree frogs sleep the day away on stalks and leaves (bottom).

The Gullah/Geechee people of the Sea Islands have a long, complex history. Despite their ethnic and linguistic diversity, slaves and freedmen in the coastal Carolinas developed a widely usable Afro-English creole and preserved many African crafts and traditions. Some escaped to Spanish Florida in the late 17th century only to be overtaken again by servitude and British authority as Georgia took shape. Some who sided with the Crown in the American Revolution emigrated to Nova Scotia and eventually founded Freetown, the capital of Sierra Leone. Others joined the Natives in what was left of Spanish territory. Most of the Black Seminoles who hadn't fled to the Bahamas after the United States took over Florida in 1821 were deported to what is now Oklahoma under the Indian Removal Act (1830). Some of *them* quickly headed for the Rio Grande.

Despite these dislocations, the Civil War, Jim Crow, and modern homogenization, Gullah/Geechee language and culture are resurgent, and the population, concentrated in eastern South Carolina, Georgia, and Florida, probably exceeds 200,000. Descendants of the Bahamian refugees ("Black Indians") survive on Andros Island, and several hundred Black Seminoles remain in Oklahoma, around Brackettville, TX, and in Nacimiento de los Negros, Mexico.

Sapelo Island, GA, was a major source of sugar, as ruins of a sugar mill attest. Cornelia Bailey, founder of the Sapelo Island Cultural and Revitalization Society, leads an attempt at reviving commercial cultivation of heirloom purple-ribbon sugarcane to support the island's dwindling population. Photograph by John Alexander.

feature of Cumberland to this day, and wild horses favor grazing on the grassy grounds.

In 1971 most of the Carnegie property was sold or donated to the Park Service. On October 23, 1972, President Nixon signed legislation to establish Cumberland Island as a 40,500-acre national seashore, making it one of the largest mostly undeveloped, barrier island preserves in the world. There were 18 retained-rights lots within the seashore boundaries deeded to allow residents to live on the land for set periods ranging from decades to life.

Today, a 9,886-acre portion of the island is federally designated wilderness, and another 10,731 acres may be added in the future. The marshes, beaches, meadows, forest, and ocean habitats teem with wildlife, and migratory birds use the island as a stopover on their journey to Mexico.

Free-roaming horses were first documented on Cumberland Island in a 1788 letter to Edward Rutledge from Phineas Miller, but we do not know whether any descendants of the early lines remain. During the Civil War, most horses were removed from the island. Some of the remainder were eaten by 900 starving soldiers and freedmen during this time. After the Civil War, Cumberland residents used most of the island for grazing free-range livestock. Records indicate that semi-gentled horses were swum to the Camden County, GA, mainland from Cumberland Island to be sold in 1866. This might have been an annual activity similar to the pony pennings on Assateague Island and the Outer Banks.

When the Carnegies came to the island in the1880s, they stabled a number of fine domestic horses in their compounds. Plum Orchard had an impressive 15-stall stable filled with high-quality animals. Farther south, the stable at Dungeness accommodated 60. The holdings of the Georgia State Archives document the Carnegies' domestic horses on Cumberland Island and the presence of feral herds at liberty all over the island. The residents held wild-horse round-ups and "rodeos" to break the latter to saddle.

Many breeds have contributed genes to the free-roaming herd. In 1896, the Carnegies purchased a white stallion from the Imperial Stud farm of the Russian Czar. From the 1880s through the 1960s, horses of numerous kinds including Appaloosas, Thoroughbreds, and retired circus horses were released at various times to add desirable genes to the herd. In 1921, a train car-load of fine Arizona mustang mares was released onto the island. In the 1950s Lucy Ferguson and

One of wildlife biologist Doug Hoffman's many duties is to secure sea turtle nests against the predations of hogs and raccoons. A simple piece of mesh allows the eggs to incubate undisturbed, and the sea turtle population continues to boom.

her staff castrated every wild male foal that they could capture, then released their own fine stallions to breed with the wild mares. As recently as 1992, a resident added four registered Arabians to the wild herd to improve conformation.

In 1991, a team led by wildlife biologist Robin Goodloe reported in the *Journal of Wildlife Management* that the Cumberland horses are genetically similar to other East Coast island populations and especially the Assateague ponies, but also resemble other breeds, including the Tennessee Walking Horse, Quarter Horse, Arabian, and Paso Fino. DNA analysis indicated that the horses descended primarily from stock associated with the Carnegie estates.

Kinship with the Assateague herd is difficult to see. In contrast with the short-legged, draft-like Assateague ponies, the Cumberland horses are much taller, longer-legged, and sleeker. While Assateague ponies are mostly pinto or sorrel, Cumberland horses range from the bays and chestnuts common at the north end of the island to the black, brown, red, and blue roans and grays in the Dungeness area. Many Cumberland horses have white markings such as blazes, forehead stars, and socks. Some have Appaloosa patterns such as roan with white blankets, dark with white "snowflake" markings, or spotted blankets across the

A white doe pauses before disappearing into the underbrush. Genetically a piebald rather than albino, she has given birth to a number of white fawns. Look for her and her offspring at the south end of Cumberland Island as you cross the forested dunes between Dungeness and the beach.

hindquarters. Some show other Appaloosa traits such as a sparse mane and tail, striped hooves, mottled skin, and a white sclera.

Other wildlife abounds on Cumberland Island. In wet years, tree frogs trill loudly for much of the night, their throats ballooning like bubble gum, at daybreak sleeping off the evening's debauchery camouflaged on palmetto leaves. Log-like alligators lurk half-submerged in the freshwater shallows, and river otters cavort in their quest for fish. Throughout the moist, steamy woods, armadillos root in rich humus. White-tailed deer, smaller than they are in northern forests, venture onto the meadows as the sun drops behind the horizon. Venomous snakes such as diamondback rattlesnakes, timber rattlesnakes and cottonmouths hunt scampering rodents.

The waters off Cumberland are critical breeding and calving grounds for endangered right whales. Manatees, up to 15 feet long and weighing as much as 3,000 pounds, graze on *Spartina* and algae in salt-marsh creeks. Groups of as many as seven manatees commonly loiter in the salty water around the ferry docks at low tide, drinking the freshwater runoff while people wash their boats

Sea turtles nest on the wild beaches. These reptiles were hunted on the island and elsewhere through the early 1900s. At one point, the Carnegies preferred turtle eggs to hen's eggs and enjoyed green turtle

A young stud wanders the beach alone. He will probably join a loosely organized bachelor group of adolescent males until he is mature and savvy enough to challenge an alpha stallion for possession of a breeding band.

soup. Eggs were found by thrusting a sharp stick into the sand of a potential site—if it was a nest, the stick would come out covered in sticky white or yolk. Over the past century, once-abundant marine turtles became endangered species. They are, however, apparently making a comeback: Cumberland Island had 336 nests in 2006, 252 in 2009, and 486 in 2010, 700 in 2012, and 561 in 2013.

Bobcats were exterminated on Cumberland in 1907 and later reintroduced. They thrive on the island, preying upon rabbits, rodents, and young fawns. Black bears and Florida panthers were also native to the island, but were hunted to extinction and not reintroduced.

The destructive, elusive, and prolific feral hogs are perpetually vexing to the Park Service. The first swine were brought to the island by Spanish colonists and missionaries in 1562, and they probably have been free-roaming since then. Feral swine are adept at evading capture and multiply rapidly, with large litters, short gestation periods, and early puberty. Their preferred habitat is palmetto forest and salt marshes. Feral hogs will eat anything from grasses, fruit, nuts, tubers, and seeds to rodents, frogs, fawns, and carrion. Weighing up to 130 pounds apiece, the pigs stand accused of consuming the eggs of

A mare teaches her young colt to descend the stairway at the Dungeness ruins on the way to the lower lawns.

ground-nesting birds and sea turtles, uprooting and destroying endangered plants, and competing with native animals for resources. Public hunts are held regularly and traps are set, but the clever hogs survive.

My June 2011 visit coincided with hog-trapping season for Doug Hoffman, wildlife biologist for Cumberland Island National Seashore. After the fall had brought a bounty of acorns and other foods, the hogs were not as tempted by the corn he used to bait his traps. We were negotiating the circuitous Grand Avenue, which was more a broad trail than a road, the when he suddenly braked and jumped out of the truck, falling to one knee to peer critically at subtle impressions in the moist soil. He moved sinuously, with the self-assurance of a man accustomed to living alone in the wilderness. His eyes cast searchingly into the forest on both sides of the road. He returned to the truck unhurriedly, brows furrowing slightly.

"What was it?" I asked from my perch in the passenger seat.

"Hog tracks," Doug drawled.

Doug's duties as a wildlife biologist on Cumberland Island National

Cumberland Island is large, but most of it is covered with thick forest. Wild horses compete for forage, and there is not always enough to go around. Foal mortality is high, and in dry years many lactating mares often become bone thin. With the thick foliage, it is difficult for the Park Service to count the horses, let alone implementing a contraceptive program. More research, more funds, and a workable management plan are sorely needed for the sake of both the horses and the environment.

Seashore keep him busy around the clock and around the calendar. His tanned, weathered skin attests to long hours spent in the sun and the wind, living like a Georgian Crocodile Dundee. At the time of our meeting, he had been awake more than 26 hours, keeping vigil on the moonlit beach and dispatching feral hogs that dared disturb sea turtle nests. At sunrise, he began loggerhead patrol, cruising the beachfront for "turtle crawls," indicators that new clutches of sea turtle eggs were deposited in the night. By the time he had collected me into his truck for a tour of the equine herds and habitats, a lesser man would be in the throes of sleep deprivation, yet somehow, his mind remained quick and his demeanor pleasant.

His duties are myriad. When he took his position on the island, 67 percent of sea turtle nests were ravaged by predators such as raccoons and feral hogs. Today, virtually every nest remains unmolested. He monitors the plight of graceful wood storks with 5-foot

The historic Plum Orchard Mansion is open for public tours on a limited schedule. Get in touch with the Cumberland Island NS to sign up. Park Service photograph via Wikimedia Commons.

wingspans, endangered manatees the size of Volkswagens, night-flying yellow bats, and red bay trees decimated by a fungus carried by the minute Asian Beetle. On one occasion, he even rescued a father and son who had been swept away by strong tidal currents after their fishing boat capsized.

Hoffman reads tracks as easily as Indiana Jones reads hieroglyphics. And we saw them everywhere—in the forest, roadways, and marshes. The cloven hoofprints of feral hogs appear similar to deer tracks, but the impression is round, whereas a deer's sharp hoof tips make tracks that are more heart-shaped.

Perhaps as foreign to this ecosystem as the hogs, but considerably more charismatic, roughly 150 horses maintain a relatively stable population on Cumberland Island. Carrying capacity is the maximum number of individuals that a habitat can support. Carrying capacity fluctuates in response to environmental conditions; a population of large herbivores can exceed carrying capacity following a dry season, and fall well below this threshold after a few weeks of rain without a change in numbers. During long periods of drought, ungulate populations naturally decline, then rebound

The humble First African Baptist Church is perhaps best known as the site where John F. Kennedy, Jr., and Carolyn Bessette were married in 1996. It is part of a cluster of buildings known as the Settlement, at the north end of the island approximately 17 miles from the Sea Camp Dock. The Church was established in 1893 and rebuilt in the 1930s. Park Service photo via Wikimedia Commons.

during wet years. You can see evidence of this natural fluctuation in the Cumberland herd. In dry years, lactating mares—those who have the greatest need for calories—become gaunt, and their foals are more likely to die in the first year of life. In wet years, lactating mares are fleshier, and foal mortality declines.

Horses will eat their favorite foods first, then the less palatable greens, only turning to poor-quality or bad-tasting forage if there is nothing else to eat. This selective grazing affects natural plant diversity. When the horse population expands until preferred forage becomes scarce, the health of both the horses and the environment is compromised. Research has indicated that overgrazing by horses occurs on the marsh and dunes, and in the pasture/lawn habitats associated with the Stafford Field area and Dungeness Historic District. Horses can live on barrier islands without destroying habitat (and in fact can improve habitat for other species), but they must be maintained below the carrying capacity of the island.

The Park Service says that if grazing pressures are reduced, the environment will eventually return to balance. There is no manage-

A mare and foal find plenty of food available in a green meadow during the wet year of 2009.

ment plan currently in place for the horses, mostly because of budgetary constraints and political pressures to give precedence to other projects. By the 1990s, the Park Service had painstakingly hammered out a horse management plan with help from biologists and environmental scientists. But in the fall of 1996, U.S. Representative Jack Kingston (GA 1) toured the island with one of the residents and concluded that the equine census had decreased and there was little evidence of horse-related damage. Without consulting the Park Service, he added a rider to the fiscal year 1997 budget bill blocking all horse-management planning at Cumberland Island NS. After the rider expired, budget cuts thwarted Park Service's ability to create a new management plan.

Even without such developments, implementing management options used on other barrier islands would be a challenge. Hoffman explained, "The forests are dense with saw palmetto understory that is difficult to penetrate, complicating roundups and immunocontraceptive administration. Some of the horses living at the south end of the island routinely travel distances of greater than two miles over the course of a day or two. A contraception program would neces-

A wild stallion trots across the Dungeness grounds, focused on defending his mares from a rival stallion.

sitate finding, vaccinating, and recording data on every mare on a yearly basis."

A few tracts of land on Cumberland Island remain privately owned, but a majority of the island is now part of the seashore. John F. Kennedy, Jr., brought Cumberland Island to national attention in the fall of 1996 when he married Carolyn Bessette in a quiet ceremony in the humble First African Church, then retreated to the seclusion of Grey-

Navy Submarine Base Kings Bay, about a mile across Fancy Bluff Creek from Cumberland Island, is home port of the Atlantic Fleet's Trident submarines. The base is thus a primary target for foreign antagonists, and its proximity to subs lurking offshore would ensure its obliteration in the opening minutes of a nuclear war. Of course, a warhead vaporizing the base would take Cumberland Island, too, probably without warning. Consolations might include setting off on an exploration of the hereafter with wild horses for company.

The compound of buildings near the Dungeness ruins provides optimal horse habitat. Consequently, the south end of Cumberland Island offers may opportunities for horse viewing.

field Inn. Cumberland Island was one of the few places on the East Coast where such a high-profile event could be held free of paparazzi and other interlopers.

Visitors can reach Cumberland Island by ferry or by private boat. Ferry tickets are often sold out, so you should make reservations well ahead of your trip—months in advance if you intend to visit during the busy season or on weekends. The operator does not take payment when you make the reservation. Instead, you will receive an invoice in the mail, which you must return with a check within a certain time. If you miss the deadline, your reservation will be canceled. Free-long term parking is in a unpaved lot a couple of blocks from the Cumberland Island NS Visitor Center. Check in upstairs in the Visitor Center at least 30 minutes before the ferry departs, or your reservation will be canceled without a refund. You will also have to pay an additional $4/person for admission to the seashore, and your campground fees if you will stay on the island. A park ranger provides a short orientation before you board. There are no stores on the island—you must carry in everything you will need and pack out all of your trash.

The majority of visitors ride the ferry to Dungeness dock and spend the day hiking, beach-combing, and touring ruins at the south end of

Cumberland Island is the only place you can see wild barrier island horses with Appaloosa coloration. These horses descend from animals owned by the Carnegie family, and can be spotted on the south end of the island.

the island. A free ranger-guided tour takes visitors from the dock to the ruins and provides historical and environmental insights.

A 3.5-mile trail loop from Dungeness dock provides an excellent introduction to the island, taking you past ruins, over dunes, to the beach, into maritime forest, and back to the dock. It takes about 4 hours to complete if you pursue a leisurely place and break for lunch, photography, and basking on the beach. In 2011, a motor tour became available that allows visitors to explore historic sites at the distant north end of the island. If you take the first ferry of the day to Cumberland and return on the last ferry, there will be time for either activity.

The Southern end of the island—from the Dungeness dock to the Dungeness compound and ruins and out to the beach—is probably the best place to watch wild horses. The horses prefer to graze on the lawn areas around the dock and ruins and in the nearby marshes, and there are typically several bands grazing along the main trail between the Dungeness dock area and the beach. They are usually easy to find. While horses at the north of Cumberland are primarily nondescript bays and chestnuts, to the south you will see a whole palette of color—

roans and Appaloosas splashed with vivid white blazes and stockings. The first foals are usually born in early to mid-March and most are born by the middle of April. Spring and summer visitors can enjoy the antics of the curious, energetic babies and watch rival males strut and clash on the open lawn of the Dungeness ruins.

Cumberland Island is a nesting site for three species of endangered sea turtles: the leatherback turtle, the green turtle, and the loggerhead turtle. Female sea turtles, weighing 200–300 pounds apiece, lay their eggs on the beach May through August. A mother turtle emerges from the ocean at night and crawls to the dry sand above the high tide line, leaving a distinctive tractor-like imprint in the sand. Using her two rear flippers, she excavates a round pit and deposits 50–170 leathery golf ball-sized eggs. She covers the nest with sand and returns to the ocean, never to see her offspring. The eggs are generally discovered the following morning by the turtle patrol, which carefully counts them, sends a representative sample to the University of Georgia for genetic testing, and places a predator-resistant mesh over the nest site. The eggs hatch an average of 60 days later, from mid-July to early October.

You can observe this natural drama for yourself by taking a stroll on the beach a few hours before dawn. You can illuminate the hauntingly beautiful beach with a red flashlight—artificial white light confuses the turtles, which navigate by the moon and stars. Flash photography and campfires on the beach can also prevent turtles from finding the ocean.

Cumberland Island offers a unique opportunity to experience a barrier island in its undeveloped state. It attracts people who seek solitude, who enjoy making their own entertainment, who love to hike and swim and use their bodies, who want to sleep close to the earth and embrace the rarity of an undeveloped island wilderness.

Cumberland Island National Seashore

113 W St. Marys St.
St. Marys, GA 31558
912-882-4335
www.nps.gov/cuis
30.720552, -81.549680

Most day-trippers arrive via the Cumberland Queen, a ferry operated by a Park Service concessionaire. Its earliest arrival to the island is 9:40 a.m., and the last return trip in the evening is 4:30 p.m., which is just enough time for a hike around the 3.5-mile loop with a good measure

of low-key relaxation as well. Bicycle access is limited, and vehicles are largely prohibited, so day trippers are geographically limited to where their feet can take them in the time between drop off and pickup . Allow at least an hour to return to the dock—if you miss the last ferry back to the mainland, you must arrange for a private charter to transport you.

Pack wisely for your day trip—you will carry your pack with you for the duration of your stay. There are no stores on the island, so you will need to pack in food and plenty of water, and carry all of your trash back to the mainland. Water, insect repellent, sunscreen, and snacks are crucial to your enjoyment of the park. The weather on Cumberland may be different from that on the mainland, and storms blow in quickly. A lightweight rain jacket with a hood may save you from an unexpected soaking. Closed toed shoes are preferable to sandals—cactus and sand burs are abundant and puncture your feet with every stride.

Restrooms with flush toilets and drinkable water are located at the ferry docks, at Sea Camp, and near the Dungeness complex. There are open showers for sandy beachgoers on the boardwalk at Sea Camp, and private cold showers located near the Sea Camp restrooms. There are no shower facilities at the Dungeness area.

The climate is subtropical—humid and warm for much of the year, and cool in the evening in spring and fall. In the warm season, the heat can be overwhelming, and the island offers few reprieves from the sun's relentless assault. Heat exhaustion is a real possibility despite the shady overhang of the live oak canopy. Bloodthirsty insects can bite through long sleeves and pants. To avoid oppressive heat and ferocious insects, plan your visit for early spring or late fall, when conditions are more pleasant and the water is still warm enough for swimming.

Babies are best packed into backpacks and front carriers. Strollers are impossible to push on the sand and shell roads and trails unless they are specifically designed for the beach. The rental bikes on the island do not have child seats. There are no garbage cans on the island, so plan to pack home your dirty diapers.

Campers have the opportunity to see more of the island. Campers disembark at the second ferry stop, the Sea Camp dock, about a mile distant from the first, and attend a mandatory orientation before site assignment.

Sea Camp and Stafford campgrounds are developed, but wilderness camping is also available—and necessary if you plan to hike to the north end of the island. The northernmost campground, Brickhill Bluff, lies about 10.6 miles from the ferry dock. Campers may stay a maximum of 7 days and must bring everything they will need for the time they are on the island.

Bicycles may be rented through the ferry deck hands at the Sea Camp Dock on a first-come, first-served basis. Bikes may only be ridden on designated roads—they are prohibited on the beach and on the trails. Bikes are not allowed on the ferry, but you may bring your own via private or charter boat.

The Park Service distributes a map of Cumberland's 50-odd miles of trails at the Visitor Center in St Marys. The distances always seem greater when you're hiking them than when you see them on the map. Some of the island is private property, and trespassing is forbidden. Most of the hiking trails of Cumberland are narrow, sandy roads. Grand Avenue, a sinuous sandy track at best, cleaves the thick forest and leads to the north end of the island. There you will find the ruins of the original Cumberland Wharf, where guests arriving by steamboat disembarked to vacation at the Cumberland Island Hotel. The First African Baptist Church stands on the northern tip of the main island.

The Parallel Trail, which runs near Grand Avenue, is a footpath closed to vehicular traffic and bicycles. The Lost Trail borders the Sweetwater Lake complex, where alligators and cottonmouth snakes lurk in an Everglades-like ecosystem. The Lost Trail merges with the Roller Coaster Trail, which threads through the dunes past the shore

Free ranger-led tours to the Dungeness ruins are offered daily under the spreading live oaks by Dungeness dock.

of freshwater Lake Whitney, where otters and mink hunt for fish. The beach is also a handy pathway to the north end of the island.

There is cell-phone reception on the island. Rangers recommend that you carry a cell and a map to help you keep track of where you are. If you call in an emergency, yours or someone else's, they need to know where to find you.

The *Cumberland Queen*
PO Box 1203
St. Marys, GA 31558
Toll free 877-860-6787
912-882-4335
Adults, $20; children 12 and under, $14; seniors (65 and over), $18 (subject to change)

Cumberland Island is accessible only by water, and most people arrive via the *Cumberland Queen*, which departs daily from St. Marys. The ride is a 45-minute scenic venture that sets the mood for your time on the island. Reservations, which can be made up to 6 months in advance, are recommended during the summer season. After Labor Day, the ferry is usually uncrowded, and reservations

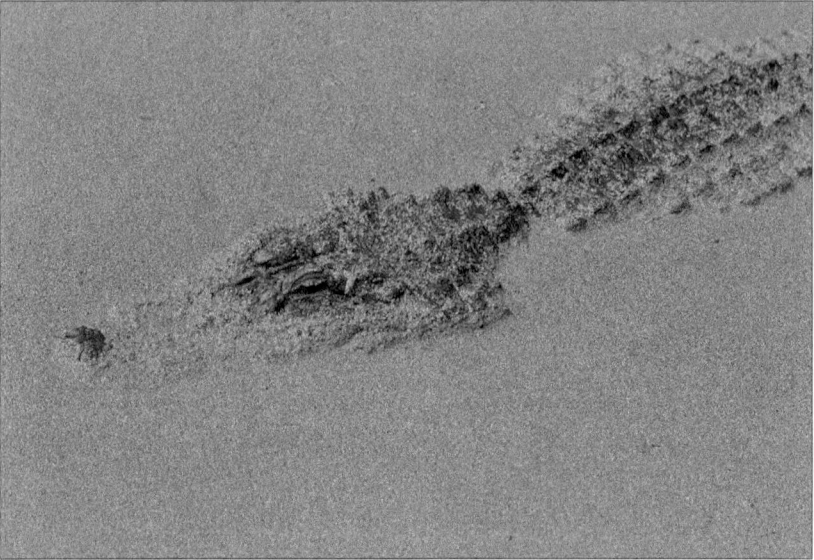

Watch out for that log! Alligators draped in duckweed are easy to miss.

are easier to obtain. The ferry does not transport pets, bicycles, or kayaks, but private boat charters will, for a fee. It is possible to kayak to Cumberland Island from Fort Clinch State Park on Amelia Island, but this undertaking involves crossing 2 shipping lanes and almost 5 miles of open water.

Schedule

March 1-November 30: departs St. Marys at 9:00 a.m. and 11:45 a.m.; departs Cumberland Island at 10:15 a.m., 2:45 p.m. (Wed.-Sat., March 1-Sept. 30), and 4:45 p.m. December 1-February 28: same as above, but no service Tuesdays or Wednesdays, and no 2:45 p.m. departure.

Guided Tours

Lands and Legacies Tour
Reserve at 912-882-4335 up to 24 hours in advance

This ranger-guided interpretive tour departs daily and from the Sea Camp Ranger Station shortly after the 9:45 a.m. ferry arrives. Park Service staff carry participants in vans or an open-air tram to historic locations around the seashore. Sites visited include the

The Park Service offers campers the use of wagons and garden carts to transport gear from the ferry to Sea Camp and back again. Back-country campers must pack in all their gear and pack out all their garbage.

106-room Plum Orchard Mansion, the Alberty House, and the First African Baptist Church, which also served as a schoolhouse and community center.

The adventure involves 6 hours of jolting over sandy, rutted single-lane roads as rippled as washboards in a noisy vehicle. You may be susceptible to motion sickness, and subject to heat, humidity, insects, and thunderstorms, and you will be required to exit the vehicle at stops and walk some distance. Once the tour has begun, you will not have the opportunity to turn back. While bathrooms are available, it will be several hours between bathroom breaks. The water at the north end of the island is not drinkable unless it is treated.

Each visitor is allowed one small personal bag if it fits on the lap or under the seat. Pack judiciously; it will have to hold all your food, water, sunscreen, and insect repellent. Large camera bags, tripods, plastic coolers, and large backpacks or duffels are not allowed.

Children between the ages of 3 and 8 are permitted if secured in car seats, which must be brought with the child and installed in the vehicle by the child's caretaker. Carefully consider whether your child can tolerate 6 hours of bouncy, jolting car ride in rough conditions, with no opportunity for free time or exploring.

It is possible to take the 9 a.m. ferry to Cumberland, take the Legends and Legacies tour, and leave the island on the 4:45 p.m. ferry the same day. Camperscannot take the tour on their first day on the island, however, because of a mandatory orientation that starts the same time as the tour. At this writing, the charge for the tour is $15 per person and $12 for seniors over the age of 62 and children under 16. This fee is in addition to the park entrance and ferry fee.

Footsteps Tour

A ranger-guided walking tour that begins about 10 a.m. and 12:45 p.m. daily and lasts about 1 hour.

Dockside Tour

Daily 30-minute cultural or natural history program at the Sea Camp Ranger Station.

Campfires and Crafts

Summer only—daily craft programs at Sea Camp Ranger Station, and evening programs on Saturday nights at the Sea Camp Campground.

Plum Orchard Tour

Two-hour tours of Plum Orchard, the historic 1898 home of George Carnegie. Tours leave at Sea Camp by ferry on the second and fourth Sunday of every month at 12:30 p.m. Ferry passengers may buy tickets for the tour for an additional $6 at check-in or at the time of the trip. Campers and hikers are welcome to meet the tour group on the steps at Plum Orchard at 1:30 p.m.

Swimming

Swimming is allowed anywhere on the island, but there are no lifeguards, and snakes and alligators live in the freshwater ponds.

Boating

A few boat slips are available to private craft at the north end of both Dungeness and Sea Camp docks on a first-come, first-served basis. The fee is $4 per person, dropped into the entrance-fee box upon arrival. Shore tying is acceptable, but overnight docking is prohibited.

Highly intelligent and resourceful raccoons are adept at filching food and other objects from campers. This enterprising bandit approached my campsite in the light of day, accustomed to foraging for scraps as soon as a camper leaves the site. The Park Service provides cages for food storage.

Hunting and Fishing

Six public deer and hog hunts are held on Cumberland Island annually. Shrimp and crabs can be harvested, and fish are abundant.

Camping

For information on ferry and camping reservations contact the *Cumberland Queen* (above) or visit www.nps.gov/cuis

Sea Camp

Sea Camp is a developed campground in a maritime-forest setting, with 16 wooded private sites accessed by individual paths. After disembarking from the ferry, you will attend an orientation session; then the Park Service will assign you a campsite. Sites are spacious and very secluded with grills, fire rings, picnic tables, food cages, poles to suspend your trash bags, hard sandy open central areas, and a canopy of shady live oaks. They are all good sites.

The dense forest understory screens you from the eyes of other campers, but voices carry, and you will become familiar with the goings-on at the sites near you. Pristine beach lies on the other side of the nearby dunes, at the end of a scenic boardwalk. The two group sites can accommodate 10-20 people each and are set away from the main campground for privacy and noise reduction.

Sea Camp is the only camping area that provides potable water. You must boil or otherwise treat your drinking water at any other spot. Near the sites are rustic but well-maintained rest rooms with sinks, flush toilets, and cold-water shower stalls open to the sky. The only electrical outlets are in the bathrooms, and campers often use them to charge cell phones and camera batteries. If the heat is overwhelming, you can take advantage of the air conditioning in the ranger station. You can buy ice from the ferry on its scheduled stops.

Although there is no limit to the gear you can bring, use restraint when packing for your camping trip. You must carry all your equipment onto the ferry and pile it on the deck, where it will become buried under the equipment of other campers. Upon docking at Sea Camp, you will have to carry all your equipment off the boat and transport all of your belongings about a half mile to the campground. The NPS provides wagons and garden carts for this purpose, which must be returned promptly to the ferry dock after you offload your gear at your site. When I last camped solo at Sea Camp, I brought an ingenious beach cart that collapsed like a stroller—easy to roll on and off the ferry and over the sandy path to the campground, and I could keep it with me.

There are no garbage cans, and you must pack out your own garbage. It is permissible to collect dead and downed wood for your campfire, but you are in competition with the other campers for this resource, and it may be scarce. Sometimes the ferry sells firewood; but if you are determined to have a campfire, bring your own.

Raccoons prowl Sea Camp with uncanny intelligence. They can open coolers secured with bungee cords, tear holes in tents, and defeat a wide variety of latches. They know the routine and watch new campers come in with the morning ferry, sizing them up to determine which might be most vulnerable to a raid. Like the boys in *Oliver Twist*, one raccoon performs for the campers while his brethren artfully dodge away, cooperatively dragging a wheeled cooler. Keep your food in the lockbox provided at each site, and

The campsites at Sea Camp are spacious and private, surrounded by woods and host to wildlife. I slept in a camping hammock, which hung easily from the live oaks. I have nothing but accolades for camping in a hammock. They are light, portable, and as comfortable as a return to the womb.

be sure nothing touches the wire mesh sides. The crafty animals use their nimble fingers to shred whatever they can reach. They can extract lunch meat by the individual slice and leave the wax paper that separated them. They consider anything on a picnic table potential food and will rip open backpacks and purses left in the vicinity.

Stafford Campground

Stafford Camp is located 3.5 miles from the Sea Camp Ranger Station, making it a reachable destination for beginner backpackers. Stafford considerably is more isolated than Sea Camp, not only because the latter is a larger campground, but also because most of the day trippers do not hike any farther north than Sea Camp. Stafford is close to an empty and primitive stretch of beach, in keeping with the unspoiled, exotic, wild character of the island. Rolling coolers, carts, strollers and wheeled conveyances are not allowed in the back country. You must carry whatever you take. Toilets and cold showers are available, and fire rings are first come first served. The Wilderness Area begins 4 miles north of Sea Camp dock.

Backcountry Camping

Backcountry camping is allowed at 3 camping areas, which are located within a National Wilderness Area. Back country sites are $2.00 per person per night, and reservations are required. The wilderness sites range from 5.5 to 10.6 miles from the Sea Camp ferry dock. The sites are assigned upon arrival on the island, and the southern sites fill first—be prepared to backpack more than 10 miles if you are placed at Brickhill Bluff. Camping is limited to seven days.

There are no toilets at the backcountry sites—human waste should be buried under 6 inches of earth at least 50 yards from the campground and any water source. There are wells, but the water must be treated. Campfires are not allowed in the backcountry, but portable stoves are. Food should be suspended out of reach of raccoons (about 8 feet from ground and trees). You must remove your ropes when you leave the site and pack out all of your trash.

A blogger on a travel message board equated wilderness camping on Cumberland Island to "living on Gilligan's Island without the head hunters or the volcano."

Hickory Hill, 5.5 miles from Sea Camp, is deep in the wilds of Cumberland Island. Birds and other wildlife are abundant at the freshwater wetlands, especially during spring and fall migrations.

Yankee Paradise, 7.5 miles from Sea Camp, deep in the center of the island, and less than a mile east of Plum Orchard mansion. The well water here has a slightly sulfurous smell.

Brickhill Bluff: Primitive camping at the northernmost campsite on Cumberland Island, on the Brickhill River 10.5 miles from Sea Camp Dock. Historically, Brickhill Bluff was a Timucuan settlement and subsequently the site of several villages.

Bed and Breakfasts

Greyfield Inn Bed and Breakfast
The Inn is on Cumberland Island
Its business office is at
4 N. Second St.
Fernandina Beach, FL 32035-0900
Toll free 866-401-8581
904-261-6408

www.greyfieldinn.com

Lodging on Cumberland is limited to two extremes—rustic camping and a 5-star mansion inn. Thomas and Lucy Carnegie built Greyfield for their daughter, Margaret Ricketson. In 1962, it was converted to an inn by her daughter, Lucy R. Ferguson. The "daily tariff" is a package rate, which includes the room, breakfast, picnic lunch, a gourmet dinner, canapés and snacks, bicycles, guided tours, and private ferry service. Greyfield Inn was once chosen one of the "Top 10 most romantic inns" by American Historic Inns. It was on the 2008 "stay list" in *National Geographic Traveler*, rated among the top 10 romantic island retreats by *Coastal Magazine*, and voted in the top 500 of world hotels by *Travel and Leisure*. Rates for double occupancy start at $395 per night. There is no television or Internet, and the inn's phone is for emergencies only.

Events

Plum Orchard Christmas

The Neoclassical Plum Orchard mansion is on the seashore's Lands and Legacies tour, but it gets all tricked out for the holidays. The special Christmas tour costs $6 at this writing, not including ferry ticket.

Nearby Points of Interest

Distances (all approximate) are in road miles to the Cumberland Island National Seashore visitor center (113 St. Marys St. | St. Marys, GA 31558 | 30.72055 - 81.5496761).

Camping

Crooked River State Park
6222 Charlie Smith Sr. Hwy.
St. Marys, GA 31558
Reservations toll free 800-864-7275
912-882-5256

http://gastateparks.org/CrookedRiver

If you want to camp, but also want access to restaurants and stores, Crooked River State Park is a 500-acre ecologically unique oasis of wildness, yet convenient to services. The park offers 62 campsites, cottages, a camp store, laundry, wood, grills, picnic tables, and fire rings. See the Ruins of the McIntosh Sugar Works mill, built around 1825 and used as a starch factory during the Civil War. Numerous hiking trails traverse various ecosystems and offer excellent wildlife viewing opportunities.

Campsites are sheltered by sprawling live oaks draped with Spanish moss. There are 11 spacious two- and three-bedroom cabins, each with a kitchen, dining and living area, screened-in porch and a bathroom. Cabin #6 is a private end unit. Cottages are well provisioned with cooking utensils, plates, glasses, cutlery, oven, stove, fridge, microwave, dishwasher, coffee pot, toaster, linens, air conditioning, and central heat—and even an electric fireplace!

As on Cumberland Island, biting insects are plentiful April through November, beginning with the onslaught of gnats in early spring. June brings vicious yellow flies. Mosquitoes can be dense and aggressive, especially in wet years and when the air is still. There are also sand gnats and no-see-ums, which are most active at dawn and dusk. 10.9 mi.

Jacksonville North/Kingsland KOA
2970 Scrubby Bluff Rd.
Kingsland, GA 31548
Reservations toll free 800-562-5220
912-729-3232
http://koa.com/campgrounds/jacksonville

RV and tent sites, cabins, cable TV, pool (April–October), fire rings, Internet, library, free breakfast. Just off I 95. 9.1 mi.

Bed and Breakfasts

Emma's Cottage House
300 W. Conyers St.
St. Marys, GA 31558
Toll free 877-749-5974
912-882-4199

The trails though the Cumberland Island wilderness wind below an angular canopy of moss-covered live oaks.

www.emmascottagehouse.com

The verdant grounds are certified by the National Wildlife Federation as a Backyard Wildlife Habitat. Five rooms with private baths. Cable TV, wireless DSL (in most), continental breakfast, complimentary bike use. During my stay I chose room 403 because of its unique layout—I loved ascending stairs to my private sleeping loft. When I visited, tree frogs were everywhere, trilling boisterously as I stalked them with my camera. 0.4 mi.

Goodbread House Bed and Breakfast Inn
209 Osborne St.
St. Marys, GA 31558
Toll free 877-205-1453
912-882-7490
www.goodbreadhouse.com/mainstreet.html
info@goodbreadhouse.com

One block to Cumberland Island ferry dock. Six air conditioned rooms, fireplaces, private baths, verandas, kitchenette, and parlor. Reconnective healing sessions, spa treatments, life coaching, couples reconnecting retreats. Pet friendly. 0.2 mi.

Spencer House Inn
200 Osborne St.
St. Marys, GA 31558
Toll-free 877-819-1872
912-882-1872
http://spencerhouseinn.com
info@spencerhouseinn.com

Historic structure (*circa* 1872) selected by TripAdvisor as the #1 bed and breakfast in St. Marys. 14 uniquely decorated guest rooms with a private baths. Full breakfast buffet, signature peach iced tea, and afternoon snacks. 0.2 mi.

Hotels and Motels

St. Marys has three hotels and motels. Kingsland has more and a greater variety, and it's almost as convenient a base for visiting the Island. It also has numerous restaurants and large department stores where you can replace items you forgot to pack. Amelia Island, FL (see Outlying Destinations, below), is farther away and has a vacationland character all its own. Jacksonville, FL, is less than an hour down the road and offers all the advantages and disadvantages of a large city.

Cumberland Island Inn & Suites
Toll free 800-768-6250
912-882-6250
www.cumberlandislandinn.com
Info@cumberlandislandinn.com
$$
Raveable 4/5, Trip Advisor #1 (in St. Marys)

85 percent nonsmoking. Complimentary breakfast, wired and wireless Internet, microwave and refrigerator in every room. 3.7 mi.

Econo Lodge Cumberland
1135 E King Ave.
Kingsland, GA 31548
912-673-7336
www.econolodge.com/hotel-kingsland-georgia-GA253
$
Raveable 3.5/5

Pet-friendly, outdoor pool, complimentary breakfast. 11.1 mi.

Fairfield Inn & Suites Kingsland
1319 E King Ave.
Kingsland, GA 31548
912-576-1010
www.marriott.com/hotels/travel/bqkkg-fairfield-inn-and-suites-kingsland
$$$
Raveable 5/5, Roadtrippers 4.5/5, Trip Advisor #4 (in Kingsland), Virtual Tourist 4.5/5
Complimentary breakfast, indoor pool, fitness center, high-speed Internet. 11.6 mi.

Hampton Inn Kingsland
102 Reddick Rd.
Kingsland, GA 31548
912-729-1900
hamptoninn.hilton.com/Kingsland
$$$
Raveable 3.5/5, Roadtrippers 4/5, Trip Advisor #5 (in Kingsland)
78 rooms, complimentary hot breakfast, pool, fitness center, free WiFi. 9.6 mi.

Hawthorn Suites by Wyndham Kingsland
1323 E King Ave.
Kingsland, GA 31548
912-882-4170
$$$
Raveable 3.5/5, Trip Advisor #6 (in Kingsland), Virtual Tourist 4.5/5
66 nonsmoking suites, each with kitchen. Pet-friendly. Children under 18 stay free. Complimentary breakfast, outdoor pool, fitness center, WiFi. The URL for the establishment's Web site is too long to reproduce here and likely to change. Fortunately, there are search engines. 11.6 mi.

La Quinta Inn & Suites Kingsland/Kings Bay Naval Base
104 May Creek St.
Kingsland, GA 31548
912-882-8010
$$

AAA 3 Diamonds, Raveable 4.5/5, Roadtrippers 4.5/5, Trip Advisor #2 (in Kingsland), Virtual Tourist 4.5/5

Smoke-free, pet-friendly. Another motel with an omitted mile-long URL. 9.5 mi.

Riverview Hotel
105 Osborne St.
St. Marys, GA 31558
912-882-3242
www.Riverviewhotelstmarys.com
Across the street from the ferry to Cumberland Island.
$$$
Raveable 3/5, Roadtrippers 3.6/5, Trip Advisor #2 (in St. Marys)

Built in 1916 and run by the same family since the 1920s, the Riverview has hosted celebrities from Willard Scott to John D. Rockefeller. (Some of the 20 rooms are named after famous guests.) The hotel includes the oldest continuously operating restaurant and bar in town, Captain Seagle's Seafood Restaurant and Saloon, which serves dinner nightly and also sells picnic lunches for the trip to Cumberland. Complimentary breakfast, WiFi. 0.1 mi.

Super 8 Motel—Kingsland
120 Robert L. Edenfield Dr.
Kingsland, GA, 31548
866-538-6194
www.super8.com
$

    9.1 mi.

Dining

Riverside Café
106 W Saint Marys St.
St. Marys, GA 31558
912-882-3466
www.riversidecafesaintmarys.com
Lunch, dinner
$
Greek-American family restaurant across the street from the

On the Dungeness grounds, wild turkeys strut by grazing horses intent on some avian mission.

ferry station with a great view of the water. When you return from Cumberland Island hot and hungry, treat yourself to spinach pie made with crispy, flaky phyllo dough, lasagna, moussaka, or fresh seafood.

Mad Hatter Tea Shop
1840 Osborne Rd., Suite A
St. Marys, GA 31558
912-576-3645
www.facebook.com/Mad-Hatter-Tea-Shop-153330864826350
Lunch Monday–Friday
$

Widely regarded as the best lunch spot in the area. The first Monday of the month it serves a specialty whiskey crab soup that garners innumerable accolades on review sites. 2.2 mi.

Pauly's Café
102 Osborne St.
St. Marys, GA 31558

912-882-3944
www.paulyscafe.net
Lunch, dinner
$

Fresh seafood, choice beef, pasta, creative salads, decadent desserts. After I visited Cumberland Island, some new friends recommended Pauly's for dinner, and we had a lovely meal. 0.1 mi

St. Marys Seafood & More
1837 Osborne St.
St. Marys, GA 31558
912-467-4217
www.stmarysseafoodandmore.com
Lunch, dinner
$

Family fare: fresh oysters, clams, shrimp, crabs, and fish =fried, grilled, blackened, or broiled. They even have frog legs! Also in Jacksonville, FL. 1.7 mi.

The Green Room Sicilian Café and Deli
2400 Saint Marys Rd.
St. Marys, GA 31558
912-882-2721
www.onthegreenroom.com
Lunch, dinner Tues.-Sat.
$
Trip Advisor #5, Yelp 4.5/5

The Green Room is a small café and deli offering sandwiches, salads, and great lasagna. 5.8 mi.

McGarvey's Wee Pub
2603 Osborne Rd.
St. Marys, GA 31558
912-467-4763
www.weepub.com
Lunch, dinner, late
$
Roadtrippers 5/5, Trip Advisor #8, Yelp 4/5, Zomato 3.4/5

Irish Pub offering shepherd's pie, fish and chips, wings . . . Good food, good service, and a good selection of beer. 3.5 mi.

Carolina Gold rice was once the predominant long-grain variety in the United States, and it was a major export of the Carolinas and Georgia in the 18th and 19th centuries. It nearly became extinct after the Great Depression, but a revival assisted by a U.S. Dept. of Agriculture seed bank began in the 1980s. Descriptions often use adjectives such as nutty, chewy, and fragrant. It's the perfect rice to use in perlow (the dialectal form of *pilau/pilaf*), a Low Country dish that may include chicken, shrimp, or sausage. A good source of information on where to find Carolina Gold and what to do with it is the Carolina Gold Rice Foundation of Charleston, SC (www. carolinagoldricefoundation.org | 843-709-7399).

For a glimpse of Low Country rice culture, visit

Hofwyl-Broadfield Plantation Historic Site
5556 US Hwy. 17 N
Brunswick, GA 31525
912-264-7333
http://gastateparks.org/HofwylBroadfield

In the early 1800s, a Charleston entrepreneur began transforming marshes and cypress swamps along the Altamaha River into a rice plantation. In its heyday, it covered 7,300 acres and required the labor of more than 350 slaves. The owners grew rice until 1913, then converted their remaining holdings into a dairy farm. The Big House is full of antique aristocratic furnishings and decorations. The site offers an introductory film and number of programs throughout the year—lectures on antebellum life, nature hikes, plein air painting, even an annual Easter egg hunt. It's also a stop on the Colonial Coast Birding Trail. Open Wednesday–Sunday, 9 a.m.–5 p.m. 52 mi.

Steffens Restaurant
550 S Lee St.
Kingsland, GA 31548
912-729-5355
http://m.mainstreethub.com/steffensrestaurant
Breakfast, lunch, dinner Monday–Saturday
Breakfast, lunch Sunday
$

Roadtrippers 5/5, Trip Advisor #2 (in Kingsland), Yelp 4.5/5, Zomato 4/5
A diner in business since 1948. 12.2 mi.

Other Attractions

Crooked River State Park
6222 Charlie Smith Sr. Highway (GA Spur 40)
St. Marys, GA 31558
Reservations toll free 800-864-7275
912-882-5256
gastateparks.org/CrookedRiver

Crooked River Park, north of St. Marys on Ga. Spur 40 and 8 miles east of I 95, is roughly 15 min from the Cumberland Island ferry. It offers cozy facilities in a beautiful setting. Campsites are surrounded by Spanish moss-draped oaks, and most cottages overlook the river. The park has a playground, a boat dock, and many trails.

Hikers can explore the Nature Trail, which winds easily through a maritime forest and salt marsh, ideal for children and the elderly. You may see alligators, armadillos, raccoons, ospreys, herons, egrets, wood ibis, white eyed vireos and other birds, dolphins, wild hogs, gopher tortoise (Georgia's state reptile), orb weaver spiders, and lots of butterflies. A large bird blind affords views of many species—even the garishly marked painted buntings.

The Palmetto Trail takes you through the Georgia pine flatwoods, a rare habitat once common in the Georgia lowlands. The Sempervirens Trail features old-growth hardwoods—oak, cherry, and hickory. The Bay Boardwalk traverses the bay forest ecosystem, where loblolly pine and swamp bay are the dominant species. The River Trail is a short jaunt along the waterfront, revealing steeply scarped bluffs and steamy marshes. The erosion-chiseled bank of the Crooked River has a stark beauty. The river relentlessly carves under the banks until trees topple onto the beach, root systems bleached and washed into tangled driftwood art forms. 9.1 mi.

Cumberland Island National Seashore Museum
129 Osborne St.
St. Marys GA 31558

912-882-4336, ext. 254
www.nps.gov/cuis/planyourvisit/museum.htm

Engaging displays depicting the island's history, culture and ecology. Not to be confused with the visitor center beside the ferry dock, which offers little in interpretive displays, this facility is located one block from the waterfront. The exhibits portray the archeological beginnings of the island, showcase local history and ecology, and illustrate the opulent lifestyle of the Carnegies. "The Forgotten Battle" exhibit includes artifacts from the last engagement of the War of 1812, fought at St. Marys' Point Peter, nearly a week after the more famous Battle of New Orleans. Open Wednesday through Sunday 1–4 p.m. 0.1 mi.

Colonial Coast Birding Trail
http://georgiawildlife.com/ColonialCoastBirdingTrail

More than 75 percent of the bird species known in Georgia have been observed on this 18-site trail, which runs from Savannah to Okefenokee National Wildlife Refuge, encompassing a wide variety of habitats including beaches, salt marshes, old rice fields, woodlands, tidal rivers, and freshwater wetlands. Crooked River State Park and Cumberland Island National Seashore are stops along the bird trail.

The Green Elephant Ghost Tours
406 Osborne St.
St Marys, GA 31558
Toll free 867-863-0342
912-576-9111

90-minute walking tour through downtown St. Marys, with spooky tales about local historical sites. Tours are available Friday and Saturday at 7 and 9 p.m. Adult price is $12.00; seniors and children under 12, $8.00. 0.4 mi.

Howard Gilman Memorial Waterfront Park
100 W St. Marys St.
St. Marys, GA 31558
912-882-4000

A peaceful place for a walk, for sunset-watching, and a great spot to look for rainbows when storms pass in the afternoon. Old-fashioned wooden swings, fountains, playground, arbors, brick walk.

Merges with the Tilden Norris Marsh Walk, which crosses a tidal marsh where waterfowl forage. 130 ft.

Lang Charters
100 E. St Marys St.
St. Marys, GA 31558
912-674-8062/882-4262
www.langcharters.com

Fishing charters, sightseeing and river cruises. Limited to six persons per cruise. 80 ft.

Orange Hall House Museum
311 Osborne St.
St Marys GA
912-576-3644
www.orangehall.org

The "Grande Dame of St. Marys," Orange Hall is an elegant 1830s mansion museum with daily tours. Reportedly the site of paranormal phenomena, Orange Hall has been investigated several times. Three ghosts said to make regular appearances are a young girl believed to be the builder's daughter, an elderly man, and a woman dressed in purple. A possible fourth spirit occasionally sighted is a soldier who, by his uniform, predates the Civil War. Visit the Southern Paranormal Research Society (http://www.southernparanormal.org/sprs_investigations_1/orange_hall_-_st_marys_ga). 0.3 mi.

St. Marys Historic Tram Tour
400 Osborne St.
St. Marys, GA 31558
Toll free 800-868-8687
912-882-4000

Meets at the flag pole on the waterfront Mon.–Sat., 11 a.m.–2 p.m.; $5 ($3 for children 12 and under); seven-person maximum.

St. Marys Aquatic Center
301 Herb Bauer Rd.
St. Marys, GA 31558
912-673-8118
www.funatsmac.com

A 7-acre water park offering varied activities for families. 1.9 mi.

Pileated woodpeckers are one of the many species that can be sighted on the Colonial Coast Birding Trail.

St. Marys Submarine Museum
102 W. St. Marys St.
St. Marys, GA 31558
912-882-2782

Submarine memorabilia, displays including a working periscope, portions of actual submarines, and replicas of torpedoes. St. Marys is home to Kings Bay Naval Submarine Base, one of only two Trident submarine bases in the world. 80 ft.

Up the Creek Xpeditions
111 Osborne St.
St. Marys, GA 31558
Toll free 877-UP-THE-CREEK
912-882-0911

Up The Creek offers a variety of kayak nature tours and specialty trips to a number of scenic waterways in coastal Georgia and Florida's. Half-day and full-day trips, kayak lessons/instruction equipment, clothing and gifts. Groups welcome. 0.1 mi.

Events

Mardi Gras
The town of St. Marys and the Downtown Merchants Association pull out all the stops with a charity fun run, a festival with entertainment and vendor booths, a parade, and a costume-optional evening ball. Festivities occur the Saturday before Fat Tuesday, which the schedule started by Dionysius Exiguus in the 6th century allows to fall on any day from February 3 to March 9, inclusive. For the exact date of the observance and other details, consult either of these sources.

St. Marys Convention & Visitors Bureau
400 Osborne St.
St. Marys, Ga 31558
Toll free 800-868-8687
912-882-4000
www.visitstmarys.com/mardi-gras-festival.html

Downtown Merchants Association
207 Osborne St.
St. Marys, GA 31558

912-882-7350
www.stmarysdma.org

Outlying Destinations

Places more than 20 road miles from the Cumberland Island National Seashore visitor center (113 St. Marys St. | St. Marys, GA 31558 | 30.72055, - 81.5496761). Distances are approximate and rounded to the nearest mile.

Camping

Osprey First In Florida RV Park
US Hwy. 17 and I 95
Yulee, FL 32097
904-225-2080
   73 sites, 13 miles from Fernandina beach. Full hookups at all sites, all pull-throughs. No tents. Pool, cable TV, dump station, showers, toilets, store, game room. 21 mi.

Fort Clinch State Park Campground
2601 Atlantic Ave.
Fernandina Beach, FL 32034
904-277-7274
www.floridastateparks.org/fortclinch
   Fort Clinch State Park is a heavily wooded, scenic park situated on the northern tip of Amelia Island. Fort Clinch itself is a brick Civil War-era Union fort designed to block ships from entering the Confederate port. The fort never saw battle. 61 campsites divided into two sections. The Amelia River section has 40 shaded sites, canopied by moss-draped oaks, and 21 sites are in the Atlantic Beach section. Toilets, showers, dump station, laundry, water and electric hookups. Well-behaved pets welcome. 32 mi.

Bed and Breakfasts

Addison on Amelia
614 Ash St.

Fernandina Beach, FL 32034
Toll-free 800-943-1604
904-277-1604
http://addisononamelia.com
$$

Located on nearby Amelia Island. Winner of Bed and Breakfast's "Top Ten Overall: U.S." and "Best of the South" awards. Three buildings, 14 guest rooms, lush gardens, brick walkways. 30 mi.

Amelia Island Williams House Bed & Breakfast Inn
103 S. Ninth St.
Fernandina Beach, FL 32034
Toll-free 800-414-9258
904-277-2328
www.williamshouse.com
$$

30 mi.

Elizabeth Pointe Lodge
98 S. Fletcher Ave.
Amelia Island, FL 32034
Toll-free 888-757-1912
904-277-4851
www.elizabethpointelodge.com
$$$
Trip Advisor #3 (among hotels)

31 mi.

Fairbanks House
227 S. Seventh St.
Amelia Island, FL 32034
Toll-free 888-891-9887
904-277-0500
www.fairbankshouse.com
$

30 mi.

The Hostel in the Forest
Off US Hwy. 82
Brunswick, Ga 31520

(31.162499999999998, -81.59583333333333)
912-264-9738
http://foresthostel.com
$

This unusual establishment combines aspects of a B&B, an ashram, a visit to grandma's, and an episode of *Survivor*. It's a collection of unheated, uncooled treehouses and geodesic domes—some with solar power, some with none—plus a sweat lodge in the teeming woods about 10 miles west of Brunswick. Staff and volunteers turn over at a rapid rate by design. Members, that is, guests are discouraged from bringing small children. The maximum group size is five. The maximum stay is three days. Members and volunteers alike have chores. There is no trash collection, so you must pack out whatever you generate. There's a long list of rules. (One worthy of general adoption: anybody using a cell phone in a common area is subject to being tossed into the pool.) The only meal provided is a vegetarian dinner cooked in the communal kitchen and likely to include produce from the on-site organic garden. The Web site includes glamor shots of chickens, which provide the only thing akin to a wake-up call. Despite its idiosyncrasies, or because of them, the hostel has been rolling along since 1975, and it remains very popular. It has its own brand of fair-trade coffee and a calendar of events that has included concerts, songwriters' summits, and a "Hula Hoop and Yoga Retreat." Rates are low (as this book goes to press, membership is $10, and lodging is $25 per night), the surroundings are lovely, the meditative tranquility of the place is certainly in the spirit of vacationing, and you can enjoy yourself even if you've never heard of the *Whole Earth Catalog*. 39 mi.

Hotels and Motels

Amelia Hotel at the Beach
1997 S. Fletcher Ave.
Amelia Island, FL 32034
904-206-5200
$
Raveable 4/5, Trip Advisor #10
29 mi.

Beachside Motel
3172 S. Fletcher Ave.
Fernandina Beach, FL 32034
904-261-4236
$$
Raveable 3.5/5, Roadtrippers 4.5/5, Trip Advisor #5
    30 mi.

Comfort Suites Fernandina
2801 Atlantic Ave.
Fernandina Beach, FL 32034
904-261-0193
www.comfortsuites.com
$
Raveable 4/5, Roadtrippers 4/5
    31 mi.

Days Inn & Suites on Amelia Island
2707 Sadler Rd.
Fernandina Beach, FL 32034
904-277-2300
$
Roadtrippers 3.5/5, Trip Advisor #11
    29 mi.

The Lodge at Sea Island
100 Cloister Dr.
Sea Island, GA 31561
Trip Advisor #1, *U.S. News* #1 (in the country)
    If the Greyfield Inn, John F. Kennedy, Jr.'s, honeymoon retreat, isn't swanky enough, this should fit the bill. Golf. Multiple restaurants and pools. Round-the-clock butler service and valet parking . . . 54 mi.

Residence Inn by Marriott Amelia Island
2301 Sadler Rd.
Fernandina Beach, FL 32034
904-277-2440• Residenceinnameliaisland.com
$$
Raveable 5.5, Roadtrippers 4.5/5, Trip Advisor #1
    29 mi.

The Ritz-Carlton, Amelia Island
4750 Amelia Island Pkwy.
Amelia Island, FL 32034
Toll free 866-538-6194
$$$
Roadtrippers 4.5/5, Trip Advisor #6
  31 mi.

Dining

Gary Lee's Market
3636 US Hwy. 82
Brunswick, GA 31523
912-265-1925
$
Lunch, dinner Tuesday–Saturday
Trip Advisor #3 (in Brunswick), Yelp 4.5/5
  Specializes in barbecue. The Web site of the Hostel in the Forest (above) proclaims it "the best BBQ on the planet." That's quite an endorsement from an institution whose staff seems to consist mostly of vegetarians. 38 mi.

Sassafras (*S. albidum*) was an important colonial export. Until the mid-20th century, it was used widely in the United States as an additive to food and other products and as the main flavoring for root beer. The U.S. Food and Drug Administration banned sassafras in 1960 because it deemed safrole (a component found at lower levels in cinnamon, basil, and black pepper) carcinogenic. Whether safrole causes cancer has since been disputed, but ingesting large amounts can cause liver damage. Safrole-free sassafras extract is readily obtainable, but since the ban most commercial root beer has been flavored with wintergreen, vanilla, and other substitutes. Sassafras grows wild throughout East Coast horse territory. If you don't fancy boiling up the roots for sassafras tea, you can dry and pulverize the leaves to make filé powder for gumbo or use the aromatic wood for grilling.

Indigo Coastal Shanty
1402 Reynolds St.
Brunswick, GA 31523
912-265-2007
www.indigocoastalshanty.com
$
Lunch Tuesday–Saturday, Dinner Friday–Saturday
Trip Advisor #1 (in Brunswick), Yelp 4.5/5, Zomato 4.5/5
   Small, eclectic, and off the Interstate. 47 mi.

Horse-Related Activities

Amelia Island Horseback Riding
Peters Point Beach Front Park
S. Fletcher Ave.
Fernandina Beach, FL 32034
904-277-7047
   Personalized horseback riding on the beach. Debbie trailers her horses to Peters Point Beach Front Park on South Fletcher Ave. Intimate rides, only 2-3 riders in a group. Open daily, morning and evening rides only during the summer. Flexible ride times in fall and winter. Experienced riders may trot or canter on the beach. 31 mi.

The Kelly Seahorse Ranch
7500 1st Coast Hwy
Fernandina Beach, FL 32034
904-491-5166
www.kellyranchinc.net
   Located within Amelia Island State Park, Kelly Seahorse Ranch offers horseback riding on the beach, walk/trot, ages 13 and up. Groups of 10-12 riders taken out 4 times daily. No experience necessary. Sunset rides and pony rides available! Very safety-minded. Do consult their web site or call for directions, they are difficult to find. Reserve well in advance in season, rides fill quickly. 36 mi.

Old Towne Carriage Company
115 Beech St.
Fernadina Beach, FL 32035

904-277-1555

www.ameliacarriagetours.com reservations@ameliacarriage-tours.com

Horse-drawn carriage tours through the historic district of Fernandina Beach. 30 mi.

Other Attractions

The Catty Shack Ranch

1860 Starratt Rd.

Jacksonville, FL 32226

904-757-3603

www.cattyshack.org

Exotic-animal rescue facility with 45-minute tours by day and night. Meet gorgeous Siberian tigers, lions, cougars, black leopards, a bobcat, a coatimundi, and foxes. Feeding time is a kick. The full-throated roar of an irate lion will send thrills of primal fear down your spine. But mostly, these animals are beautiful to behold. Highly recommended, great for kids. 31 mi.

Amelia Island Museum of History

233 S Third St.

Fernandina Beach, FL 32034

904-261-7378

Permanent exhibits include artifacts from the native Americans who settled this region, as well as the industries, wars and missions that shaped Florida's history. 30 mi.

Amelia River Cruises and Cumberland Sound Ferry Service

1 S Front St.

Fernandina Beach, FL 32034-4295

904-261-9972

www.ameliarivercruises.com

The Amelia Island River Cruise is a 2-hour narrated water tour of Cumberland Island which highlights the history and local folklore. This is a great way to visit Cumberland Island with young kids in tow. Children enjoy the storytelling, and get to see wild horses, wild turkey, waterfowl, and dolphins galore. 31 mi.

Egan's Creek Marina
997 Egan's Creek Lane
Fernandina Beach, FL 32034
904-206-1762

Private guided nature tours of Amelia and Cumberland Island. Offering two hour, half-day, and full-day trips aboard a 26' center-console Panga boat. 32 mi.

The Folkston Funnel Platform
3795 Main St.
Folkston, GA 31537
912-496-2536

Most rail traffic bound to or from Florida passes through downtown Folkston, GA. Dozens of trains a day, every day, attract rail enthusiasts, who sometimes seem to outnumber residents. To accommodate train-watchers, the town built a covered viewing platform in 2001. This isn't just a roof on poles. It has ceiling fans to mitigate the South Georgia heat, electric outlets, a scanner that monitors two CSX Railroad frequencies, and floodlights to illuminate the tracks all night. The site also offers chairs, benches, rest rooms, picnic tables, grills, even WiFi. Admission is free of charge. In addition, the town operates the Folkston Railroad Transportation Museum inside the restored Atlantic Coast Line depot nearby. 31 mi.

Fort Clinch State Park
2601 Atlantic Ave.
Fernandina Beach, FL 32034
904-277-7274
www.floridastateparks.org/fortclinch

The federal government built Fort Clinch in 1847, and Confederates used it until they concluded it was obsolete. Union forces reclaimed it in 1862, but it never saw battle. Interpreters in period costume answer questions, and a small museum runs a short movie about living conditions in the fort during the Civil War.

Fort Clinch State Park is a heavily wooded, scenic park situated on the northern tip of Amelia Island, just south of the Georgia state line. The verdant spreading trees form a living archway that shades hiking and biking trails. The beach is wide, clean, and fairly empty. Catch the sunset off of the long fishing pier, and bed down

Beautiful big cats and other exotics wait for you at the Catty Shack in nearby Jacksonville, FL. Proceeds go to support the exotic rescue animals in their keeping.

in a campsite under the canopy of moss—garnished trees. There is a snack bar, camp store, and bike rental. The spacious campsites have full electrical hook-up, a fire pit, a picnic table and are well concealed. 31 mi.

Georgia Sea Turtle Center
214 Stable Rd.
Jekyll Island, GA 31527
912-635-4444
http://gstc.jekyllisland.com
   A sea turtle rehabilitation facility with a wide range of educational programs, from daily patient feedings, sunrise beach walks, and behind-the-scenes tours to summer camps. 50 mi.

Timucuan Ecological & Historic Preserve
12713 Fort Caroline Rd.
Jacksonville, FL 32225
904-641-7155
   Includes the 600-acre Theodore Roosevelt Natural Area, with nature trails though grasslands, forest and wetlands. Also includes Fort Caroline and Kingsley Plantation. Rich archeological area—humans have lived here for 6,000 years. 42 mi.

More Information

Bullard, M. (2003). *Cumberland Island: A history*. Athens: University of Georgia Press.

Dilsaver, L.M. (2004). *Cumberland Island National Seashore: A history of conservation conflict*. Charlottesville: University of Virginia Press.

Gruenberg, B.U. (2015). *The wild horse dilemma: Conflicts and controversies of the Atlantic Coast herds*. Strasburg, PA: Quagga Press.

Kirkpatrick, J. (1994). *Into the wind: Wild horses of North America*. Minocqua, WI: Northword Press.

Mills, D.S., & McDonnell, S.M. (Eds.). (2005). *The domestic horse: The evolution, development and management of its behaviour*. Cambridge, United Kingdom: Cambridge University Press.

Seabrook, C. (2002). *Cumberland Island: Strong women, wild horses*. Winston-Salem, NC: John F. Blair.

The One Thing You'll Never Forget

Plum Orchard. Photograph courtesy of the National Park Service via Wikimedia Commons; public domain image.

The Lands and Legacies motorized tour to the north end of Cumberland Island offers the most comprehensive overview of the significant cultural and natural landmarks of the island. This 30-mile, 5–6-hour expedition will take you to the Stafford Plantation, Plum Orchard Mansion, Cumberland Wharf, The Settlement, the First African Baptist Church, and more! You will feel a real sense of adventure as you bump down jarring dirt roads and cope with whatever the elements bring—rain, wind, dust, heat, cold, and storms. It is an astonishing value at any price.

Getting to Cumberland Island

Distances (all approximate) are in road miles to the Cumberland Island National Seashore visitor center (113 St. Marys St. | St. Marys, GA 31558 | 30.72055, -81.5496761).

Boston, MA, 1,130 mi.; New York, NY, 910 mi.; Philadelphia, PA, 830 mi.; Pittsburgh, PA, 810 mi.; Washington, DC, 680 mi.; Raleigh,

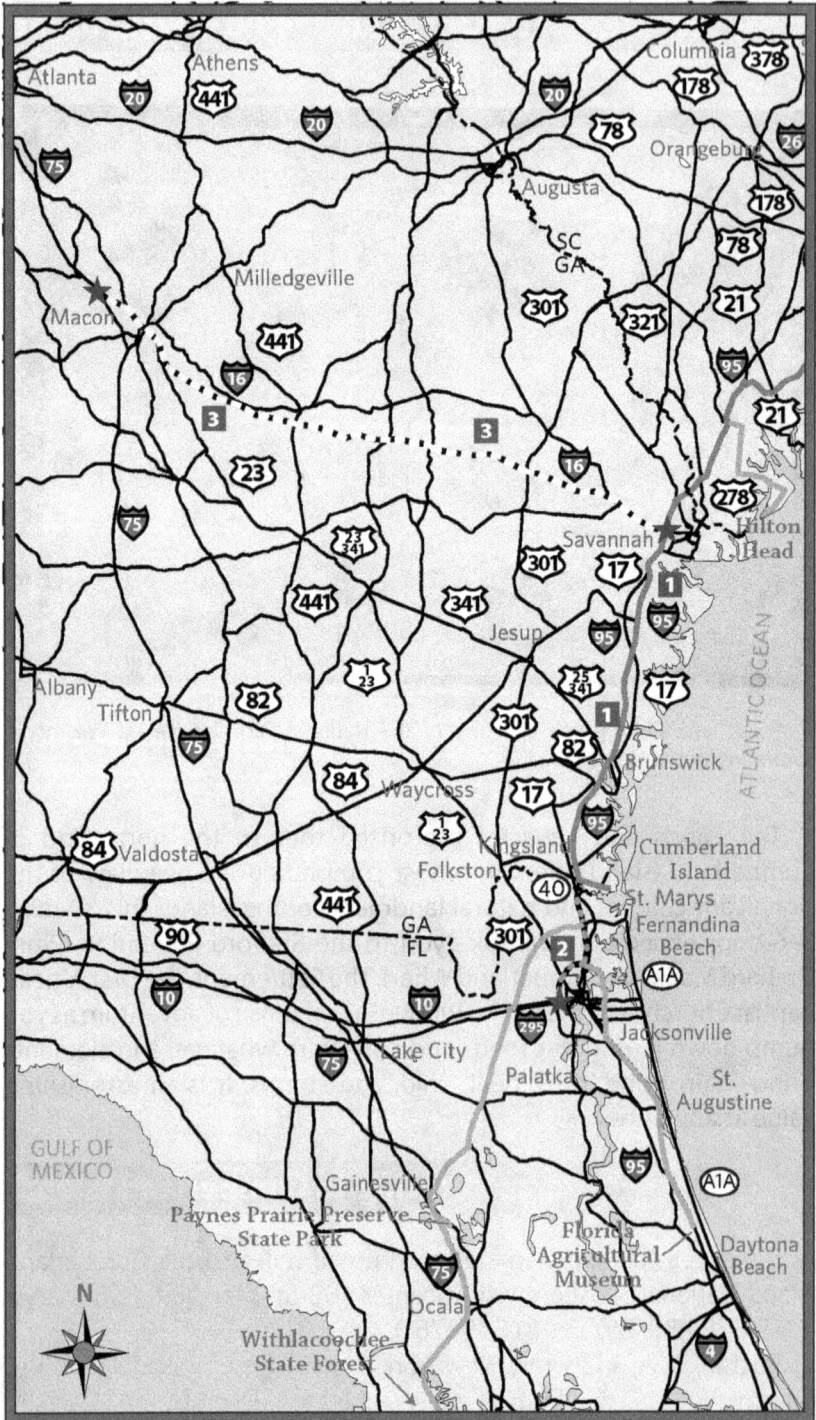

NC, 430 mi.; Columbia, SC, 270 mi.; Atlanta, GA, 345 mi.; Orlando, FL, 180 mi.

1. From Savannah, GA

I 16/I 95 interchange (32.075593,-81.246643); 105mi.

- Take I 95 S 95.2 mi.
- At Exit 3 (Kingsland/St. Marys), exit right, then turn left on GA 40 E (King Ave., which turns into Osborne Ave.); go 9.3 mi.
- Turn right on St. Marys St.; go about 100 yards. The visitor center and the dock for the ferry to Cumberland Is. are on the left.

Day and overnight parking are allowed behind the Park Service administrative building (Bachlot House), on the right, across from St. Marys Waterfront Park. Bus and RV parking are allowed in marked spots along the east side of Seagrove St., the second street on the right.

2. From Jacksonville, FL

I 10/I 295 interchange (30.318359,-81.77124); 43mi.

- Take I 295 N 14.3 mi.
- At Exit 35 B, take I 95 N; go 20.7 mi., passing into Georgia.
- Take Exit 1 (St. Marys Rd.); turn right on St. Marys Rd. and go 2.9 mi.
- Turn left on GA 40 E (King Ave., which turns into Osborne Ave.); go 5 mi.
- Turn right on St. Marys St.; go about 100 yards. The visitor center and the dock for the ferry to Cumberland Is. are on the left.

3. From Macon, GA

I 75/I 16 interchange (32.955961,-83.812637); 275mi.

- Take I 16 S; go 156 mi.
- Take Exit 157 A to I 95 S; go 95.3 mi.
- At Exit 3 (Kingsland/St. Marys), exit right, then turn left on GA 40 E (King Ave., which turns into Osborne Ave.); go 9.3 mi.
- Turn right on St. Marys St.; go about 100 yards. The visitor center and the dock for the ferry to Cumberland Is. are on the left.

Several more southerly routes combining I 16 and US 23 or I 75 and US 82, for example, are shorter by 20–30 miles; but they take roughly the same time, and they require more route changes and more driving on surface roads.

Cumberland Island Ferry
Toll free 877-869-6787
912-882-4335

March–Nov.: Leaves St. Marys daily at 9 and 11:45 a.m.; leaves Cumberland at 10:15 a.m. and 4:45 p.m. Also leaves Cumberland at 2:45 p.m. Wed.–Sat. through Sept. 30. Dec.–Feb.: Leaves St. Marys Thurs.–Mon at 9 and 11:45 a.m.; leaves Cumberland at 10:15 a.m. and 4:45 p.m. Adults $20; seniors $18; children 12 and under $14; park user fee $4. The run usually takes about 45 min.

Note: At this writing, the contract to operate the ferry is about to expire, and the long-time concessionaire faces a competing bidder who proposes to move the terminal from St. Marys, GA, to Fernandina Beach, FL. A predictable interstate quarrel has resulted. Changing the route would have far-reaching implications not only for the two towns, but also for the seashore, whose headquarters and visitor center would presumably remain in St. Marys no matter where the ferry terminal happened to be.

A wild Cumberland horse eats Spanish moss from the boughs of a live oak near the Dungeness dock.

Side Trip 5
The Okefenokee

The celebrated Okefenokee Swamp covers roughly 438,000 acres in southern Georgia and northern Florida, a small portion of the vast swampland that European settlers found when they arrived. From here the Suwanee River, popularized by Stephen Foster (who never visited) and George Gershwin, flows south to the Gulf of Mexico, and the sluggish St. Marys River, which forms part of Florida's northern boundary, flows east to meet the Atlantic just below Cumberland Island. The Okefenokee contains not only the largest blackwater swamp in North America (most of it on the west side), but also wet and dry prairie (most of it on the east), pine and hardwood forest, and floating peat mats. (Okefenokee means "trembling earth," and if you stomp over the peat deposits, the trees will quiver.) It supports a great variety of plant life, including several carnivorous species, and more than 400 kinds of vertebrate. Although none of the Okefenokee's flora, fauna, or habitats is unique, its diversity is.

More than 400,000 acres of this natural wonder are in Okefenokee National Wildlife Refuge, which offers a wide range of recreational opportunities and educational programs. The main refuge entrance, is off GA 121, about 11 mi. southwest of Folkston, GA, and 41 mi. from St. Marys. This area includes the 5,000-square-foot Richard S. Bolt Visitor Center, the restored 1920s Chesser Island Homestead, Swamp Island Drive, hiking trails, and a picnic area. It is also the locale of most events listed below. Okefenokee Adventures, an official concessionaire, provides guided boat tours and rents boats, bicycles, and camping equipment.

Winter in the Okefenokee is generally mild, but lows below 20°F do occur. Spring and fall weather is erratic, and preparing for it involves packing extra clothes. All things considered, spring may be the best time to visit. Many creatures are stirring, but pests and heat are tolerable. Summer, which is also the rainy season, tends to be very hot and humid; thunderstorms are common, and lightning is probably a greater hazard than predators. Lightning also causes fires. About 600,000 acres in the swamp and the surrounding area burned in the human-caused Bugaboo Scrub fire (April–July 2007), and about 300,000 acres, most of it in the refuge, burned again in the Honey Prairie fire (April 2011–April 2012). Countless plants and animals perished in these conflagrations, and the damage is still being studied. The Okefenokee is evidently very resilient, though, and repeat visitors can watch it regenerate.

Distances, rounded to the nearest whole number, are in road miles from the Cumberland Island National Seashore visitor center (113 St. Marys St. | St. Marys, GA 31558 | 30.72055, -81.5496761).

1. Okefenokee National Wildlife Refuge
2700 Suwannee Canal Road
Folkston, GA 31537
30.72055, -81.5496761
General information 912-496-7836 9 a.m.–5 p.m. daily except Christmas
www.fws.gov/okefenokee

A green tree frog sleeps the day away on the underside of a saw palmetto. At dusk, he will wake to lend his voice to the chorus of trills and croaks.

There are three major entrances and two secondary entrances to Okefenokee NWR, each with its own facilities and special character. To visit from the east, use the Folkston entrance. Intrepid visitors can canoe the waters unguided and camp on the sleeping platforms at night. Guided boat tours take visitors through cypress forests, historic canals, and open prairies. Water trails and platforms allow people to canoe for the day or stay overnight deep within the 354,000-acre wilderness. Winding boardwalks and trails lead through unique habitats to observation towers and viewing platforms. From the west, enter through Stephen C. Foster State Park (below).

Open from 30 min. before sunrise to 7:30 p.m. March–October and until 5:30 p.m. November–February. Admission: weekly pass (good for 7 days from purchase date), $5; annual pass, $12; interagency senior pass, $10 (lifetime); interagency annual pass, $80; overnight wilderness canoe permit, $10/person per night; commercial passes, $5-50. 41 mi.

2. Okefenokee Swamp Park (private, nonprofit)
5700 Okefenokee Swamp Park Rd.

Waycross, GA 31503
912-283-0583
www.okeswamp.com
okefenokee@btconline.net

For those who prefer a more structured introduction to the Okefenokee, this nonprofit attraction at the north entrance to the refuge may be just the ticket. It offers a reconstructed pioneer village; a serpentarium; a boardwalk and viewing areas for alligators, river otters, turtles, deer, and bears; an observation tower; a 1.5-mile train ride; an exhibit on Walt Kelly's popular comic strip *Pogo*, set in the Okefenokee; and numerous activities for families with small children. Admission $15 for adults (ages 12–62), $14 for everyone else except children under 2 (free). Boat tours (5 and 10 mi.) are offered when water levels permit at extra charge. Open 9:00 a.m.–5:30 p.m. daily except Thanksgiving, Christmas Eve, and Christmas. 62 mi.

3. Stephen C. Foster State Park
17515 Hwy. 177
Fargo, GA 31631
912-637-5274
www.gastateparks.org/info/scfoster

This isolated park is a primary entrance to Okefenokee from the west. Hike the elevated boardwalk or take a guided pontoon boating trip, rent canoes, kayak or motor boats. Abundant wildlife includes alligators, raccoons, black bear, deer, and array of birds. Stay in the park's campground or cabins. 102 mi.

4. Newell Lodge
661 Ozzie Rowell Rd.
Folkston, GA 31537
912-496-2838
www.newellresort.com
info@newellresort.com

A 60-acre equine resort 7 mi. north of Folkston that offers summer horse camps, lessons for all ages above 6, trail rides, 26 horses for various skill levels (BYOH if you prefer), event hosting, six on-site rental cabins, 106 RV sites (for event attendees only), and the "Hold Your Horses Café" (that is, the proprietors cook for you). 39 mi.

Events

- Earth Day/National Wildlife Week (late April). A day of programs starts with a litter pickup on the refuge and along GA 121.
- Banks Lake NWR Youth Fishing Derby (early June): Flatlanders Lake, Lakeland, Georgia. For children ages 3–15. Includes knot-tying demonstrations, fish printing, ranger-led interpretive programs, and free refreshments. (Banks Lake NWR is an unstaffed satellite refuge administered by Okefenokee NWR.)
- International Migratory Bird Day (May). The Okefenokee is a birding hot spot, and the refuge marks this occasion with guided walks and other programs.
- National Public Lands Day Celebration (September): An observance that includes volunteer maintenance on the historic Chesser Island Homestead and free refreshments for workers.
- Okefenokee Festival/National Wildlife Refuge Week (second full week in October): Programs at the Chesser Island Homestead focus on how swampers lived and made a living in the early 20th century, before the refuge was created. Topics include traditional cooking, crafts, and entertainment (such as shape-note singing).
- Sugar Cane Grinding and Syrup Boil (fall): Participants cut their own cane from the garden and grind it in a traditional mule-powered grinder. Staff and volunteers boil the juice down to syrup.
- Christmas on Chesser Island: includes cider, cookies, tours, a hayride, traditional decorations, caroling, and musical performances.

Side Trip 6

Crackers

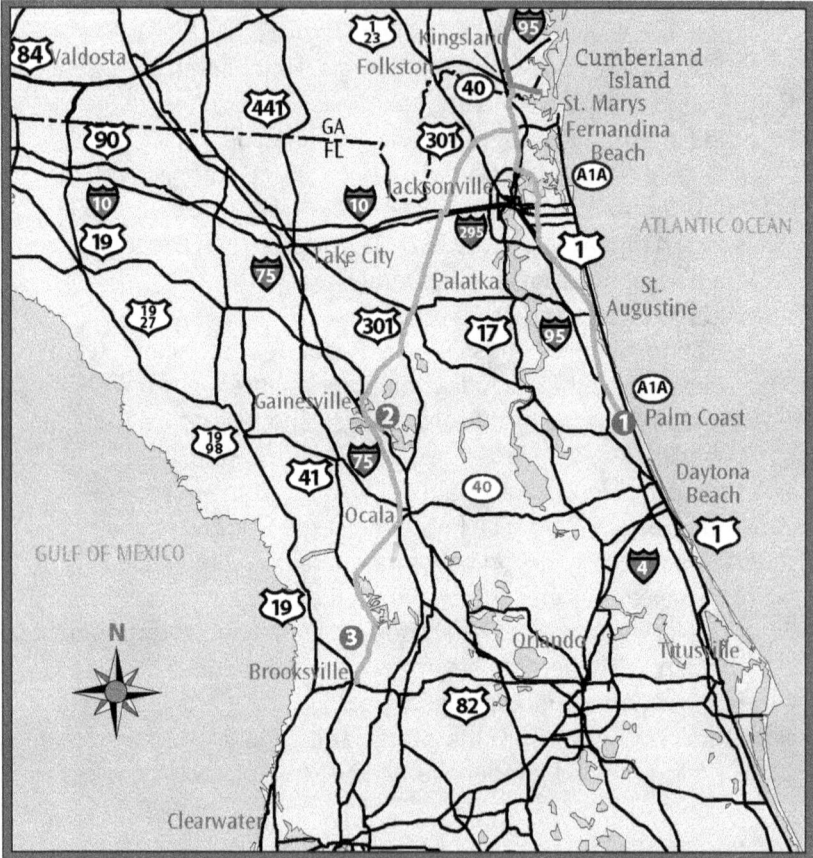

The Florida Cracker Horse, a Colonial Spanish breed with many physical and genetic similarities to Marsh Tackies and Banker Horses, is rare and endangered. The Florida Cracker Horse Association registry contains fewer than 900 individuals. The following destinations afford chances to see and appreciate Cracker Horses without long searching, private appointments, or other difficulties.

1. Florida Agricultural Museum
7900 Old Kings Rd. N.

A Florida Cracker horse grazes on the lush foliage at Paynes Prairie State Preserve in Gainesville, FL. Photograph by Geoff Gallice via Wikimedia Commons.

Palm Coast, FL 32137
29.642948, -81.282486
386-446-7630
www.myagmuseum.com
info@myagmuseum.com

The museum's heritage livestock include Cracker Horses, Cracker Cattle, and Piney Rooter Hogs. It also conducts guided trail rides, riding lessons, and summer riding camps. Open 9 a.m.–5 p.m. Wednesday–Sunday. Admission: $9 (adults), $7 (children 6–12).

2. Paynes Prairie Preserve State Park

100 Savannah Blvd.
Micanopy, FL 32667
29.521835, -82.293229
352-466-3397
www.floridastateparks.org/paynesprairie

The 22,000-acre park, located just south of Gainesville, maintains a small herd of bison reintroduced from Oklahoma in the 1970s, 40–50 rare Florida Cracker Cattle, and 16–30 Florida Cracker Horses. The last-named are essentially wild because they run loose and receive no veterinary care or supplemental feeding, though the park staff does control the herd's population by selling off horses that it considers excess.

"Cracker Cart," from a collection of stereoscopic views made between 1870 and 1885, Here a man rides a Cracker horse as it pulls a cart with a female passenger. Photograph by J.A. Palmer via Wikimedia Commons

Besides the opportunity to observe Florida Crackers, the park offers a visitor center (open 9 a.m.-4 p.m. daily), tours guided by cell phone, boating, hiking, camping, picnicking, fishing, geocaching, birdwatching (the park is on the Great Florida Birding Trail), and horseback riding.

Open 8 a.m.-sunset 365 days a year. At this writing, admission is $6 per vehicle (2-8 occupants), $4 single-occupant vehicle, $2 pedestrians, bicyclists, and extra passengers.

3. Withlacoochee State Forest
15003 Broad St.
Brooksville, FL 34601
850-488-4274
www.freshfromflorida.com/Divisions-Offices/Florida-Forest-Service/Our-Forests/State-Forests/Withlacoochee-State-Forest

The preserve keeps a small breeding population of Cracker Horses—a stallion and three mares in 2009—and it hosts the Cracker Cattle and Horse Auction every November. The official Web site, however, says virtually nothing about either. The preserve, 157,000-acres in several discontinuous tracts, has campsites, stables, corrals, and miles of riding trails. All horses brought in must have proof of a recent negative Coggins test for equine infectious anemia.

Florida Cracker Horse Assn., Inc.
2992 Lake Bradford Rd. S.
Tallahassee, FL 32310
www.floridacrackerhorses.com

Side Trip 6.1

St. Augustine Alligator Farm Zoological Park

The St. Augustine Alligator Farm Zoological Park is one of Florida's oldest continuously running attractions, having opened on May 20, 1893. Besides the zoo and the zip lines, this park is the site of a natural rookery for wild herons, egrets, ibises, spoonbills, and wood storks. From March through June, native wading birds nest by the hundreds in the trees over the Alligator Swamp, where predators are unlikely to threaten them. You can follow wooden walkways that bring you within a few feet of nesting water birds that are usually too shy and secretive to approach. It is easy to get amazing photographs with a basic camera, and the park holds an annual photography contest to showcase extraordinary images taken within its boundaries.

St. Augustine Alligator Farm Zoological Park
999 Anastasia Blvd.

St Augustine, FL 32080
904-824-3337
www.alligatorfarm.com

Wood storks with bare, vulture-like heads tend gangly chicks a few feet from the boardwalk. The St. Augustine Alligator Farm Zoological Park is a remarkable natural rookery for wading birds, where hundreds of wild herons, egrets, roseate spoonbills, wood storks, and other water birds congregate to breed. They feel safe raising chicks over the alligator swamp, where they are protected from predators.

Side Trip 7

Marsh Tackies

The Marsh Tacky, a hardy, gaited Colonial Spanish Horse once common in the Low Country of the Carolinas and Georgia, is on the verge of extinction. Only about 300 remain, none in the wild. They no longer own the marshes, and chances to see or interact with them are few. Fortunately, the 68-acre Coastal Discovery Museum in Hilton Head, SC, has a living Marsh Tacky exhibit comprising 19-year-old Comet and a changing cast of companions on loan. At this writing, his only equine buddy is a young mare descended from the last known Tacky on Daufuskie Island, SC (the Yamacraw Island of Pat Conroy's memoir-novel *The Water Is Wide* and its screen adaptation, *Conrack*).

Brookgreen Gardens in Murrells Inlet, SC, is worthy of a visit on its esthetic merits. An added attraction is the Dalton and Linda Floyd Domestic Animals of the Plantation Exhibit, which includes several heirloom livestock breeds, such as Marsh Tackies, Dominique chickens, Red Devon cattle, and Tunis sheep.

The Carolina Marsh Tacky Association held well-attended annual beach races on Hilton Head in winter or spring from 2009 to 2012 and

Carolina Marsh Tackies race before a cheering crowd at Hilton Head, SC. Photograph by Anthony Surbeck via Wikimedia.Commons.

on Daufuskie in 2013. The organization canceled the 2014 and 2015 races, however, and the future of the event is unclear though plans are afoot at this writing to hold a race on Hilton Head in November 2016.

1. Discovery Museum
   70 Honey Horn Drive
   Hilton Head Island, SC 29926
   32.211580, -80.743884
   843-689-6767
   www.coastaldiscovery.org
   info@coastaldiscovery.org
   Admission free, though some programs and tours may not be. Open Monday–Saturday 9 a.m.–4:30 p.m., 11 a.m.–3 p.m. Sunday. Holiday hours vary.

2. Brookgreen Gardens
   1931 Brookgreen Garden Dr.
   Murrells Inlet, SC 29576
   33.521682, -79.094684
   Toll free 800-849-1931
   843-235-6000
   https://www.brookgreen.org
   info@brookgreen.org
   Admission: adults 13–64, $14; 65+, $12; children 4–12, $7. Tickets are good for a week. Discount for groups of 15 or more. Open daily 9:30 a.m.– 5 p.m. (8 p.m. in April).

Carolina Marsh Tacky Association
P.O. Box 1447
Hollywood, SC 29449
843-726-8845
http://marshtacky.org
marshtacky@gmail.com

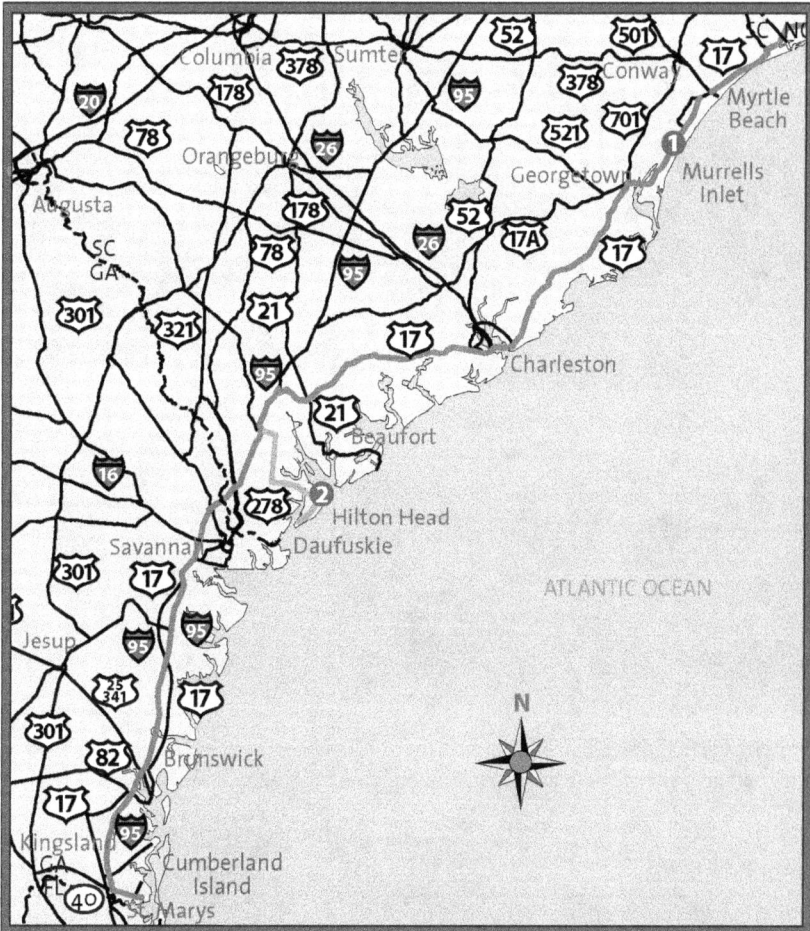

Appendix 1

Riding with the Herd

Two women ride their Arabians up the beach at Assateague Island National Seashore, after camping overnight in an Oceanside site.

Beach Riding

Assateague (Maryland)

Despite potential hostility between wild and domesticated horses, Assateague Island National Seashore allows day riding Oct. 9–May 14 and horse camping Oct. 16–April 14. Although the equine visiting season is timed to minimize transmission of equine infectious anemia and eastern equine encephalitis from visitors to natives or vice versa, the biting insects that carry these diseases don't always observe human schedules. Although there are no documented cases of a visiting horse acquiring equine infectious anemia from a native animal, the wild horses of Assateague Island National Seashore have not been Coggins tested. Horses from other barrier island herds, including the herd at the south end of Assateague, have historically tested positive for equine infectious anemia, so the possibility of transmission must be considered.

The fee for horse camping is $30 per site per night. It's possible to reserve sites up to 6 months in advance by calling (toll free) 877-444-6777 or visiting www.recreation.gov. Day riders need no extra permit and incur no charge beyond the usual entrance fee. They should use the North Ocean Beach parking lot, however; check in at the ranger station; cross to the beach unmounted at the old ranger station (the walk is about 1.5 mi.); and ride only on the beach east of the white posts from there south. That is, they're restricted to the Over-Sand Vehicle zone.

Assateague (Virginia)

Chincoteague National Wildlife Refuge forbids pets even in vehicles—a dangerous place for them, especially in hot weather—and horseback riding. But it does let visitors trailer horses through its property to ride on the Virginia end of Assateague Island NS during the off-season. There's no extra fee for horse or trailer, but riders must park in the southernmost oceanfront lot and ride only in the OSV zone. Like beach vehicles, horses must stay seaward of the black and white posts, and they are not allowed south of the Coast Guard station from March 15 through August 31. The nearest wild horses are fenced a good distance away. They leave their enclosure now and then, but there's virtually no likelihood of a confrontation.

Corolla

Currituck County ordinance 10-55 forbids merely having a domestic horse in the wild horse sanctuary, from the end of the paved road at Corolla north to the Virginia line. Riding there is out of the question.

Shackleford Banks and Vicinity

Cape Lookout NS doesn't allow horseback riding. Neither does the Rachel Carson North Carolina National Estuarine Research Reserve. The Cedar Island wild horse sanctuary is private property.

Cumberland Island

Cumberland Island NS doesn't allow visitors to bring horses, never mind riding them.

In summary, it's legal for you and your mount to romp through the wild horse ranges on the north end of Assateague. You can still thunder along the beach within a mile or so of Chincoteague Ponies on the far south end of Assateague. Romping or thundering anywhere else may result in a court date.

Mountain Riding

Mt. Rogers National Recreation Area
3714 Highway 16
Marion, VA 24354
Toll free 800-628-6202
www.fs.usda.gov/detail/gwj/specialplaces/?cid=stelpr
db5302337

Hundreds of miles of beautiful scenic trails are open to equestrians. The Virginia Highlands Horse Trail (orange paint blazes) extends over 67 miles through the high country of the Mount Rogers National Recreation Area Parking facilities for horse trailers and overnight stables are available at the park. Equestrians may use nearly every trail in the Mount Rogers National Recreation Area (except where signs indicate that horses are prohibited). Remain at least 100 feet from streams or springs when camping, bathing, washing dishes, and tethering horses. Always stay on the trail; it is illegal to shortcut across switchbacks. Pack out what you pack in. All trails close at dusk. Secure your horses by hobbling them or tying them to a picket line. The park warns, "NEVER tie them to a tree, even for a few minutes."

Raven Cliff Horse Camp

The camp is about a mile east of Raven Cliff Campground, just south of Highway 642. Its features include hitching rails, chemical flush toilets and horse trailer parking. The camp offers year-round access to Virginia Highlands Horse Trail.

Fox Creek Horse Camp
3714 Hwy 16
Marion VA 24354
(800) 628-7202
www.recreation.gov/camping/fox-creek-horse-camp/r/camp-groundDetails.do?contractCode=NRSO&parkId=132691

Located almost 4,000 feet above sea level, with 32 campsites located in open fields on either side of the creek, Fox creek is

Grayson Highlands State Park and Mt. Rogers Recreational Area offer hundreds of miles of equestrian trails, which take you through a mountaintop wild-pony range.

part of the George Washington & Jefferson National Forest. This campground offers pit toilets and garbage and manure collection. It offers hitching posts, rather than stalls. There is no potable water. Most of the campsites are first-come, first-served except for two designated sites available for reservations

Grayson Highlands State Park
829 Grayson Highland Ln.
Mouth of Wilson, VA 24363
276-579-7092;
www.dcr.virginia.gov/state-parks/grayson-highlands#general_information
GraysonHighlands@dcr.virginia.gov

Grayson Highlands offers more than nine miles of bridle paths which connect with bridle trails in Jefferson National Forest. Horseback riders must ride only on orange-blazed horse trails. Hiking trails are for pedestrians only. There is plenty of parking for horse trailers.

Chestnut Hollow, the equestrian campground, provides a stable with 67 stalls (38 covered, 29 uncovered) as well as 50-amp electrical service and water hookups for horse trailers, a dump station, and a bathhouse. Day-use riders access Virginia Highlands Horse Trail from the Chestnut Hollow parking lot. Sawdust provided for stalls; bring your hay bag and water bucket. All horses must be tied into specific stalls and have valid Coggins papers. Campsites are $27 per night, covered stalls are $9, open stalls are $7 a $5 transaction fee applies to each reservation. There are 23 campsites that can accommodate either tents or trailers. A second campground, Hickory Ridge, for non-equestrian campers offers 42 sites with water and electric and 32 tent sites without utilities.

Iron Mountain Horse Camp
4449 Arrowhead Dr.
Ivanhoe, VA 24350
276-744-2056 / 744-7677
or text 276-235-1162 276-237-2600
http://ironmountainhorsecamp.com
info@ironmountainhorsecamp.comsheila@ironmountainhorse-
camp

All campsites have water and electric hookup. Bath house, dump station. Dogs with up-to-date rabies vaccinations are welcome. Barn with 78 10 ft. x 12 ft/ stalls, wash bay with hot and cold water, tack room, and tack shop. If your horse loses a shoe, management can arrange for a farrier. Ride right out the gate onto hundreds of miles of horse trails.

Rocky Hollow Horse Campground
40 Camp Dr.
Troutdale, VA 24378
Toll free 888-644-0014
www.ridemtrogers.com
rockyhollow@wildblue.net

Family run equestrian campground since 2003. Offers 10 ft. x 10 ft. stalls with shavings and a wash pit. Bring your own hay and grain, water/feed containers, and hay nets. Stalls must be stripped upon departure. Valid negative Coggins required. 42 campsites are available with power and water and a central bathhouse. Cabin and RV rental available.

High Country Horse Camp
6866 Whitetop Rd.

Troutdale, VA 24378
276-.388-3992
www.highcountryhorsecampva.com
info@highcounryhorsecampva.com
   Offers basic campsites, sites with and without tie lines, water, electric, and covered stalls.

Appendix 2
Beachcombing

On the Chincoteague National Wildlife Refuge, visitors have decorated an ancient snag with gifts from the sea.

What washes up on Cumberland Island, GA, alone provides more than enough raw material for Janet "Gogo" Ferguson's popular line of jewelry (www.gogojewelry.com). A sample of one local woman's littoral gleanings was sufficient to fill the Outer Banks Beachcomber Museum in Nags Head, NC (www.oldnagshead.org), closed at this writing. You may be astonished by what litters the beach—crab carapaces, fish bones, fulgurites (treelike glass tubes formed when lightning strikes sand), alligator osteoderms (Ferguson turns them into earrings) . . .

Almost as great and variable as the bounty of the beach is the mass of laws and regulations that govern collecting it. How you're allowed to find and remove one thing or another depends on where you are and who's in charge. For example, Assateague State Park allows use of metal detectors, but the adjacent Assateague Island National Seashore doesn't. What you may keep differs from item to item, agency to agency, and place to place. Even on Currituck Banks, where most of the wild horse sanctuary is owned by absentee private parties or managed by absentee government and nonprofit agencies, numerous laws and regulations are in effect. When in doubt, ask.

A few general observations:

- The best times for beachcombing are around low tide (especially near new and full moons), after storms, and during the off season.
- In 2014 the National Resources Defense Council ranked the beaches of Maryland, North Carolina, and Virginia 4th, 5th, and 6th, respectively, in cleanliness among the 30 eligible states. Contrary to complaints about wild horses' degradation of water quality, all the beaches where they roam have generally low bacteria counts. Storms can release sewage and other pollutants, however; so the water may be dirtiest when beachcombing is at its best.
- The most promising spots are usually the hardest to reach, for example, the middle of Assateague.
- The most desirable shells may lie in or under clumps of seaweed or a few inches of water.
- The Institutes of Justinian recognized the public right of access to beaches in 530 AD, and the United States inherited this protection of free movement from the Roman Empire by way of English common law. Occupants of oceanfront property (often renters) may try to chase you off "their" beach; but if you're below the high-tide mark, they can't legally do much to you in most states. Delaware, Maine, Massachusetts, Pennsylvania, and Virginia don't own their intertidal zones, however; and about three quarters of Delaware's beaches are private. Fortunately for the purposes of this book, they don't have wild horses. Note that there's no public domain along estuaries or rivers.
- The probability of getting into trouble for routine beach-combing is usually low; but policies, Web sites, and brochures can be unclear, and stories of official overreach and overreaction are numerous. It's unwise to take anything off federal or state property without explicit permission. Of course, private citizens don't often welcome unauthorized use, destruction, or removal of their property.

Booty

Coins from Spain and elsewhere sometimes turn up in the surf at Assateague SP. Another treasure trove is Currituck Banks near the Virginia line, where Currituck Inlet once accommodated oceangoing vessels. Though unusual and valuable, old coins probably aren't connected with pirates or early explorers. Spanish currency circulated around the globe for centuries, and some European money was legal tender in the United States until 1858.

Fossils

Spectacular discoveries such as the 36,000-year-old walrus skull found in 1990 on Hatteras Island occur once in a lifetime, but old fish vertebrae and woolly mammoth teeth are common enough to go unnoticed. Black shells of oysters and other mollusks, hundreds or thousands of years old, are plentiful where a barrier chain has migrated over an ancient estuary. Some homely, worm-riddled shells, notably those of *Mercenaria* clams and extinct giant oysters, may go back 750,000 years. Blackened shark teeth may be 10–15 times older. The last-named can turn up in dredge spoil, so look for them around artificially nourished beaches and on the gravel roads of Cumberland Island.

Junk

Even on remote beaches, the number and variety of castoff items boggle the mind. Cleanup campaigns aren't completely effective, so you may find anything from medical waste to discarded appliances. Watch out for ordnance, too. The U.S. Navy used Assateague for aerial target practice during World War II and Currituck Banks for the same purpose until the early 1960s.

Sea Glass

Broken glass can puncture bare feet; but after several years' tumbling in the surf, it becomes smooth, frosted, and suitable for use in jewelry and other crafts. Assateague has its share, though the most productive beaches in Maryland are on Chesapeake Bay. (Glass abraded naturally in brackish or fresh water or mechanically in a studio tumbler is usually referred to as "beach glass.") The Outer Banks is sporadically rewarding, as is the south end of Cumberland Island. Collectors have taken tons of the stuff, and replenishment is slowing as Americans use less glass and recycle a higher percentage. Though sea glass is becoming rarer, it's still out there. If you find any in blue, yellow, orange, or black, you're fortunate.

Shells

Usual finds on Assateague include whelks (common, knobbed, and lightning), clams (razor, jackknife, quahog, and ponderous ark), moon snails (northern and Atlantic), bay scallops, delicate angel wings, and translucent jingle shells. The Park Service limits the take to 1 gallon of unoccupied shells per person per visit and prohibits commercial use.

Shells common on Assateague also appear around Corolla and elsewhere on the Outer Banks north of Cape Hatteras. In addition, you'll probably find many small conical univalves, such as augers, oyster drillers, periwinkles, fantastically patterned olive shells, and Scotch bonnets, the surprisingly rare North Carolina state shell. You may find moon snails (locally known as "shark eyes") and the spindle-shaped banded tulip shells. Large univalves include the queen or emperor helmet and occasionally the fragile giant tun, which despite its name seldom exceeds 7" in length. The most colorful bivalves are delicate pen shells and the tiny coquina clams (1" or less), often found in large beds.

Ocracoke makes many top-10 lists of American shelling beaches. Because it's less dynamic than some other barrier islands, intact shells last a bit longer. Because it's less crowded, competition for prize specimens is less fierce. But all of the North Carolina coast from Cape Hatteras to Cape Lookout is first-rate shelling territory because the warm and cold currents meeting offshore bring northern and southern species together. Cape Hatteras National Seashore, which includes most of Ocracoke, prohibits taking shells with animals inside, but apparently sets no limit on empty ones.

Portsmouth Island and Core Banks, both in Cape Lookout NS, are good places to look for Scotch bonnets. They're uninhabited, so rivalry is often nonexistent. This seashore limits collectors to 2 gallons of empty shells per person per day. But it also allows off-road vehicles, which help collectors cover more territory, remove more shells than regulations allow, and crush shells not taken.

Vehicles are not a problem on Shackleford Banks, which is also part of Cape Lookout NS. Although traveling on foot limits the range of your shell collecting, it makes for a more relaxed pace.

Cumberland Island has many of the shells found along the southern Outer Banks along with heart cockles, ark shells, and disc clams. The national seashore allows collecting up to 2 gallons of unoccupied shells per person per day. You may also take dead starfish, sand dollars, and sea urchins, but not bones, feathers, or plants.

Wreckage

Since European exploration began in the early 16th century, thousands of shipwrecks have taken place all around the areas where wild horses roam. One idea that takes getting used to is that old vessels and their parts can disappear for centuries, reappear, and move around. For example, in October 1889 the schooner *Frances E. Waters* ran aground near the Nags Head, NC, Lifesaving Service station. In May 1978, a nor'easter refloated the buried hulk, which cut a fishing pier in two before settling on the beach near Oregon Inlet, several miles south. What's left of the Waters now adorns the Nags Head town hall. Many wrecks are clustered around inlets, which also come and go. The Abandoned Shipwreck Act of 1987 puts most civilian wrecks, even on federal property, under state control and forbids looting mostly intact ones. The legal status and archaeological significance of small wreck fragments are hard to ascertain at a glance.

Appendix 3

Handicapped Access

The Chincoteague National Wildlife Refuge has paved roads and trails that allow the visitor to observe the beauty of nature from a wheelchair or from inside a vehicle. This photo was taken from the side of Wildlife Loop at sunset.

Observing large wild animals that can't be handled safely, approached legally, or heard clearly at appropriate distances is an activity strongly biased toward those with unimpaired vision and hearing. Appreciating a wild place, scenic spot, or historic structure can challenge anyone with limited mobility. Making attractions more accessible, when technically possible, can also make them less wild or scenic or historic and partially defeat the purpose of improving access. But within these stark limits many kinds and degrees of accommodation are possible. The East Coast preserves where wild horses roam cover most of the accessibility spectrum, from inviting to forbidding.

Assateague

While it is impossible to predict where to watch wildlife on any given day, wild horses wander freely across the northern end of Assateague, and can usually be observed from the comfort of your vehicle. My strategy is to drive up and down the paved roads until I find a band, then pull into a nearby parking area to watch.

- Assateague State Park has an accessible visitor center, campsites, floating boat dock, playground (between the accessible bath house and the accessible camp shower building), fishing and crabbing pier, camper registration office, picnic areas and pavilion, shelters, and food and beverage concessions. A "surf" wheelchair is available.
- Assateague National Seashore (MD): A roll-out mat that lets wheelchairs reach the water's edge is offered from Memorial Day to Labor Day. Beach wheelchairs with balloon tires, a bathhouse with accessible rest rooms and roll-in shower, and wheelchair-accessible picnic tables (36 in. high) beside beach parking lots are also available.
- Assateague National Seashore (VA): The Toms Cove Visitor Center has a ramp, ADA-compliant doors, and accessible rest rooms. The Park Service also offers accessible portable toilets, an accessible public phone, program transcripts for the hearing-impaired, hands-on exhibits, and large-print or non-glossy documents.

Chincoteague National Wildlife Refuge

The Chincoteague National Wildlife Refuge offers 7 mi. of paved trails with no steep grades. The Wildlife Loop has wheelchair-accessible parking spaces and portable toilets and two accessible observation decks overlooking Snow Goose Pool. The Herbert Bateman Visitor Center is not only green, but also accessible from the parking lot to the rest rooms, and it offers two closed-captioned movies. The Wildlife Loop is open to vehicular traffic after 3pm, allowing visitors to watch birds, deer, and other wildlife (and occasionally, ponies!) from the comfort of their vehicles.

Corolla

Some wild horse tours in 4-wheel-drive vehicles are well-suited for some visitors with mobility limitations.

The wild horse sanctuary on Currituck Banks is in four parts:
- The 965-acre Currituck Banks component of the North Carolina National Estuarine Research Reserve borders

Shackleford Banks is a wilderness area without roads, buildings, flush toilets, or improved trails. People with impaired mobility are likely to have trouble navigating the grassy dunes and overwash flats.

the horse-exclusion fence just north of Corolla, so it's the southernmost spot where you should be able to see wild horses regularly. The site has a parking lot, a handicapped-accessible boardwalk, and a not-very-accessible 1.5-mi. trail.

- Having helped establish the reserve and the Currituck National Wildlife Refuge, the Nature Conservancy retained a small ocean-to-sound slice of Currituck Banks just north of the NCNERR. Nothing is accessible except by four-wheel-drive vehicle or boat, and there are no boat ramps.
- Like the NCNERR and Nature Conservancy tracts, Currituck NWR is a minimalist operation. Unlike the other federal preserves with wild horses, the Currituck Refuge makes virtually no attempt to serve the handicapped. Its discontinuous holdings are reachable only by boat or over-sand vehicle. It makes no allowance for those who have trouble walking on the beach. It forbids trespassing nearly everywhere else, and it has lately reinforced this prohibition with barbed wire, which is as hazardous to horses, deer, and other wildlife as it is to errant people. It has little signage that could be made more inclusive. It has no visitor center, exhibit, marked trail, observation deck, picnic table, gazebo, audio tour, or program schedule. Its only formal attempt

at conciliating the mobility-impaired is letting them hunt waterfowl in Currituck Sound from boats instead of blinds.
- The remaining half of the sanctuary is privately owned and generally less off-putting if only because few individual landowners purposely block access and none has the mischief-making resources of the federal government. If you have your own OSV, you can drive along the beach and explore many back roads more or less as you please. If you don't, several wild-horse tour companies can oblige. A number of accessible rental houses beyond the end of the paved road are available. Prepare for high prices.

Shackleford Banks Area

- Shackleford has no boardwalk, and all trails are soft sand. Composting toilets are located at the west-end ferry landing area and at Wades Shore.
- A quarter-mile boardwalk with benches does connect the ferry landing on Core Banks to the Lighthouse Keepers' Quarters, an overlook deck, and the beach; but it's across Barden Inlet from the horses. The size and kind of your boat and the state of the tide will affect how easily you reach the boardwalk. Stairs connect it to the beach, and the Light Station Visitor Center supplies conventional and beach-adapted wheelchairs on a first-come, first-served basis. You may need assistance getting the latter to the intertidal zone.
- The Rachel Carson Reserve makes no attempt at improving accessibility. Its holdings are marsh islands, and you're on your own if you visit.
- The Cedar Island sanctuary is private, and accommodations are whatever you can arrange with the owners.

Cumberland Island

Environmentalists expressed hope that as a national seashore, Cumberland would remain safe from exploitation and eventually revert to a "natural" state. Although the wilderness area designated in 1982 is legally closed to vehicular traffic, most private property owners on the island were allowed to use the main road until 2010. Without vehicular access through the wilderness area, visitors unable or unwilling to hike 17 miles from the ferry landing were barred from the historic sites at the north end of the island. The Greyfield Inn provided vehicle tours despite the constraints of the Wilderness Act, Park Service regulations, and even a 2004 ruling by the 11th U.S. Circuit Court of Appeals.

In 2004, island residents persuaded U.S. Rep. Jack Kingston (GA 1) to address their concerns in a rider to the Consolidated Appropriations Act of 2005. Without a public hearing or other open discussion, his amendment removed the wilderness designation from 25-ft. corridors around three dirt roads (Main Road, North Cut Road, and Plum Orchard Spur) and required the Park Service to keep the roads drivable. It set a precedent by rolling back a federal wilderness designation, but it also tried to reconcile that designation with the seashore's other missions, such as recreation and historic preservation. Opponents were incensed, but unable to reverse the change.

Conservationists argued that the prevailing vision for Cumberland Island NS was for wilderness, not vehicular traffic, and that these changes would detract from the native beauty of the island. The Park Service, however, has a statutory and regulatory duty to make its publicly funded holdings accessible to the public and not to discriminate against mobility-challenged visitors.

To comply with this mandate, the National Park Service offers daily Lands and Legacies interpretive tours via passenger van to historic locations around the Seashore, including Plum Orchard Mansion, the Settlement (including the First African Baptist Church), Cumberland Island Wharf, and other sites along the main road. The trip covers 30 miles and lasts for 5-6 hours. While, a van with a lift and space for 2 wheel chairs is available if requested while making reservations, the Park Service emphasizes that these trips are long and arduous, and involve dusty, bumpy roads, walking, exposure to heat, cold and rain, and limited access to rest rooms.

Appendix 4

Laws, Regulations, and Their Discontents

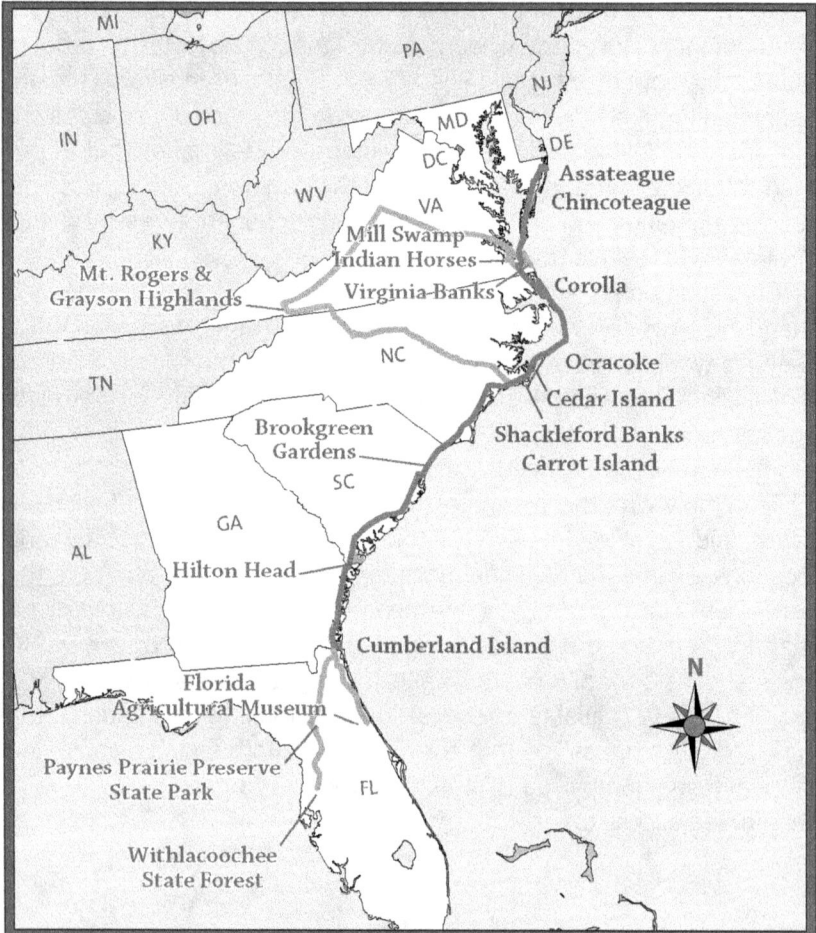

Restrictions and requirements that you may encounter in your travels to and within the seven states near the wild horse ranges are innumerable, and many are thoroughly baffling. A passenger who opens a beer in one state may be unable to finish it lawfully in another state a mile down the road. Application is often inconsistent. A law-enforcement officer may ignore the drivers zipping past you and cite you for speeding. Overlapping jurisdictions and mutual-aid agreements add to the excitement. In Pea Island National Wildlife Refuge, at the north end of Hatteras Island, NC, you're subject to being stopped by LEOs from at least eight agencies singly, serially, or in any combination: the U.S. Fish and Wildlife Service; the National Park Service; the North Carolina Department of Transportation, Division of Marine Fisheries, Highway Patrol, State Bureau of Investigation, and Wildlife Resources Commission; and the county sheriff's department.

Although you can't stay abreast of everything on the books, you can avoid a lot of trouble by driving sober, obeying regulatory signs, turning off the cell phone, and giving all stopped vehicles plenty of room. If you leave the Lamborghini and wads of Benjamins at home, you're less likely to lose them to the mystifying phenomenon of civil asset forfeiture. In short, fortune favors the prudent and inconspicuous.

Alcohol

The minimum age for public possession of alcoholic beverages in all 50 states is 21.

All seven states along the Atlantic Horse Trail set a legal intoxication threshold of 0.08 g/dL blood alcohol content for drivers 21 and over. Intoxication limits vary for minors. Delaware and Virginia allow open alcoholic beverages in automobiles, but all seven states forbid drivers to drink at the wheel.

Cell Phones

Delaware, Maryland, and North Carolina prohibit drivers from using hand-held cell phones. Maryland, North Carolina, and Virginia forbid drivers under 18 to use any kind. Florida allows using cell phones with headsets, but prohibits headsets (see below). All seven states prohibit texting by drivers, and all but Florida and South Carolina allow LEOs to stop drivers for texting.

Emergency Vehicles

All seven states have a move-over law that requires motorists to slow down and, where possible, change lanes when approaching law enforcement, fire, or other emergency vehicles stopped on or beside the road. The laws in Delaware and Virginia add tow trucks. North Carolina adds tow trucks, utility and construction vehicles, and road crews. It also prohibits driving over fire hoses or parking within 400 feet of fire trucks.

Maryland requires drivers to pull as far right as possible and stop for emergency vehicles approaching from ahead or behind. Delaware requires pulling over, but not stopping. North Carolina requires stopping, but not for oncoming vehicles. Maryland also forbids passing an emergency vehicle that's in motion with signals on.

Violators usually get noncriminal citations; but in Virginia, a second or subsequent offense is a misdemeanor. In North Carolina, an infraction causing property damage or injury is a misdemeanor, and one resulting in serious injury or death is a felony. In Delaware, any move-over violation causing injury is a felony.

Firearms

Traveling with firearms grows less simple by the day. The federal Firearm Owners' Protection Act of 1986 allows interstate transport of unloaded firearms if they're inaccessible from the passenger compartment. In some cases, it also guarantees safe passage with such firearms through states with tight gun laws. State and local laws govern *unsecured* firearms, though. In some states or cities, you may lose safe passage if you stop for gas or directions. In others, you may invoke FOPA protections, with no guarantee of success, only after you've been arrested.

Concealed-carry permits increase the confusion. Forty states have reciprocity with all or some other states. California, Connecticut, Hawaii, Maryland, Massachusetts, New Jersey, New York, Oregon, Rhode Island, Washington, and the District of Columbia have none. LEOs checking your license plate can find out whether you're permitted to carry; if you have a concealed-carry permit, they may stop you for that reason alone. If the state you're driving in has no reciprocity with your state of residence, expect problems even if you're not packing. Maryland Transit Authority police made national news in early 2014 for ransacking a Florida traveler's SUV in search of a concealed-carry weapon sitting hundreds of miles away. How many similar incidents go unreported is anyone's guess. You're not exempt from difficulty even in the state that issued your permit. In New York, for example, cities and counties that issue permits for various weapons, concealed or not, don't always honor one another's permits.

If you must travel armed and can't detour around problem states, follow the federal guidelines. Keep registration documents, highlighted copies of federal and state laws, and other relevant-looking paperwork handy. Expect trouble and delay no matter what you do.

The Credit Card Accountability Responsibility and Disclosure Act of 2009 (yes, really) loosened restrictions on firearms in national parks and wildlife refuges, but regulations still forbid firearms in "federal facilities." Individual agencies define "facilities" as they see fit and don't always clearly identify places where firearms are not allowed.

Headphones and Headsets
Maryland prohibits them except for the hearing-impaired. Virginia adds an exception for motorcycle-helmet earphones.

James Bond Stuff
Radar detectors are prohibited in Virginia and on naval and military bases, and Virginia LEOs will confiscate them. Maryland forbids them in commercial vehicles.

Using a radar jammer is a federal felony. There's no national law against laser jammers, but using them is illegal in Virginia.

Maryland, Virginia, and North Carolina forbid television, video player, and computer screens visible to drivers. Delaware doesn't.

Motorcycles
Delaware requires drivers and passengers under 19 to wear helmets and eye protection. Maryland and Virginia require everyone to wear a helmet, but let a windshield take the place of eye protection. North Carolina requires wearing helmets and using lights at all times.

School Buses
All seven states require traffic in both directions to stop for a stopped school bus with signals activated. Maryland, Virginia, and North Carolina make an exception for oncoming traffic on divided highways. North Carolina's law also covers church buses. Regardless of the law, keep a sharp eye out for passengers approaching or leaving a bus.

Seat Belts and Child Restraints
Delaware: Children under 12 years or 65 inches in height may ride in a front seat only if the airbag is disabled. Children under 8 yr./66 lb. must be in a child restraint.

Maryland: Children under 8 and shorter than 57 in. must be in a child restraint; children 8–16 must use seat belts.

Virginia: Children under 1 must be in a rear-facing child restraint. Children ages 1–8 must be in a child restraint or booster seat. Children ages 8–18 must be in a child restraint, booster seat, or seat belt.

North Carolina: Children less than 8 years and 80 lb. must be in a rear-seat child restraint if there's a front-seat passenger-side air bag unless the restraint is designed for use with air bags. Children ages 8–16 must be in either a child restraint or a seat belt.

Tinted Windows

All seven states limit aftermarket tint on a vehicle's glass. South Carolina allows dark windows (27% minimum visual light transmittance). Delaware (70%) doesn't. The other states fall somewhere between. Finding out whether you're legal before you travel is a good idea.

Additional Local Issues

Delaware

- Delaware State Police were named the "best-dressed state law-enforcement agency" in 2005, but they stand out mainly because of their numbers. Delaware has the highest ratio of state police officers to residents in the country.
- Speed traps include Harrington (35 mph), on US 13 south of Dover, and Bridgeville (25 mph), at the junction of US 13 and DE 404, a popular route from Greater Washington to the beaches.
- Restaurants and bars may operate 9 a.m.–1 a.m. seven days a week. Liquor stores (all privately run) may sell 9 a.m.–1 a.m. Mon.–Sat. and noon–8 p.m. Sunday.

Maryland

- Although Maryland State Police are most active within 5 mi. of their barracks in Easton, Salisbury, Princess Anne, and Berlin, any vehicle anywhere at any time may be an unmarked MSP unit.
- Citations are common around the intersection of US 50 and the Ocean City Expressway and on Stephen Decatur Highway (MD 611) from Berlin to Assateague.
- Grocery stores in most of the state don't sell alcoholic beverages. Distilled spirits of 190° proof or higher are

unavailable. Many restrictions on alcohol sales differ between counties and even within them. For example, the bar in the Casino at Ocean Downs in Berlin is open for business 8 a.m.–4 a.m.; but other seven-day licensees in Worcester Co. operate 9 a.m.–2 a.m., and some establishments are limited to six days a week.

Virginia

- The speed limit on VA 175, the only road to Chincoteague, bounces around. The new bridge over Chincoteague Channel is Y-shaped. LEOs park on the dead-end southern branch (Marsh Island Rd.) to catch drivers on the northern branch who don't notice that the speed limit drops from 55 to 40 to 25 over a short distance.
- Speed traps on US 13 include Eastville; Exmore, which gets about 25% of its budget from lead-footed drivers; and both ends of the Chesapeake Bay Bridge-Tunnel. Gunning it *on* the CBBT is also inadvisable.
- Grocery and convenience stores may sell beer and wine of 14% ABV or less 6 a.m.–midnight. State-run ABC stores sell the stronger stuff. Most ABC stores are open 10 a.m.–7 p.m. or later Mon.–Sat. and 1 p.m.–6 p.m. Sun. Bars may sell until 2 a.m. Ten western counties prohibit sale of mixed drinks, but they're hardly dry.

North Carolina

- State law-enforcement agencies conduct frequent license and sobriety checks, one reason North Carolina has more than four times as many impaired-driving arrests per capita as New York. Be mindful around the sites of large events. In May 2013, mainland Highway Patrolmen flocked to Ocracoke and issued so many tickets that they all but shut down a fishing tournament.
- Speed traps include Ocracoke Village, where the limit on NC 12 drops abruptly from 55 mph to 20; the western approach to Morehead City, where the limit on US 70 goes from 55 to 35; and around Columbia, where a 3-mile section of US 64 is a 70-mph expressway, a 55-mph surface highway, a 35-mph main street, and a 45-mph gotcha zone.

More Information

The AAA's Digest of Motor Laws is a good source of the latest on many topics covered above: http://drivinglaws.aaa.com/

The National Rifle Association offers a useful tool for researching firearm issues at www.nraila.org/gun-laws/articles/2010/guide-to-the-interstate-transportation.aspx

A consortium of nonprofit groups maintains a site on move-over laws at www.moveoveramerica.com

Appendix 5

Electronic Sources of Travel Information

511

Forty-one states are fully or partially integrated with the Federal Highway Administration's national travel-information system, which you can reach by dialing 511 from any land line or cell phone. Each participating state has a 511 Web site with maps, advisories, and traffic cams. Some states also have sites for mobile devices, and all have back-door phone numbers, usually toll free. At this writing, Delaware isn't on the network; but its Web sites are useful.

New Jersey
www.511nj.org
866-511-6538

Delaware
www.deldot.gov
Mobile: www.deldot.gov/mobile

Maryland
www.md511.org
Mobile: http://m.chart.maryland.gov/home
855-466-3511

Virginia
www.511virginia.org
800-578-4111

North Carolina
www.ncdot.gov/travel/511
Mobile: www.ncdot.gov/m
877-511-4662

South Carolina
www.511sc.org

877-511-4672

Georgia
www.511ga.org
877-694-2511

Florida
www.fl511.com
866-511-3352

There's an App for That

Several government agencies, nonprofit entities, and private companies offer potentially beneficial applications for Android (available from Google Play), Apple (from the App Store), and other mobile devices. Some apps are better than others, but all listed here are either inexpensive or free.

Delaware
DelDOT
Android 2.33 up
iPhone, iPad, iPod; iOS 6.0 up

Virginia
VDOT 511
Android 2.3 up
iPhone, iPad, iPod; iOS 5.0 up

South Carolina
SCDOT 511
Android 2.3 up
iPhone, iPad, iPod; iOS 6.0 up

Georgia
GDOT 511
Android 2.3 up
iPhone, iPad, iPod; iOS 6.0 up

Florida
Florida 511

Android 2.33 up
iPhone, iPad, iPod; iOS 4.0 up

Eastern Nat'l. Park & Monument Assn.
Passport to Your National Parks
(maps, Web sites, phone numbers, etc.)
Android 2.33 up
iPhone, iPad, iPod; iOS 5.0 up

NOAA
NOAA Weather Free
(no alerts)
Android (various)

NOAA Weather Radio
iPhone, iPad, iPod; iOS 5.0 up

National Geographic Society
National Parks by National Geographic
iPhone, iPad, iPod; iOS 5.0 up

WMDT-TV (Salisbury, MD)
WMDT 47 News
(News, weather, fuel prices)
Android 2.2 and up
iPhone, iPad, iPod; iOS 5.0 up

WVEC-TV (Norfolk, VA)
WVEC 13 News
(News, weather, radar, traffic cams; also for Kindle and Black-
berry)
Android (various)
iPad; iOS 6.0 up

WCTI-TV (New Bern, NC)
News Channel 12 Mobile
(News, weather, radar, traffic cams, scores;)
Android 2.3 up
iPhone, iPad, iPod; iOS 6.0 and up
Also for Kindle and Blackberry

WTEV-TV (Jacksonville, FL)
ActionNewsJax.com
(News, weather radar, scores)
Android 1.6 up
iPhone, iPad, iPod; iOS 4.3 up

The Weather Channel
The Weather Channel
Android (various)
iPhone, iPad, iPod; iOS 6.0 up

WAZE

The Israeli app acquired by Google combines GPS with crowdsourcing to provide up-to-the-minute maps, driving directions, and traffic information. Like Wikipedia, it has turned tradition on its head. Whereas some of the apps listed above deliver information from broadcast stations to mobile users, WAZE delivers traffic information from mobile users to broadcasters—more than two dozen so far.

Controversy is vigorous and ongoing. One complaint is that the two-way flow of information makes WAZE unusually distracting to drivers. Another is that its police-locator feature not only helps motorists in trouble, but also identifies speed traps and contributed to the murder of two New York City officers in 2014. The app is free of charge, but it places information about users' location, itineraries, speed, and habits in the hands of a large, secretive for-profit company that probably sells that information and has reportedly cooperated with the federal government in domestic surveillance.

WAZE is available for Android, iPhone, Blackberry, Windows Phone, and other devices directly from www.waze.com

TIS/HAR and Other On-Air Resources

Travelers' Information Stations and Highway Advisory Radio stations are low-power government AM transmitters individually limited to ranges of a few miles, but sometimes networked for broader coverage. Not all licensed stations have or transmit call signs. Some don't broadcast consistently. Temporary TIS/HAR stations for construction projects and disaster areas come and go with little publicity. Easy-to-miss highway signs and scans of the upper and lower AM band can sometimes reveal new and reactivated stations. Small broadcast stations may be community-focused, but still news-poor. Some urban commercial stations issue useful traffic reports.

SiriusXM Travel Link (www. siriusxm.com/travellink) packages weather, fuel prices, speed-trap alerts, etc. SiriusXM Traffic (www. siriusxm.com/siriusxmtraffic) offers graphic representations of average speeds on major and some minor roads in 130 markets, including Philadelphia-Camden-Wilmington, Hampton Roads, Savannah, and Jacksonville. Neither is free, and neither is compatible with all onboard navigational equipment.

Pennsylvania
- Philadelphia
  KYW, 1060, commercial

New Jersey
- Cape May
  WQEL632, 1700, city

Delaware
- Wilmington
  WTMC, 1380, DelDOT

Licensed as an AM broadcast station. Four repeaters on 1380 provide statewide coverage.

Maryland
- Assateague Island NS
  KPC756, 1610, USNPS
- Cambridge
  WPED444, 530, 1610, 1640, state
- Easton
  WNQA290, 530, 1610, 1630, state
- Kent Narrows
  WNAL786, 530, state
- Ocean City
  WPFE399, 1290, city
- Ocean City
  WQKF629, 1670, city
- Ocean City
  WPFJ882, 530, 1610, 1630, state

- Queenstown
  WNQA289, 530, 1610, 1630, state
- Salisbury
  WNQA283, 1250, 1610, 1630, state
- Salisbury-Pocomoke City
  WICO, 1320, 92.5 FM, commercial

Virginia

- Hampton Roads
  WQOQ385, WQOQ596, 1680, VDOT
- Chincoteague
  WCTG, 96.5, commercial
  Streaming audio at http://965ctg.com
- Chincoteague NWR
  1610, USNPS
- Norfolk
  WNIS, 790, commercial
- Tasley
  WESR, 1310, commercial
   Streaming audio at www.shoredailynews.com
- Wallops Flight Facility
  760, NASA

North Carolina

- Cape Hatteras NS
  KPC710–711, KPC713–714, KPC755, 1610, USNPS
  The seashore has licenses for five transmitters from the
  Wright Memorial to Ocracoke, but service is intermittent.
- Nags Head
  WQJN500, 1610, NCDOT
- Ocracoke
  WOVV, 90.1 FM, nonprofit
  Operated by the Ocracoke Foundation. Streaming audio at
  www.wovv.org

Georgia

- **Brunswick**
  WPQB293, 530, county

Appendix 6

Gluten-Free Sustenance

Dozens of nationwide and regional restaurant chains call attention to their gluten-free dishes—Boston Market, McDonald's, P.F. Chang's, Qdoba, Red Robin . . . This summary is limited to those with outlets near the wild-horse ranges. Current lists of national scope are available at several locations on the Web, such as http://glutenfreeguidehq.com/chain-restaurants

Policies and implementation differ substantially. Some companies maintain separate gluten-free menus in print or online. Others use symbols or notes on their general menu. Some go out of their way to prepare gluten-free versions of dishes that normally contain gluten. Others merely point out the obvious absence of gluten in foods such as lettuce. Not every franchise owner, cook, or server knows about advertised provisions for customers with gluten sensitivity or other concerns. Not every restaurateur who offers gluten- (or meat- or dairy- or peanut-) free options lets on. Many Subways gladly serve the Veggie Max/Veggie Patty, made of non-vegan vegetable protein, but decline to put it on the menu. Other chains bury extensive alternate menus in their Web sites. The burden of due diligence and the joy of discovery belong to the patron.

Applebee's
http://www.applebees.com/~/media/docs/Applebees_Allergen_Info.pdf
- 12849 Ocean Gateway
  Ocean City, MD 21842
  410-213-7396
- 5002 S. Croatan Hwy.
  Nags Head, NC 27959
  252-441-3652
- 5183 Highway 70 W.
  Morehead City, NC 28557
  252-727-0409
- 113 The Lake Blvd,
  Kingsland, GA 31548
  912-729-9515

Arby's
http://cds.arbys.com/pdfs/nutrition/gluten-free-menu.pdf
- 10633 Ocean Gateway
  Berlin, MD 21811
  410-641-1124
- 2322 Stockton Rd. .
  Pocomoke City, MD 21851
  410-957-3770
- 5158 Hwy. 70
  Morehead City, NC 28557
  252-240-3800
- 2518 Osborne Rd.
  St. Marys, GA 31558
  912-882-3200

Blimpie
https://www.blimpie.com/assets/pdf/BlimpieAllergensChart.pdf
- 1884 NC Hwy. 24 E.
  Newport, NC 28570
  252-727-5444

Carrabba's Italian Grill
https://www.carrabbas.com/menu/under-600-gluten-free/
gluten-free
- 12728 Ocean Gateway
  Ocean City, MD 21842
  410-213-0037

Chili's
http://www.chilis.com/en/locationspecificpdf/menup-
df/001.005.0000/chilis%20allergen%20generic.pdf
- 463725 SR 200
  Yulee, FL 32097
  904-225-8666

Chipotle Mexican Grill
http://chipotle.com/allergens?format=aspx
- 12909 Ocean Gateway Ocean City MD 21842
  410-213-9704

KFC
http://www.kfc.com/nutrition/food-allergies-and-sensitivities
- 12641 Ocean Gateway
  Ocean City, MD 21842
  410-213-2553
- 101 Newtowne Blvd.
  Pocomoke City, MD 21851
  410-957-6813
- 7320 S. Virginia Dare Tr.
  Nags Head, NC 27959
  252-441-3028
- 3414 Arendell St.
  Morehead City, NC 28557
  252-726-6033
- 107 Miller Blvd.
  Havelock, NC 28532
  252-447-8144
- 1155 E. Boone Ave. Ext.
  Kingsland, GA 31548
  912-729-7311
- 117 Sidney Pl.
  Yulee, FL 32097
  904-225-8643

LongHorn Steakhouse
http://media.longhornsteakhouse.com/en_us/pdf/longhorn_allergen_guide.pdf
- 5120 Hwy. 70
  Morehead City, NC, 28557
  252-222-0396
- 121 Crown Pointe
  Kingsland, GA, 31548
  912-576-2811

Olive Garden
http://www.olivegarden.com/menu-listing/gluten-sensitive
- 5152 Hwy. 70
  Morehead City, NC, 28557
  252-240-0250

Outback Steakhouse

http://www.outback.com/docs/default-source/Gluten-Free/Gluten-Free

- 12741 Ocean Gateway
  Ocean City, MD 21842
  410-213-2595
- 5220 S. Croatan Hwy.
  Nags Head, NC 27959
  252-441-3981
- 4937 Arendell St.
  Morehead City, NC 28557
  252-247-6283

Ruby Tuesday

https://www.rubytuesday.com/assets/menu/pdf/informational/allergen.pdf

- 5227 Hwy. 70
  Morehead City, NC
  252-726-3144

Subway

https://www.subway.com/Nutrition/Files/AllergenChart.pdf

- Berlin, MD—15 outlets within 20 mi.
- 6448 Maddox Blvd.
  Chincoteague, VA 23336
  757-336-2480
- 6496 Lankford Hwy.
  Oak Hall, VA 23416
  757-824-0094
- 2146 Old Snow Hill Rd., Ste. 6
  Pocomoke City, MD 21851
  410-957-0090
- Corolla, NC—nine outlets within 20 mi.
- Beaufort, NC—6 outlets within 20 mi.
- St. Marys, GA—19 outlets within 20 mi.

Wendy's

https://www.wendys.com/redesign/wendys/pdf/en_US_gluten_free_list.pdf

- 12641 Ocean Gateway #580

Ocean City, MD 21842
410-213-1911
- 25403 Lankford Hwy.
Onley, VA 23418
757-787-8598
- 1503 S Croatan Hwy.
Kill Devil Hills, NC 27948
252-441-1417
- 4006 Arendell St.
Morehead City, NC 28557
252-726-2769
- 557 US Hwy. 70 W.
Havelock, NC 28532
252-444-2050
- 2442 Osborne Rd.
St. Marys, GA 31558
912-882-7009
- 2607 Scrubby Bluff Rd.
Kingsland, GA 31548
912-729-8020
- 1350 Hwy. 40 E.
Kingsland, GA 31548
912-729-5620

Appendix 7

Fueling Around

Deviation of state average prices, in cents per gallon, from the national average price of regular unleaded gasoline ($1.82 when the map was made). Gasoline prices are also a usable proxy for price of diesel., though one is often more expensive than the other. Although absolute fuel prices change minute by minute, *relative* prices are stable to a degree. Unless refineries open, pipelines move, or state legislators drastically change tax rates, average pump prices in South Carolina will probably remain lower than those in Georgia and Pennsylvania no matter whether crude oil costs $50 or $150 a barrel. or the federal government mandates new additives nationwide.

Gasoline

Buying a national brand ensures consistent quality and reliable results, doesn't it? Yes and no.

In 2016, AAA published results of a test showing that gasoline sold by the 46 TOP-TIER™ manufacturers, from 76 to Valero, leaves significantly less gunk in engines. The reason: these brands contain high levels of detergents (required by federal law since 1996), metal inhibitors, oxygenators, and other additives in all grades. Unfortunately, making use of this finding isn't as simple as it seems.

Gasoline sold under one oil company's brand may start with several refiners' distillates mixed together in a pipeline or a bulk-storage terminal. At this early stage, gas is just gas.

Differences emerge when distributors introduce additives for national brands and independent customers. Branded stations don't always sell their parent company's gas. Unbranded stations, which make up about one-third of the 162,000 fuel outlets in this country, sometimes *do* sell branded gas, though it may differ slightly from the gas sold at branded stations nearby. Today a Gas Giant station and a mom-and-pop convenience store across the street may sell the same stuff, which may have been formulated for a third retailer. Tomorrow, offerings may change. Knowing what's for sale at which station is labor-intensive when it's even possible, and you can run dry searching for your preferred formulation in unfamiliar territory; so there are three main considerations

- Inventory turnover. Busy stations are less likely to have water or trash in their storage tanks.
- Price. Other things being equal, lower prices are better.
- Safety. Paying a little more down the road is usually preferable to using an unattended pump in the middle of nowhere at 3 a.m.

Diesel

Brand differences are slight, but there are other distinctions.

No. 1 diesel is kerosene with additives. *No. 2 diesel* is augmented home heating oil. No. 1 is less efficient, harder to find, and more expensive, but it burns cleaner and doesn't turn into glop at first frost. You can fill up with it if nothing else is around, but it doesn't lubricate the engine as well, and long-term use probably isn't a good idea. No. 2 is less pricy and nearly ubiquitous, but it pollutes more and jells at a higher temperature.

Some distributors make *winter diesel* by diluting No. 2 with No. 1; others tinker with additives to No. 2. Fuel-filter heaters on most personal vehicles can keep summer diesel usable down to -20°F. The record low temperature for any wild-horse island is only -5°F, on Assateague, so you're probably safe with summer diesel even if you drive up from Florida in January with a really big auxiliary fuel tank.

Dyed diesel exists for the benefit of tax collectors. Red diesel is untaxed and intended for tractors, bulldozers, and generators. Blue, also untaxed, is for federal-government vehicles. The clear diesel sold at nearly all gas stations for on-road use is taxed. A retailer can get into big trouble by selling dyed diesel for unauthorized purposes, and you can get in trouble for buying it, though the IRS will probably never inspect the contents of your tank.

Rudolf Diesel's 1893 prototype engine ran on peanut oil, and *biodiesel*, made from vegetable oil or recycled animal fat, is becoming more popular in the United States. Some stations offer blends of bio- and petrodiesel, usually B2 (2 percent bio) to B20 (20 percent). B 99 and B100 are less common and may harm engines not modified for them. Using anything higher than B5 may void some car makers' warranties.

Filling up at high-volume stations such as truck stops is important for diesel users because bacteria (sometimes referred to as "black algae") can grow in diesel contaminated with water. Biodiesel is especially vulnerable to bacterial attack.

Prices

Politicians and pundits get high oratorical mileage from the price of fuel, whether it's up or down, whether it's fair or rigged, whether Americans should pay what Europeans pay, and on and on. Public discourse on the subject tends to be simplistic because there's no single national price for fuel. In fact, Congress and state legislatures have spent more than 100 years passing laws that expressly forbid, or coincidentally obstruct, uniform pricing of nearly everything. Major corporations have paid nine-figure fines and executives have gone to prison for price-fixing all manner of goods.

Most other factors of pump prices are equally beyond our control.

- *Crude-oil prices* account for about two-thirds of the price of fuel. Since World War II, the annual average price of domestic

crude oil in constant 2015 dollars has ranged from $17.26 a barrel in 1998 to $100 in 2008.

- The *federal excise tax* is another big bite. There was none for gas until 1932 and none for diesel until 1951. At this writing, the rate has been 18.4 cents a gallon for gas and 24.4 cents for diesel since October 1997.
- *State taxes* differ substantially. Pennsylvania's taxes are the highest (50.4 for gas/65.1 for diesel), though its average pump prices rank 10th. Alaska's taxes are the lowest (12.25/12.75), but its prices are third highest.
- *Supply* varies. If a hurricane destroys oil rigs in the Gulf of Mexico or OPEC increases production, prices change.

Still it's possible to cut costs by being choosy about what to buy, when, and where.

If the price of super premium is insane on the road, a couple of tanks of regular won't ruin an engine or a vacation.

Pump prices traditionally rise around holidays and in summer, when people drive more. Since 1995, the federal Reformulated Gas Program has exaggerated the summer increase by requiring everyone to use a warm-weather formulation that evaporates more slowly and burns cleaner, but costs more to make. State and local mandates have raised the total of distinct recipes to 20, some of which are more expensive to produce than others. In spring, when refineries perform maintenance and switch to making summer blends, supply falls, and prices rise. In the fall, when refineries begin changing back, prices usually drop. Horse-watching at off-peak times may not easily mesh with your schedule, but filling the tank then is usually more economical.

Average pump prices can differ sharply from state to state (see the accompanying map), but they don't accurately depict the chaos of local prices. Gas and diesel usually cost more around the Maryland end of Assateague than across the border in Virginia or Delaware. If you pass through the Hampton Roads region of Virginia heading north or south, you may wish to fill up there. Prices are sometimes 10-20 cents a gallon lower there than on the Eastern Shore and 20-40 cents lower than on the Outer Banks. Prices are often lower between Raleigh and Shackleford or between Atlanta and Cumberland than in either capital or along the coast.

Sometimes you can find lower prices by venturing a few miles off the Interstate. A little comparative shopping over the course of a trip may save enough money to pay for a fancy breakfast.

Alternative Fuelishness

At this writing, about 19,000 places in the United States offer alternative fuel. This figure includes nearly 12,000 electric-vehicle charging stations (with about 30,000 total connections) and smaller numbers offering biodiesel, hydrogen, propane, and other combustibles with or instead of gasoline and petrodiesel. Alternative fuels can turn up in unexpected places. Car dealerships, stores, restaurants, bars, motels, and B&Bs offer EV charging. Some Tractor Supply and U-Haul outlets sell propane.

Despite the wild-horse islands' undeserved reputation for remoteness and backwardness, it's possible to enjoy worry-free horse watching even in an electric vehicle. Other fuels may require more thought and preparation, but they're not out of the picture for a wild horse vacation.

More Information

- Gas Buddy (www.gasbuddy.com) offers up-to-date price information, a trip calculator, a blog, and an app for iPhone, iPad, and iPod Touch running iOS 7.0 or higher.
- AAA (http://fuelgaugereport.aaa.com) provides online price information, e-mail price updates, a trip calculator, a blog, travel guides compatible with mobile devices, and an app that lets you read AAA magazines and other publications with iOS 6.0 or higher .
- TruckMiles (http://www.truckmiles.com/) focuses on diesel prices.
- Mapquest has current gas prices and apps for a variety of mobile devices.

For current locations and particulars on sources of alternative fuel, visit

- The U.S. Energy Department's Alternative Fuels Data Center (note: some entries are cryptic) www.afdc.energy.gov/fuels/electricity_locations.html
- Open Charge Map, a nonprofit that maintains a global directory of EV charging stations http://openchargemap.org
- or any of the following for-profit entities:
- Plugshare (www.plugshare.com)

- Chargepoint (www.chargepoint.com)
- Car Stations (http://carstations.com)

Catch a Wave

Assateague

The beach breaks (left or right) are sometimes intermediate level in spring and fall, and you have to paddle a ways. The island has a little southwest-northeast tilt, so waves are better when swells are from the south or southeast. Surfing is allowed outside lifeguarded areas in the state park and in the national seashore in Maryland and Virginia. The beaches at both ends are jammed in summer, but the middle is often deserted. If you escape the crowds, your only spectators may be horses, who'll never laugh if you wipe out. There are plenty of surfing-related businesses in the area, e.g.,

Dr. Shred's Surf Adventures
25 Walnut Hill Dr.
Berlin, MD 21811
443-397-0186
https://www.facebook.com/DrShredsSurfAdventures#_=_

Atlantic Shoals Surf Shop
6758 Maddox Blvd.
Chincoteague, VA 23336
757-336-1305
If you'd rather rip it up in complete obscurity, most of Virginia's other

barrier islands are owned by the Nature Conservancy and uninhabited. Parramore and several other islands in the Virginia Coast Reserve are off-limits, however, and access to others is often restricted. For the latest information, visit http://www.nature.org/ourinitiatives/regions/northamerica/unitedstates/virginia/placesweprotect/virginia-coast-reserve.xml

On the other hand, if you're an exhibitionist, you can show off at the East Coast Surfing Championship. The world's second-oldest surfing event started in 1963 as the Virginia Beach Surfing Carnival. Its first winner, Jack "Murph the Surf" Murphy, soon achieved wider fame by stealing the Star of India sapphire from the American Museum of Natural History and going to prison for murder. Despite its awkward beginning, the ECSC routinely draws more than 100,000 spectators a day in late August. In recent years, it has grown to include volleyball, skimboarding, and other competitions.

Outer Banks

Some of the features that made the Outer Banks deadly to mariners in the age of sail—strong winds, colliding currents, frequent hurricanes—make it one of the top surfing spots on the East Coast. Cape Hatteras is the prime location, especially around the jetties that once protected the lighthouse, but you can find a good beach break nearly anywhere.

The Army Corps of Engineers Pier in Duck is a hot spot on the northern Banks. Note: stay at least 100 yards from this or any other pier on the Banks. Despite stumps in the water, Carova, near the Virginia line, has gained popularity because crowds tend to be thinner than around Corolla. Waves break close to shore around Milepost 4 in Kitty Hawk because of an old inlet channel. Unfortunately for property owners, this also contributes to rapid erosion and frequent overwash. The days of parking in the sand along NC12 and surfing all day on the undeveloped Epstein Tract in Nags Head are long gone, but you can still find decent action at Jennette's Pier, near the former site of Roanoke Inlet.

Most of Hatteras Island is owned by the U.S. Fish and Wildlife Service or the U.S. National Park Service. The Code of Federal Regulations allows the Park Service to prohibit surfing in any place designated as a swimming beach; but the agency doesn't always make much noise about them. In practice, you're probably all right as long as you avoid areas with lifeguards and don't plow through hordes of bathers or fishermen. Irene's Inlet and the S-curves, both north of Rodanthe, have a growing fan base. Although you can't watch horses while you surf along the south-facing beaches of around Frisco, on sparsely-populated Ocracoke, and on unpopulated Portsmouth Island, these places have characteristics in common with Assateague and with Shackleford Banks, which *does* have horses.

Bonuses:
- The water's bearably warm in winter, especially around Cape Hatteras.
- Wind—the main reason the Wright brothers spent so much time there—makes for great wind-surfing and kiteboarding. A popular location for these activities is Pamlico Sound just north of Buxton. This alarmingly narrow section of Hatteras Island is an historic inlet-formation zone. John White showed an opening here in 1585, and Hurricane Isabel put one in nearly the same location in 2003. Locals used to call this area the Haulover because they used it for moving their boats overland between ocean and sound, thus avoiding the long, dangerous water route around the cape and through the inlet. The deep water in the relict inlet channel west of the Haulover attracts so many Northern wind-surfers, especially in spring, that it acquired the unofficial name Canadian Hole.

Drawbacks:
- Summer crowds can be bothersome on the developed parts of Hatteras Island and from Nags Head north.
- In many places, you can't see across the sound, and in heavy weather it can look like the ocean. Geographically challenged surfers sometimes go looking for big waves in the sound. Laugh as heartily as you please. It happens.

Cumberland

Great tidal range, wide continental shelf, and other things make really exhilarating surf rare anywhere on the Sea Islands. Cumberland isn't Maui or even New Hampshire; but neither of those places has wild horses, and Cumberland doesn't have big rocks or a history of shark attacks. Take your board, though you may not need a GoPro to record your exploits. If you're not expecting 30-foot waves, you can still have fun or at least get wet.

This rugged adventurer tried his luck in the breakers off the Virginia portion of Assateague on a brisk December day.

Conclusion

Horse watching along the Atlantic Wild Horse Trail is an activity that can bring a new dimension of fun and understanding to your vacation. Our family has taken great pleasure in visiting the wild horse islands over the decades, and I hope this book marks the trail so that you can embark on your own life-changing adventures.

The rewards are many. Horse watching engenders a sense of calm and awareness, the perfect antidote to a hectic workplace and the cumulative stresses of daily living. Shared activities promote family bonding and build common ground that supports relationships through life's upheavals. Horse watching integrates beautifully with creative activities such as photography, scrapbooking, drawing, blogging, and journaling. It is as inexpensive as you want it to be: we have enjoyed trips camping in leaky tents and pampered in elegant bed and breakfasts.

The horses that survive along the Atlantic Wild Horse Trail are the subject of intense conflict and controversy. Some of the herds are in danger of extinction. Many are threatened by land-use conflicts, restrictive regulations, political machinations, bureaucratic inertia, and the actions of careless or abusive people. If you believe that wild horses should remain forever free on their East Coast ranges, please support the government agencies and nonprofit organizations that are responsible for their welfare and safeguard their wildness. Use your all-important voice and political influence to improve wild horse management policies, and demonstrate that the American public wants wild horses to remain on our public lands. Ultimately, we hold their future in our hands.

Acknowledgments

Throughout my research on the herds of the Atlantic Coast, many people have given their time and expertise.

Dr. Jay F. Kirkpatrick, senior scientist at the Science and Conservation Center at Zoo Montana in Billings and author of *Into the Wind: Wild Horses of North America*, was unfailingly helpful when I wrote *The Wild Horse Dilemma: Conflicts and Controversies of the Atlantic Coast Herds*. I carried what I learned from him forward into this book, adding to the scientific accuracy of this project.

Karen McCalpin, director of the nonprofit Corolla Wild Horse Fund, Inc., has been consistently helpful and supportive throughout my years of research. She and the other members of the organization—mostly volunteers—have upended their lives to secure protection for these horses.

Dr. Sue Stuska, the wildlife biologist at Cape Lookout National Seashore who oversees the Shackleford Banks herd, has corresponded regularly about the horses and helped me to understand them better.

Doug Hoffman, wildlife biologist at Cumberland Island National Seashore, helped me to understand the Park Service perspective on the horse herd and corrected my assumptions and misinformation. He generously drove me to key parts of the island that I could not otherwise reach, and my time with him was the highlight of the trip.

Steve Edwards, by day an attorney for Isle of Wight County, VA, works magic in rehabilitating injured Corolla and Shackleford horses and preserves the rare Banker horses through an off-site breeding program at Mill Swamp Indian Horses in Smithfield, VA.

Carolyn Mason, president of the Foundation for Shackleford Horses, Inc., and Woody and Nena Hancock took me to see the herds on and near Cape Lookout National Seashore.

Laura Michaels, the Park Service ranger in charge of pony care at Cape Hatteras National Seashore, took me behind the scenes to meet the Ocracoke horses.

Roe Terry and Denise Bowden of the Chincoteague Volunteer Fire Company supplied me with useful information. Besides managing the herd of free-roaming ponies, these dedicated people donate their time to provide tax-free fire suppression, search and rescue, and emergency medical services in a town of 2,700 permanent residents that receives roughly 1.5 million visitors a year. Roe granted me access to the optimal vantage point for the world-famous Chincoteague Pony Swim: whereas most onlookers stood in a field behind an orange fence, out of harm's way, I was able to stand directly on the grassy landing where the horses regained solid ground after swimming the channel from Chincoteague National Wildlife Refuge.

And once again my husband, Alex Gruenberg, Tabetha Fenton, and my mother, Joyce Urquhart have been invaluable proofreaders who caught errors that others missed.

About the Author

Bonnie Gruenberg, MSN, CRNP, is a midwife and nurse practitioner working in rural Pennsylvania. For more than 20 years, she has studied, photographed, painted, and written about the controversial wild herds of the Atlantic coast. Her seminal work, The Wild Horse Dilemma (2015) Dilemma won the Eric Hoffer, Next Generation Indie, and Independent Publisher book awards, and won second prize for best nonfiction book in the American Horse Publications 2016 Equine Media Awards. Reviewers have praised it as "the best work ever written about East Coast wild horses (or wild horses period!)" and "an in-depth read not to be missed by serious wild horse enthusiasts." She is also the author of the popular six-volume *Hoofprints Guides to the Wild Horses of the Atlantic Coast,* and *Hoofprints in the Sand.*

Her award-winning *Birth Emergency Skills Training : Manual for out-of-hospital midwives* (Birth Guru/Birth Muse, 2008) has been translated into Russian and developed into a hands-on workshop (www.birthemergency.com). She also has published *Essentials of Prehospital Maternity Care* (Prentice Hall, 2005); *Hoofprints in the Sand: Wild Horses of the Atlantic Coast* (as Bonnie S. Urquhart; Eclipse, 2002), and numerous other books, e-books and articles Prior to her career in obstetrics, she worked as an urban paramedic in Connecticut. More information and an assortment of her photographs and artwork can be found at her Web sites

www.BonnieGruenberg.com
www.BonnieGphoto.com
www.WildHorseIslands.com

EXPOSE YOURSELF!
1 Get listed for FREE
Send a brief description of your business or organization. We'll list it on the Web site and try to work it into the next edition of the book.
2 Buy an ad
Sizes range from a 1/3-page coupon to a full-page attention-grabber.
3 Get personalized copies
If you buy 100+ books to sell or give to your customers, we'll put your name and logo on the cover FREE—in addition to our great volume discount.
If you report a typo, you'll win an apple.
Nay. You'll be entered in a yearly drawing for a really cool print from bonniegphoto.com
For rates, options, and other information, e-mail
info@wildhorseislands.com

www.ingramcontent.com/pod-product-compliance
Lightning Source LLC
Chambersburg PA
CBHW062200270326
41930CB00009B/1598